Using the
Schoolwide
Enrichment
Model With Technology

Using the Schoolwide Enrichment Model

With Technology

Angela M. Housand, Ph.D.,
Brian C. Housand, Ph.D., &
Joseph S. Renzulli, Ed.D.

PRUFROCK PRESS INC.
WACO, TEXAS

Library of Congress catalog information
currently on file with the publisher.

Copyright © 2017, Prufrock Press Inc.

Edited by Lacy Compton

Cover design by Raquel Trevino and layout design by Allegra Denbo

ISBN-13: 978-1-61821-593-2

At the time of this book's publication, all facts and figures cited are the most current available. All telephone numbers, addresses, and website URLs are accurate and active. All publications, organizations, websites, and other resources exist as described in the book, and all have been verified. The authors and Prufrock Press Inc. make no warranty or guarantee concerning the information and materials given out by organizations or content found at websites, and we are not responsible for any changes that occur after this book's publication. If you find an error, please contact Prufrock Press Inc.

Prufrock Press Inc.
P.O. Box 8813
Waco, TX 76714-8813
Phone: (800) 998-2208
Fax: (800) 240-0333
http://www.prufrock.com

Table of Contents

PART I
Getting Started

CHAPTER 1

The Schoolwide Enrichment Model (SEM)

Introduction

This book is designed to provide teachers with specific strategies and resources for infusing technology into any and all aspects of the curriculum. The approaches discussed in the chapters that follow are based on a general model for talent development entitled The Schoolwide Enrichment Model (SEM; Renzulli & Reis, 2014). The SEM (Renzulli & Reis, 1985, 1997, 2014) is designed to challenge and meet the needs of high-potential, high-ability, and gifted students, while providing challenging learning experiences for *all* students. This is the primary difference between the SEM and other models in gifted education: The SEM advocates enriched learning opportunities for *all* students and advanced-level follow-up for students who show high levels of interest, ability, and motivation that may result from positive reactions to general enrichment experiences, the regular curriculum, or nonschool experiences. The three major goals of the SEM are to:

1. maintain and expand a continuum of special services that will challenge students with demonstrated superior performance or the potential for superior performance in any and all aspects of the school and extracurricular program;

2. infuse into the general education program a broad range of activities for high-end learning that will challenge all students to perform at advanced levels, and allow teachers to determine which students should

be given extended opportunities, resources, and encouragement in particular areas where superior interest and performance are demonstrated; and

3. preserve and protect the positions of gifted education specialists and any other specialized personnel necessary for carrying out these goals.

The SEM Identifies Potential and Talent

Every learner has potential strengths that can be used as a foundation for learning. Within the SEM approach, potentially high-performing students are recognized and provided with advanced opportunities, resources, and encouragement based on their aptitudes, motivation, and creative behaviors. In addition to or in replacement of traditional test-based assessment, teachers and content-area specialists can observe students using technology tools, conducting research on the Internet, interacting with concepts, and creating products for authentic audiences in any subject or extracurricular area. This provides opportunities for performance-based assessment and allows educators to make instructional decisions about individuals and small groups accordingly. In a performance-based identification system, classroom observations play an equal part in selecting students for advanced services. Utilizing a performance-based approach is critical in locations where students experience disadvantages that may limit their achievement on standardized tests (Cooper, Baum, & Neu, 2004). By recognizing and developing the unique strengths of children, students can develop a sense of self-efficacy that promotes a growth mindset (Dweck, 2006), which often carries over to higher success rates in other areas.

DID YOU KNOW?

Delcourt (2008) found that students who participated in specific content-area lessons designed to promote engagement and enhance inquiry skills, like the SEM approach, were more successful in advanced follow-up pursuits. These activities focused on recognizing potential and aptitude in a specific area rather than measuring the amount of training already acquired, and allowed teachers to rate student performance using criteria such as "displays complexity of ideas," "uses materials effectively," "recognizes patterns in the content," and "utilizes specialized vocabulary."

In the SEM, a talent pool of approximately 10%–15% of above-average ability and high-potential students is identified through a variety of measures, including achievement tests, teacher nominations, assessment of potential for creativity and task commitment, as well as alternative pathways of entrance (e.g., self-nomination, parent nomination, etc.). High achievement test scores or high IQ scores automatically include a student in the talent pool. This enables educators to focus the majority of their talent search efforts on finding those students who are underachieving in their academic schoolwork.

The structure of the SEM, outlined in Figure 1, has three service delivery components: The Total Talent Portfolio, Curriculum Modification and Differentiation, and Enrichment Pedagogy. These three services are delivered through the regular curriculum, a continuum of special services, and a series of enrichment clusters. First, a comprehensive strengths and interest assessment portfolio, The Total Talent Portfolio, is created for each student to inform the kinds of learning opportunities that students will be encouraged to pursue. With interests and learning style preferences tracked in equal measure to cognitive abilities, a strong foundation for effective learning and creative productivity is identified for each student. A second service delivery component is curriculum compacting. This differentiation strategy identifies the parts of the regular curriculum that talent pool students have already mastered and then eliminates or streamlines the curriculum, enabling these students to avoid repetition of previously mastered work. The curriculum compacting strategy guarantees mastery while simultaneously finding time for more appropriately challenging activities (Reis, Burns, & Renzulli, 1992; Reis, Renzulli, & Burns, 2016; Renzulli, Smith, & Reis, 1981). Once students have been identified for talent development and arrangements have been made that free up time for students to work on something different, advanced learning opportunities can begin.

These opportunities are organized around the Enrichment Triad Model, which is the curricular foundation at the heart of the SEM and the primary focus of this book, *Using the Schoolwide Enrichment Model With Technology* (SEM:*Tech*). The Enrichment Triad Model provides the framework for teaching and learning within the broader components of the SEM and is comprised of three indivisible parts called Type I, Type II, and Type III. These three types of experiences function interdependently to create learning that engages students using their interests and passions to drive instruction.

This chapter discusses the theory and practices of the SEM, which has been used in schools for decades and is the basis for *Using the Schoolwide Enrichment Model With Technology* (SEM:*Tech*).

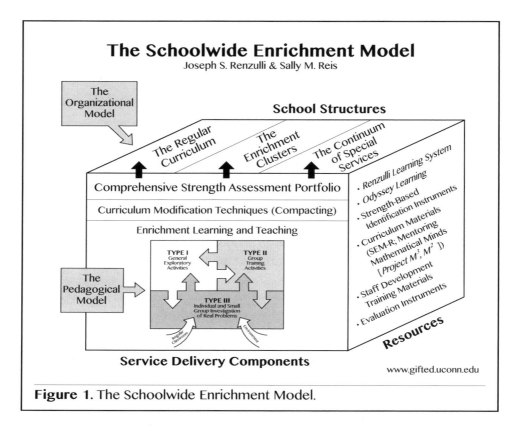

Figure 1. The Schoolwide Enrichment Model.

The Total Talent Portfolio

In the SEM, teachers help students better understand three dimensions of their learning: their abilities, interests, and learning styles. This information, focusing on their strengths rather than deficits, is compiled into a management form called the Total Talent Portfolio. The portfolio can be used to make decisions about talent development opportunities in general education classes, enrichment clusters, and in the continuum of special services. The major purposes of the Total Talent Portfolio are to:

1. collect information about students' strengths on a regular basis;
2. *classify* this information into the general categories of abilities, interests, and learning styles;
3. periodically *review and analyze* the information in order to make decisions about providing opportunities for enrichment experiences in the general education classroom, the enrichment clusters, and the continuum of special services; and

4. use this information to make decisions about acceleration and enrichment in school and in later educational, personal, and career decisions.

This expanded approach to identifying talent potentials is essential if we are to make genuine efforts to include a broader, more diverse group of students in enrichment programs. This approach is also consistent with the more flexible conception of *developing* gifts and talents that has been a cornerstone of the SEM, addressing concerns for promoting more equity in special programs.

Curriculum Modification and Differentiation Techniques

The second service delivery component of the SEM is a series of curriculum modification techniques that: (a) adjust levels of required learning so that all students are challenged, (b) increase the number of in-depth learning experiences, and (c) introduce various types of enrichment into regular curricular experiences. Essentially, these curriculum modification techniques help to ensure that all students' needs are being met within instructional settings. The procedures that are used to carry out curriculum modification include curriculum differentiation strategies, such as curriculum compacting, and increased use of greater depth into regular curricular material (Reis et al., 1993; Renzulli, 1994).

Curriculum compacting, for example, is an instructional differentiation technique that allows students to skip or be accelerated through content that has already been mastered. The process allows teachers to make appropriate curricular adjustments for students in any curricular area and at any grade level, through (a) defining the goals and outcomes of a particular unit or segment of instruction, (b) determining and documenting which students have already mastered most or all of a specified set of learning outcomes, and (c) providing replacement strategies for material already mastered through the use of instructional options that enable a more challenging and productive use of the students' time. An example of how compacting is used is best represented in the form, The Compactor, which serves as both an organizational and record-keeping tool (see Figure 2). Curriculum compacting provides a unique opportunity for teachers. Instead of simply replacing compacted regular curriculum work with more advanced material that is solely determined by the teacher, students' interests can and should be considered. If, for example, a student loves designing video games or smartphone apps, that option may be used to replace material that has been

Individual Education Program Guide		
The Compactor		
Student Name(s):	Grade:	School:
Participating Teachers:		
Name it.	Prove it.	Change it.
Curriculum Area	Assessment	Enrichment/Acceleration Plans
Name or insert the subject area, unit or chapter, or learning standards that are the focus for compacting.	List the assessment tools and related data that indicate student strengths or were used for preassessment, the results of the preassessment data, and learning standards that have not yet been mastered. Identify pertinent student interests that emerged from inventories or interviews.	Briefly describe the enrichment or acceleration tasks that will be substituted for the compacted curriculum, and any strategies used to ensure student mastery of learning standards and objectives that have not been met through enrichment and acceleration. Explain which strategies will be used to support or coach student learning at more advanced levels.

Figure 2. The Compactor.

compacted from the regular curriculum. With curriculum compacting, we can ensure that the challenge level of the material being substituted is sufficiently rigorous. This helps us ensure that gifted students understand the nature of effort and challenge.

Enrichment Learning and Teaching

The third service delivery component of the SEM, based on the Enrichment Triad Model, is enrichment learning and teaching, which has roots in the ideas of a small but influential number of philosophers, theorists, and researchers such as Jean Piaget (1976), Jerome Bruner (1960, 1966), and John Dewey (1913, 1916). The work of these theorists, coupled with research and program development activities, has given rise to the concept of enrichment learning and teaching. The best way to define this concept is in terms of the following four principles:

1. Each learner is unique, and therefore, all learning experiences must be examined in ways that take into account the abilities, interests, and learning styles of the individual.

2. Learning is more effective when students enjoy what they are doing, and therefore, learning experiences should be constructed and assessed with as much concern for enjoyment as for other goals.

3. Learning is more meaningful and enjoyable when content (i.e., knowledge) and process (i.e., thinking skills, methods of inquiry) are learned within the context of a real and present problem; and therefore, attention should be given to opportunities to personalize student choice in problem selection, the relevance of the problem for individual students at the time the problem is being addressed, and authentic strategies for addressing the problem.

4. Some formal instruction may be used in enrichment learning and teaching, but a major goal of this approach to learning is to enhance knowledge and thinking skill acquisition that is gained through formal instruction with applications of knowledge and skills that result from students' own construction of meaning (Renzulli, 1994).

The ultimate goal of learning guided by these principles is to replace dependent and passive learning with independent and engaged learning. Although all but the most conservative educators will agree with these principles, much controversy exists about how these (or similar) principles might be applied in everyday school situations. Truly, a danger exists that principles and theories developed in the ivory towers of academe often do not translate into real classroom settings, but the SEM and the Enrichment Triad Model were not only developed in classrooms, but they have been implemented in thousands of schools across the county and around the world. We do not present an idealized list of glittering generalities, but rather concrete strategies and processes that can and will enrich the lives of students in *any* school setting. Developing a school program based on these principles is not necessarily an easy task, but with the clear and easily understandable structures within the Enrichment Triad Model and subsequently the SEM, the implementation becomes accessible for any school willing to take the time to make an even better learning environment for their students. Example after example demonstrate how schools have achieved success by gaining faculty, administrative, and parental consensus on a small number of easy-to-understand concepts and related services, and by providing resources and training on the Enrichment Triad and SEM processes and service delivery procedures. Additionally, numerous research studies and field tests have shown that the SEM can be implemented in a wide variety of settings with various populations of students, including high-ability students with learning disabilities and high-ability students who underachieve in school (Renzulli & Reis, 1994).

School Structures of the SEM

There are several school structures that, when in place, support the implementation of the Schoolwide Enrichment Model. These structures work in harmony to ensure students' experiences are connected to life that occurs beyond the school walls while still providing rich, meaningful, and appropriately challenging learning opportunities.

The Regular Curriculum

The regular curriculum consists of everything that is a part of the predetermined goals, schedules, learning outcomes, and delivery systems of the school. The regular curriculum might be traditional, innovative, or in the process of transition, but its predominant feature is that authoritative forces (i.e., policy makers, school councils, textbook adoption committees, state regulators) have determined that the regular curriculum should be the "centerpiece" of student learning. Application of the SEM influences the regular curriculum through the differentiation of the challenge level of required material using curriculum compacting, and through enrichment teaching and learning like that of the Enrichment Triad Model (Renzulli, 1977). The goal of the SEM is to influence rather than replace the regular curriculum, but the application of certain SEM components and related staff development activities can substantially alter both the content and instructional processes of the entire regular curriculum.

The Enrichment Clusters

The enrichment clusters, a second component of the SEM, are nongraded groups of students who share common interests, and who come together during specially designated time blocks during school to work with an adult who shares their interests and who has some degree of advanced knowledge and expertise in the area. Typically, enrichment clusters occur at a specific time each week for an entire marking period (trimester, semester, quarter, etc.). Using information gathered via interest inventories, themes are identified across students' interests. Then, adults from the faculty, staff, parents, and community are recruited to facilitate enrichment clusters based on the identified interests, such as video game design, robotics, LEGO construction, vlogging, and other areas. After a little training, facilitators develop their enrichment clusters and students are provided with the opportunity to select their top three choices for the clusters. When scheduling is complete, students are placed into their first, or in some cases, second choice. Like extracurricular activities and programs such as FIRST LEGO League, Makerspace, or Future Problem Solving Program, the main rationale for participation in one or more clusters is that *students and teachers want to be there.* All teachers (including music, art, physical education, etc.) are involved in teaching the clusters, and their involvement in any particular cluster is based on the same type of interest assessment that is used for students in selecting clusters of choice.

The model for learning used with enrichment clusters is based on an inductive approach to solving real-world problems through the development of authentic products and services. Enrichment clusters promote real-world problem solving, focusing on the belief that "every child is special if we create conditions in which that child can be a specialist within a specialty group" (Renzulli, 1994, p. 70).

Enrichment clusters are organized around various characteristics of differentiated programming, including the use of major disciplines, interdisciplinary themes, or cross-disciplinary topics (e.g., a theatrical/film production group that includes actors, writers, technical specialists, costume designers). The clusters are modeled after the ways in which knowledge utilization, thinking skills, and interpersonal relations take place in the real world. Thus, all work is directed toward the production of a product or service. Cluster facilitators do not prepare a detailed set of lesson plans or unit plans in advance; rather, direction is provided by three key questions addressed in the cluster by the facilitator and the students:

1. What do people with an interest in this area (e.g., filmmaking, computer programming, hardware engineering, etc.) do?
2. What knowledge, materials, and other resources do they need to do it in an excellent and authentic way?
3. In what ways can the product or service be used to have an impact on an intended audience?

Enrichment clusters incorporate the use of advanced content by providing students with information about particular fields of knowledge and requiring students to use the methods and conventions of the field. Enrichment clusters are not intended to be the total program for talent development in a school or to replace existing programs for talented youth. Rather, they are one component of the SEM that can stimulate interests and develop talent in the entire school population. They can also serve as staff development opportunities as they provide teachers with an opportunity to participate in enrichment teaching, and subsequently to analyze and compare this type of teaching with traditional methods of instruction. In this regard, enrichment clusters promote a spillover effect by encouraging teachers to become better talent scouts and talent developers, and to apply enrichment techniques to general education classroom situations.

The Continuum of Special Services

A broad range of special services is the third school structure targeted by the Schoolwide Enrichment Model. Although the enrichment clusters and the SEM-based modifications of the regular curriculum provide a broad range of services to meet individual needs, a program for total talent development still requires supplementary services that challenge our academically or intellectually talented students who are capable of working at the highest levels. These services, which cannot ordinarily be provided in enrichment clusters or the regular curriculum, typically include individual or small-group consultations; acceleration; direct assistance in facilitating advanced-level work; arranging for mentorships; and making other types of connections between students, their families, and the persons, resources, and agencies that exist beyond the school setting.

Direct assistance also involves setting up and promoting student, faculty, and parental involvement in special programs such as Future Problem Solving, Science Olympiad, Destination Imagination, National STEM Video Game Challenge, FIRST LEGO League, Makerspace, and other state and national competitions in robotics, mathematics, art, and history. Another type of direct assistance consists of arranging out-of-school involvement for individual students in summer programs, on-campus courses, special schools, theatrical groups, scientific expeditions, and apprenticeships at places where advanced-level learning opportunities are available. Provision of these services is one of the responsibilities of the Schoolwide Enrichment teaching specialist or an enrichment team of teachers and parents who work together to provide options for advanced learning.

The Enrichment Triad Model

The kinds of learning that are addressed in a schoolwide enrichment approach to school improvement are based on a learning theory called the Enrichment Triad Model. This plan for enrichment learning and teaching is designed to encourage creative productivity on the part of young people by: (1) exposing them to various topics, areas of interest, and fields of study; (2) teaching them how to integrate advanced content, thinking skills, and investigative and creative problem solving methodology to self-selected areas of interest; and (3) providing them with the opportunities, resources, and encouragement to apply these skills to self-selected problems and areas of interest. Accordingly, three types of enrichment are included in the Enrichment Triad Model (see Figure 3).

The Triad Model is based on the ways in which people learn in a natural environment rather than the artificially structured environment that characterizes most classroom learning conditions. External stimulation, internal curiosity, necessity, or combinations of these three starting points cause people to develop an interest in a topic, problem, or area of study. Children are, by nature, curious, problem-solving beings, but in order for them to act upon a problem or interest with some degree of commitment and enthusiasm, the interest must be a sincere one in which they see a personal reason for taking action. Essentially, the Enrichment Triad Model was developed to motivate and engage students by exposing them to various topics and areas of interest, offering instruction in thinking skills, creative problem solving, and investigative methodology, and providing them with the opportunities, resources, and encouragement to *apply* these content and process skills to selected areas of interest.

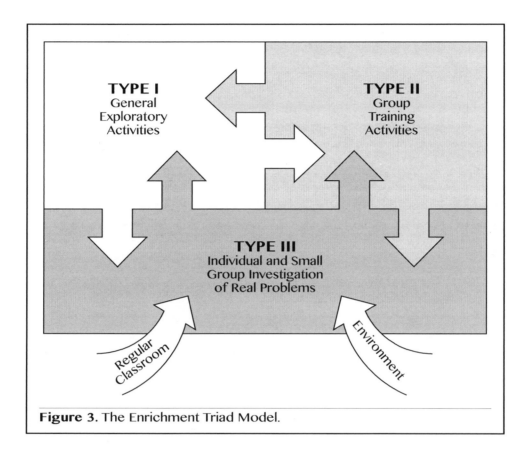

Figure 3. The Enrichment Triad Model.

The Enrichment Triad Model is designed to promote the *interaction* between and among the three types of enrichment depicted in Figure 3. The arrows in Figure 3 are as important as the individual cells because they give the model dynamic properties that cannot be achieved if the three types of enrichment are pursued independently or sequentially. A Type I exposure experience may, for example, have value in and of itself, but it achieves maximum payoff if it leads to Type II or III experiences for one or more students. And the backward arrows in Figure 3 are intended to convey paths through which the Type III productions of some students can serve as both Type I and Type II training for other students. In other words, these two types of general enrichment serve to fulfill both awareness and instructional purposes, and they produce maximum payoff when they also stimulate potential new interests on the parts of other students. For example, in one school, a group of fourth-grade students designed an online learning module to make advanced learning content accessible to younger learners.

The Schoolwide Enrichment Model is rich with opportunities to identify students who might not otherwise be recognized for enriched learning experiences. The SEM is an excellent means to provide gifted students with rich and challenging learning, *and* it serves the needs of *all* students, particularly in the Type I and Type II learning within the Enrichment Triad Model. Types I and II Enrichment should be provided to larger groups of students than those formally identified as gifted. In some cases, this enrichment can be provided to all students and in other cases, it might be for targeted groups (e.g., advanced math groups, students with a special interest in coding). The reason for this change is because formal identification obviously helps us select students with high cognitive and/or achievement levels; however, we may miss students who have great potentials for higher level performance because of high interest and motivation, task commitment, and creativity—traits that are frequently overlooked in formal test-based identification procedures for gifted programs. This change is especially important if we want to examine the potentials of underachieving students, twice-exceptional students, low-income students, English language learners, and minority group students who typically do not do as well on standardized tests as middle class students. In this regard, it is a good idea to view Types I and II Enrichment as *identification situations*[1] that may lead to Type III experiences, which are the most advanced type of enrichment in the model.

The Enrichment Triad Model is the pedagogical core for the organizational structure of the Schoolwide Enrichment Model. The Triad has also been used in a variety of gifted programs, regular classroom curriculum enrichment approaches, and as charter and magnet school themes. The Triad has been adapted and adopted in diverse suburban, rural, and urban schools throughout the country, and it is widely used in schools around the world.

Type I Enrichment: General Exploratory Experiences

Type I Enrichment is designed to expose students to a wide variety of disciplines, topics, occupations, hobbies, persons, places, and events that would not ordinarily be covered in the regular curriculum. In schools using this model, an enrichment team of parents, teachers, and students often organizes and plans Type I experiences by contacting guest speakers, previewing films, or arranging mini-courses, demonstrations, or performances. Type I experiences are designed to motivate students to such an extent that they will act on their interests in creative and productive ways or seek out more information to satisfy their curiosity. The major purpose of Type I Enrichment is to include, within the overall school program, selected experiences that are purposefully developed to be

---

1 This concept has gained a good deal of popularity in recent years under the designation of "performance based assessment."

motivational. This type of enrichment exposes students to a wide variety of disciplines, topics, ideas, and concepts in a way that allows for connections across domains and to the world that exists beyond the school walls.

Type I Enrichment experiences can be based on regular curricular topics, innovative outgrowths of prescribed topics, or stand-alone topics in which teachers believe students would have an interest. But in order to qualify as a bona fide Type I experience, any and all planned activities in this category must be designed to stimulate new or present interests that may lead to more intensive follow-up on the parts of individuals or small groups of students. In Type I experiences, students are aware that the activity is an *invitation* to various kinds and levels of follow-up. The most successful Type I experiences are dynamic in nature, include some hands-on activities rather than a "straight lecture" approach, and demonstrate investigative and creative opportunities in the topic area. A systematic debriefing of the experience will enable students to envision further involvement and the ways that follow-up might be pursued.

An experience is clearly not a Type I if every student is required to follow up on an activity in the same or similar way. Required follow-up is a regular curricular practice, and although prescribed follow-up certainly has a genuine role in general education, it almost always fails to capitalize on differences in students' interests and learning styles. To make Type I experiences exciting to students, guest speakers, for example, should be selected for both their expertise and passion about a particular area *and* their ability to energize and capture the imagination of students even when presenting via digital means. Guest speakers or any Type I experience has to help students explore the realms and ranges of opportunity for further involvement that are available, while still being developmentally appropriate for their age or intellectual capacity.

It is important to incorporate Type I activities into the regular classroom curriculum because this helps connect these activities to classroom instruction, which highlights the importance of learning within the Type I experience. Following any Type I activity, an assessment of the levels of interest of all students can be conducted, and advanced Type I activities that pursue the material in greater depth might be planned for highly interested students. This helps support the implementation of interest-based learning opportunities like special groupings for Internet research or even field trips. This ensures that opportunities to go deeper are provided for all students when appropriate, not just intellectually advanced learners.

The Type I dimension of the Enrichment Triad Model can be an extremely exciting aspect of overall schooling because it creates a legitimate slot within the curriculum for bringing the vast world of knowledge and ideas that are above and beyond the regular curriculum right into the school setting. It helps students connect what they are learning to what happens in the world outside the school and, as a relatively easy-to-implement component of the model, it is an excellent vehicle for getting started on a path to enriched learning for the entire school.

Type II Enrichment: Group Training Activities

Most educators agree about the need to blend into the curriculum more training in the development of higher order thinking skills. Type II Enrichment is a systematic approach for organizing process skills, specifically developing both thinking and feeling processes. Some Type II Enrichment is general, consisting of training in areas such as creative thinking and problem solving, learning how to learn skills such as classifying and analyzing data, and advanced research, reference, and communication skills. And some Type II training is very specific because it focuses on work a student is doing in a particular discipline or on a specific project. Type II training is usually carried out both in classrooms and in enrichment programs, and includes the development of skills outlined in Figure 4.

Typically, implementation of Type II instruction cannot be planned in advance because it is designed to be responsive to students' need for information as they engage in advanced learning in an interest area. When we refer to these strategies, we use the term *process skills*, and include examples of specific skills within each of the six general categories listed in Figure 4.

In general, Type II training provides students with various learning opportunities designed to improve their independent learning skills as well as the quality of their personal assignments, projects, and research. Type II enrichment also includes a broad range of affective training activities designed to improve social and emotional development, develop interpersonal and intrapersonal skills, and to promote greater degrees of cooperation and mutual respect among students. By placing this instruction within the framework of the regular curriculum, enrichment clusters, and any other special groupings of students, teachers can offer these valuable training activities without the risk of having the training viewed as an end in and of itself. This category of enrichment has generally been well received by students because it usually involves more hands-on activities and students can begin to see the relevance of these skills for projects that they may want to pursue.

Developing a Type II library of resources should be a major responsibility of the Schoolwide Enrichment Team, but the entire faculty should always be on the

---

Taxonomy of Cognitive and Affective Processes (The Type II Matrix)

I. Cognitive Thinking Skills
   A. Creative thinking skills
   B. Creative problem solving and decision making
   C. Critical and logical thinking

II. Character Development and Affective Process Skills
   A. Character development
   B. Interpersonal skills
   C. Intrapersonal skills

III. Learning How to Learn Skills
   A. Listening, observing, and perceiving
   B. Reading, note taking, and outlining
   C. Interviewing and surveying
   D. Analyzing and organizing data

IV. Using Advanced Research Skills and Reference Materials
   A. Preparing for research and investigative projects
   B. Library and electronic references
   C. Finding and using community resources

V. Written, Oral, and Visual Communication Skills
   A. Written communication skills
   B. Oral communication skills
   C. Visual communication skills
   D. The acquisition and appropriate application of digital literacy skills and just-in-time knowledge

VI. Metacognitive Technology Skills
   A. Identify trustworthy and useful information
   B. Selectively manage overabundant information
   C. Organize, classify, and evaluate information
   D. Assess web-based information
   E. Use relevant information to advance the quality of one's work
   F. Communicate information effectively

Figure 4. Type II Matrix (Renzulli, 2001).

lookout for materials and resources that they believe would be worthwhile additions to a broad and comprehensive library of source material. Type II resources go beyond a series of material sources. Do not forget that teachers who have become proficient in any set of process skills can share their expertise with other members of the faculty. The material selection process and development of process skills by teachers should be considered a long-term and ongoing undertaking. As materials are collected and teachers identified, it is important to classify the resources for easy retrieval. For example, it is much easier to go to a database where materials are catalogued and listed by grade-level appropriateness than it is to send out an e-mail every time you have a need. For the most part, all of the process skills that are part of the Type II Matrix can be introduced in the early grades, but they will need reinforcement and practice at more advanced levels as students progress through the grades. Do not hesitate to find out which materials and resources are working well using teacher and student feedback. This allows the resource library to be curated over time as effective materials and resources are maintained for Type II training and replacements are made for those materials that are not doing the job well.

Type III: Individual and Small-Group Investigations of Real Problems

Works of theorists such as Jean Piaget (1976), Jerome Bruner (1960, 1973), Leta Hollingworth (1926), and John Dewey (1910) provided part of the rationale for the original Enrichment Triad Model (Renzulli, 1976), but the ways that people learn in the outside-of-school world were the impetus for the Type III in the Enrichment Triad Model. Type III Enrichment is based on the ways in which people learn in a natural environment, rather than the artificially structured classroom and prescribed curriculum environments that characterize most school learning situations. Type III Enrichment incorporates investigative activities and the development of creative products in which students assume roles such as firsthand investigator, writer, artist, blogger, app developer, or game designer—the roles of practicing professionals. Although students pursue these kinds of involvement at a more junior level than adult professionals, the overriding purpose of Type III Enrichment is to create situations in which young people are thinking and feeling like practicing professionals and doing what practicing professionals do, even if at a less sophisticated level than adult researchers, writers, or entrepreneurs. Bona fide Type III experiences incorporate the following four characteristics of what makes a problem real (Renzulli, 1982):

1. Personalization of interest
2. Use of authentic methodology

3. No existing solution or "right" answer
4. Designed to have an impact on an audience other than or in addition to the teacher

Type III Enrichment is the vehicle through which everything from basic skills to advanced content and process skills blends together into student-developed products and services. This kind of learning represents a synthesis and an application of content, process, and personal involvement. The student's role is transformed from one of lesson-learner to firsthand inquirer, and the role of the teacher changes from an instructor and disseminator of knowledge to a combination of coach, resource procurer, mentor, and "guide-on-the-side."

A few examples of Type III Enrichment projects. The best way to understand what Type III Enrichment is all about is to look at a few examples that point out roles that teachers, students, and even parents play in the Type III process.

› A multilingual girl whose first language is Spanish felt it was important that students learn Spanish just as she had learned English. She conducted research on the Internet to determine the best way to learn a language. She then created an instructional blog on Blogspot [now called Blogger], which she shared on the Internet.

› After a curricular unit on Greek mythology in their gifted pull-out program, a group of fourth-grade students used GoAnimate to tell the stories of Greek gods and goddesses through animation in a K–2 friendly version. These videos were shared with teachers and younger students in their school.

› A group of third-grade students produced, created, and acted in an original film about perspective taking. The film was screened by the school community and later entered into a highly competitive film festival.

› A group of third graders interested in electronics and computer hardware used a Makey Makey (http://www.makeymakey.com) device to create an *Operation* board game for their class to use as a review for a unit on human anatomy. Players had to correctly identify the names of bones and successfully remove them from the game board that they designed.

› A group of elementary students wanted to learn to design their own apps and investigated the use of Appy Pie (http://www.appypie.com). The students partnered with local businesses to design mobile apps.

› Middle school students fascinated by the film industry used the Internet to research tax incentives provided by the state of North Carolina for film production. The students created a series of public service announcements advocating for the continued support of the incentives to benefit the local economy. The public service announcements were posted on YouTube.

› In a gifted elementary class, students felt that people did not understand them and their giftedness. They then examined the characteristics of giftedness and created a conception of what it means to be gifted, based on the extant knowledge on giftedness and their own experiences. The students utilized photography and personal narratives to capture the essence of being gifted. Student photographs were displayed at a local gallery as part of an art exhibit.

Each Type III topic and product idea is almost inevitably germinated by an enrichment experience about something that happens to trigger the interest, either in or out of school. Many excellent resources are available to help students consider their interests and the potential Type III Enrichment projects they might like to pursue. Thanks to the Internet, young students in almost any part of the world can have access to a wealth of resources that were previously available to only a very small group of scholars and adults. In excellent Type III studies, students select both the topics and the products they wish to pursue. And in a certain sense, the teacher builds the curriculum around the child. Rather than define each product and determine the content and outcomes in advance as is typically done with prescribed curriculum, teachers help guide and facilitate the learning process of individuals and small groups. Teachers provide support and guidance for planning, organization, decision making, resource procurement, audience finding, and editorial assistance to bring product quality to its highest level. The experience becomes a dynamic learning environment where a student's gifts and talents emerge in creative and investigative ways, but the student (not the teacher) is in charge of his or her own learning. Each student's unique blend of interests is developed and celebrated.

DID YOU KNOW?

Follow-up studies with numerous young adults who participated in Triad-based programs (Brigandi, 2015; Delcourt, 1988, 1994; Hébert, 1993; Schack, 1986; Schack, Starko, & Burns, 1991; Starko, 1988; Westberg, 2010) have almost always revealed that one or more of their Type III experiences have been determining factors in making decisions about college majors and career choices. And many respondents to follow-up inquiries point out how their own professional contributions can be traced back to work carried out in Triad programs.

The *most important thing* students have "taken away" from their Type III Enrichment projects is a greater interest in and expertise for examining a topic of their own choosing in a rigorous and highly professional way. They have also developed a set of advanced-level thinking skills and a creative and investigative mindset that is transferable to a much broader range of competencies essential for future work and careers that place a premium on creative productivity. These skills include increased self-efficacy, which is a belief in themselves that they can do something that is bigger, more robust, and more challenging than what they have previously done in school. They have developed important executive function skills, such as organization and time management, self-regulation, task commitment, goal orientation, a strong work ethic, the ability to work cooperatively with others, and the communication skills that allow them to share their work with target audiences. Most importantly, however, they experience learning as a process that is joyful and worthy of their time.

CHAPTER 2

From the SEM to Using Technology

The Purpose of Education

The first purpose of gifted education is to provide young people with maximum opportunities for self-fulfillment through the development and expression of one or a combination of performance areas where superior potential may be present. The second purpose is to increase society's reservoir of persons who will help to solve the problems of contemporary civilization by becoming producers of knowledge and art rather than mere consumers of existing information (Renzulli & Reis, 2014; p. 16–17).

Think for a moment about how you plan your instruction. What is the first thing you do? Have you been told that it is important to "start with the end in mind"? Most educators conceive the outcomes of learning as students meeting a set of standards. This likely explains why almost every educator we talk to starts his or her planning with the standards. Educators select several standards and then proceed to find a lesson that meets those standards or they design their own lesson around those standards. Either way, the lesson is *about the standards*, and when instruction is designed around a set of standards, the outcome is didactic instruction. This kind of instruction shifts students' relationship to learning processes. In didactic instruction, the standards are imposed on the student rather than inviting the student to participate in processes of learning that ultimately result in meeting the standards. This interaction is more than semantics.

Now, think about what "the end" of instruction really is. When you think about what you want for your students, do you want them to check the boxes next to a list of standards or do you want them to grow—emotionally, intellectually, and socially? Do you want them to succeed on a rubric or do you want them to exceed your expectations and surprise you with what they are capable of accomplishing? Do you want them to score well on a test or do you want them to find success and fulfillment in learning and life? When we define the end goal of instruction, we have to be careful how we define it or we might just get exactly what we envision.

So, when we design lessons with the end in mind, we should avoid defining the end as achieving the standards, because when we start our lesson development centered on the standards, the instruction is prescribed by the teacher and presented to students without their input. They are forced to participate in lessons that may do little to consider the interests, desires, or needs of the student. Teachers fail to consider whether or not the student would *want* to participate in the lesson. Within these lessons, the pathways for success are predetermined and the products are outlined in advance. There is little room for innovation and the potential for growth is limited. The primary goal of the lesson is to ensure that students have demonstrated mastery of the standards rather than the goal of supporting the development of individuals who will solve society's most pressing problems.

Don't misunderstand us; we are not suggesting you throw out the standards! Standards are important, as they set a minimum expectation for learning. We cannot deny the reality that we are living in an educational climate that is governed by accountability and is guided by standards. Our point is that while the standards are in service to improving education, we cannot forgo innovation and enjoyment in learning for the sole purpose of improving test scores. Otherwise, outside of classrooms, technology will continue to advance at an unprecedented rate and the United States will lose its entrepreneurial edge. Instead, we are suggesting that students, particularly gifted students, can *exceed the standards* and that students achieve at a higher level because they are asked to solve *real problems*.

We know that when students are engaged in solving real problems and creating authentic products, they do more than just meet the standards; they enthusiastically engage in learning. That is why, like the original SEM (Renzulli & Reis, 1985), *Using the Schoolwide Enrichment Model With Technology* espouses an approach to pedagogy that focuses on broad concepts and principles and seeks to illustrate the importance of curriculum that connects knowledge across disciplines. Curriculum focusing on multidomain connections provides students with numerous points of entry and the opportunity to connect their interests to the academic content, and allows for the combination of information from a variety of fields to develop novel and insightful solutions to *real* problems.

DID YOU KNOW?

Experts agree that curriculum is relevant for students when it (Eccles & Wigfield, 1995; Kaplan, 1986; Renzulli, Leppien, & Hays, 2000; Renzulli & Reis, 1997; Tomlinson et al., 2009; VanTassel-Baska, 2011):

›   connects with their lives;
›   seems useful in contexts beyond the classroom;
›   allows for meaningful collaboration;
›   is sensitive to global concerns; and
›   is authentic, is focused on real problems and processes, uses the conventions of the discipline, and is guided by habits of mind.

Education must emphasize the "whole child" and address subjects beyond the core curricular areas of math, science, language arts, and history. In an effort to bring up test scores, many schools have eliminated instruction in music, the arts, physical education, foreign language, design, speech, self-regulation skills, and communication skills; the kind of skills that lead to success in college, career, and life. When we shift the focus of instruction from teaching content to teaching processes, the richness of curriculum that parallels the richness of life can be reintroduced as we ask students to solve *real problems*. In essence, to solve the most pressing problems of our global society, all of these life skills will come to bear on the outcome, and the richness of life will be reflected in the richness of the problem and the skills necessary to solve it. Therefore, we invite you to join us in the alternative: A pedagogical approach to instruction that enriches students' lives and maximizes the opportunity for fulfillment, not only for the students, but for you as well.

INTRODUCING CHRISTY'S CORNER

Christy Howe has quite a vita for her 16 years of teaching experience. This K–5 gifted education specialist holds an M.Ed. in elementary education and reading from Boston College. She has specialization in gifted education through the North Carolina Academically and Intellectually Gifted Licensure, and Christy was named the 2015–2016 Gifted Educator of the Year for her district. This National Board Certified Teacher has taught up and down the east coast: Boston, Washington, DC, and Wilmington, NC. Reading specialist, classroom teacher, curriculum author, and staff development consultant are just some of the titles she has held, but her most important attribute is that she cares deeply about learning, for both her students and herself.

"Christy's Corner" is the story of Christy's work in a school where the majority of the students receive free and reduced lunch and English language learners make up a significant portion (40%) of the school's population. Christy's Corner sections of this book share with you the challenges she faces as she implements the Schoolwide Enrichment Model and the joy she experiences in watching her students learn and grow beyond where they are now or where they have been before. Christy's focus for her gifted pull-out program is to expand the program so that she is serving the entire school. Slowly but surely, she continues to expand her services to include talent development for students based on interest. She seeks out students who might want to participate in the enrichment clusters that occur in her school or participate in ThinkLab in her K–2 nurturing potential program. Christy is the kind of teacher who inspires her students and challenges them to be better, both academically and in becoming the people they will be when they grow up. In her classroom there is a sign that says, "You are a genius, the world needs your contribution." Everyday it inspires students to be more than they were yesterday. Christy's classroom was the ideal choice because her work demonstrates how one committed teacher can change an entire school culture and find the value every student brings to the learning experience. Of education generally and her teaching specifically, she says:

> I always come back to: What's the purpose of school? The purpose of school is not to do well on tests. The purpose of school is to create these lifelong learners who have the capacity to pursue their interests and dreams. I feel like student-driven projects, like the Type III Experiences in the Schoolwide Enrichment Model, really equip them to do that well. There is tremendous value in

these experiences, and students learn a lot. I can clearly see how the Common Core State Standards are met through the Type II processes embedded in the projects. So, I know we are teaching and reaching those skills, but I think it makes people nervous to see it. When I am teaching in this way, I feel like others are thinking: Are you really teaching?

We hope Christy's experiences inspire you to take the first steps in *Using the Schoolwide Enrichment Model With Technology*.

When we are thinking about pedagogy mirroring the richness of life, we also have to think about how the use of technology must also mirror how technology is used in the solving of real problems. One of the questions we have to ask ourselves when we consider using technology in educational settings: Can we achieve the instructional goal without using technology? This question is important because it highlights the fact that good pedagogy should come first and that technology should be the tool used to achieve the instructional goal. In an ideal setting, the technology would virtually disappear because it is so integrated into the process, and the effective pedagogical approach would be the thing that stands out. So, if the answer to the question, "Can we achieve our instructional goals without using technology?" is "yes," then the instruction will likely be focused on processes and skills that are transferrable and lead to success in life and career. If the answer to the question is "no," then the instruction may be focused on technology as an "event."

To illustrate, consider the use of games as instructional "tools." Sure, you can have students practice skills like reading or math facts while they play a game on the computer. This kind of drill and practice instruction often starts with the phrase, "Go to the computer and . . ." The allure of these games is short-lived because they quickly become rote exercises, and the money invested ultimately becomes a waste because the games are not complex or engaging enough to keep students' attention. Using games for skill practice is essentially providing students with electronic worksheets. Technology is a powerful tool and must be treated as such—as a tool used to support processes that involve critical thinking and problem solving. Technology affords us the opportunity to move away from didactic instruction to a more constructivist approach, where the teacher becomes a guide and coach in the learning process and at times learns alongside the student rather than being a content-area expert and imparting knowledge to students.

DID YOU KNOW?

The more constructivist the teacher's beliefs, the more technology use was reported in the classroom (O'Dwyer, Russell, & Bebell, 2004). The constructivist approach to learning is based on students taking responsibility for their own learning and requires teachers to take on the role of guiding, mediating, and modeling learning as they coach students (Henson, 2004; Sharp, 2006).

A Little Bit About Technology

"Any sufficiently advanced technology is indistinguishable from magic."—Arthur C. Clarke

The first mobile phone was made on April 3, 1973 and the first personal computer, the IBM PC, was introduced in 1981. In the subsequent decades, we have gone from technologies that were virtually inaccessible due to cost and size to ubiquitous access—complete integration into our daily lives. For many of us, it is difficult to get away from e-mail and the Internet because we are always connected via a smartphone. Already, we can control thermostats, lights, doors, and locks from our smartphones, but this barely illustrates the ways technology is becoming increasingly integrated into our daily lives.

Connectedness will be pushed even further into our day-to-day lives, while at the same time becoming increasingly less discernible as separate. Take, for example, your behaviors when you use Google to search the Internet. Google tracks your behavior over time and collects personal information to build a profile of your interests. This tracking is done using "cookies," which carry information about your search, the sites you click on, the time you spend on each site, and the content you view on those websites. These "cookies" are packets of information that are easily carried from one Internet search session to another, and the goal of using "cookies" to track you while you search online is to provide targeted advertising so that the ads you see correspond to your potential needs and wants.

As the Internet of Things arrives, this tracking will be taken even further as it connects your patterns of behavior to information that might be useful. Take, for example, a morning notification that there will be rain today and you should take an umbrella to work, but this notification happens before you wake up or check the weather report. The Internet of Things will connect our homes seamlessly with our mobile devices. It will allow us to locate people and everyday objects, permit hospitals and emergency responders to share our health information, enable us to monitor and control distant objects, and provide security as it tracks vehicles and inventory autonomously. Machines will talk to machines via "the cloud" and networked sensors will gather data and instantly share it with the machines. What makes the Internet of Things unique is that sensors will talk to machines, without human intervention, enabling the machines to interpret and transmit the data. Ultimately the sensors will provide machines with information so that they can take action without being instructed to do so. Imagine your driverless car changes course on your way to work after receiving a notification from sensors about an accident on the normal route ahead. Your route changes without a single command from you.

What we now perceive as ubiquitous will be more omnipresent in the future, and the lines between humans and technology will continue to blur. We can make educated guesses about the future of technology and what it will enable us to do. However, there is no way to truly know what the future holds. We are left preparing students for the unknown. One thing we can be certain of: Technology is not going away. Therefore, we must move beyond a 21st-century skills mindset and seek a "change and innovation" mindset. To be competitive now and in the future, individuals will have to take more initiative, be more responsible, and produce more than ever before. They will have to be flexible, comfortable with ambiguity, and continually create and recreate to stay viable in a world that will, evermore, be in a state of flux. They will have to go where no one has gone before.

What Is Technology?

When we talk about technology and using technology in K–12 educational settings, it can be confusing because there are a series of terms used to define technology and technology use. For example, technology education and educational technology (a.k.a. instructional technology) are often used interchangeably;

however, they are not the same thing. Educational technologies are the technology tools like computers, audiovisual equipment, graphing calculators, and software that are used to support instruction, deliver curriculum, assess learning, or otherwise enhance teaching and learning environments (ITEA, 2000, 2007), whereas technology education is the study of technology.

In this book, we set out to combine what we know about best practices for integrating technology into classroom settings with what we know about best practices for developing talent in educational settings. To accomplish this we have to start with a common vocabulary and a clear understanding of what we mean by technology. The term *technology* is often used in myriad ways and can refer to anything from developing new technologies to using a technology tool like the computer. In Table 1, we set out to clarify the differences so as to avoid any confusion.

Technology Know-How

As educators of the gifted and talented, we have tremendous power and responsibility to define the future by preparing students to participate in society, yet we find that we are preparing them for jobs that do not currently exist using technologies that have yet to be imagined. We can inspire students to pursue answers to civilization's most pressing problems as we seek to support the development of their maximal potential. To truly develop students' talents, we must seek to go beyond textbook-style instruction, consider the many and varied ways that talent manifests, and be willing to take risks in our instructional settings. As a result, it is important that we master some technology skills, but we do not have to be experts in technology to effectively use it within our classrooms. As a matter of fact, research suggests that teachers who are most successful implementing technology as learning tools for their students do not act as experts but as guides and themselves maintain a disposition of learning alongside the students when necessary (Jonassen, Peck, & Wilson, 1999; Keengwe, Onchwari, & Wachira, 2008). You have taken an important step toward effectively using technology to develop talent in your classroom or school. How do we know? You have picked up this book and have just demonstrated that you are motivated, interested, and willing to learn how to integrate technology into your instructional practice.

TABLE 1

SEM:*TECH* GLOSSARY OF TERMS

Technology-Related Term	Definition
Instructional technology	The use of technology tools within the classroom setting. The level of technology integration varies from school to school and classroom to classroom.
Technology tools	Any device used to carry out a particular digital function. Examples include computers, notepads, graphing calculators, smart boards, 3D printers, audiovisual equipment, software, applications, etc.
Technology innovation	Entire system of people and organizations, knowledge, processes, and devices that go into using and creating technological artifacts.
Technology	Technology is the collection of techniques, skills, methods, and processes used in the creation of products or in the accomplishment of objectives. Technology is "the innovation, change or modification of the natural environment in order to satisfy perceived human wants and needs" (ITEA, 2000, p. 242).
Technology skills	A broad set of knowledge, skills, work habits, and character traits that are necessary for success in today's world. These skills are transferrable and can be applied across all domains of inquiry.

DID YOU KNOW?

Teachers' beliefs about the positive impacts of technology integration are the strongest positive predictor of their willingness to use technology tools to deliver instruction, have students use technology tools during class, or have students create products using technology tools (O'Dwyer et al., 2004).

To gain confidence in using technology, it really just takes a willingness to try and an understanding that many mistakes will be made along the way. Modeling this for students can be very powerful. One of the things we address in Chapter 3 is having students develop a personal website. The first time we asked students to build their website, we had very little experience or knowledge of our own. Together, we had only developed *two* websites, yet we embarked on having 50 students create their own website for the first time. Call us crazy, but it was magical. We were learning alongside our students and we modeled "clicking around" for them. "Clicking around" is a phrase we use to mean that we modeled *not* having all of the answers, but trying anyway. When students asked us, "How do you (insert the phrase you hear most often when students are trying something new on a computer)?" we often did not know the answer, but we were willing to make mistakes and seek help, in front of students. So, we would search for the answer as we clicked around. In this process, we were making our best guess and we were often wrong. So we simply undid what we had just done, and then tried clicking on other items within the website creation software until we found the right answer. If a few attempts at clicking around within the software did not work, we would seek out the help section within the software. When that did not work, we would open another tab in our search engine and seek the answer to our question there, using web forums, and YouTube tutorials. If all of that failed, we might have contacted the software developers directly, but it never came to that. By demonstrating that we did not have all of the answers and that we were just trying things until we figured it out, we empowered most students to click around on their own. We demonstrated how to employ self-regulatory skills like perseverance, self-direction, help seeking, and maintaining comfort with ambiguity (see Chapter 8, Table 4, which shares processes and skills for consuming information using technology).

We do not mean to suggest that you should learn all of this on your own or that you do not need training and support in developing your own technology skills beyond that provided in this book. We are simply suggesting that the first step is your willingness to learn and make mistakes along the way and that picking up this book was great idea. What other kind of learning opportunities might you seek out?

Hopefully your principal provides the necessary time to develop your technology know-how—time to plan and participate in professional learning communities, and opportunities to attend conferences, workshops, and seminars, or take college courses.

DID YOU KNOW?

Exposure to technology-based learning opportunities for teachers supports the development of positive dispositions toward technology use. Also, creating time and opportunities for teachers to share ideas can accelerate the use of instructional technology in the classroom. Moreover, effective integration of new technologies into classroom settings is supported by professional development when it (Keengwe et al., 2008):

1. explicitly connects the use of technology to student learning outcomes,
2. provides hands-on technology use,
3. engages teachers in a variety of learning experiences,
4. utilizes applications that are curriculum specific,
5. defines the role of teacher as a guide rather than an "expert,"
6. requires the active participation of teachers,
7. occurs multiple times to ensure an ongoing technology integration process, and
8. provides sufficient time for learning and developing comfort.

It is also helpful to take time to get comfortable with technology in informal settings and to learn alongside colleagues and friends. Seek out those who care deeply about learning, are willing to take risks, and are not afraid to be wrong. Finding those who respect and value perspectives other than their own will go a long way toward creating a cadre of committed teachers who want to grow. The goal is to challenge yourself and be challenged to continually build your capacity for effectively using technology. The most important thing to remember, however, is to have fun with the process!

Providing Opportunities for TLC

Developing your knowledge by seeking professional development on the latest skills, tools, and resources related to technology is important, but be prepared to learn from your students as well. Most students are facile with technology, many have had tablets and smartphones in their hands from a very early age, and many have daily access to the Internet—making them excellent consumers and users of technology. This poses a challenge for educators: How do we stay ahead of the technology advances so that we can teach students the requisite skills to effectively use technology for learning? The reality is that we cannot be experts in technology and expert teachers.

DID YOU KNOW?

44% of elementary age children use smartphones regularly and roughly 66% report regularly using tablets (Pearson, 2014).

The only option is to learn alongside our students. In doing so, we empower students to effectively leverage technology for learning and productivity. Taking a learning disposition as the teacher can be challenging. It may feel as though there is a fine line between honoring what students can teach you and relinquishing authority, but valuing students' real contributions will go a long way toward building trusting teacher and student relationships. Just think, it took a long time for you, as a teacher, to develop your expertise. Students will not be able to surpass you in that regard, because you are the professional. So, learning alongside your students is not relinquishing authority, but rather a demonstration of the fact that learning is a lifelong process.

Now, imagine a school community that sends the message to students, everyday, that they have something valuable to contribute, not someday in the future, but rather something valuable to contribute right now. Imagine creating a community of sharing and collaboration-centered teaching and learning technology. You guessed it! We are talking about creating a Technology Learning Community (TLC) that includes teachers and students as equal contributors! Think of it as a group of "professionals" who meet regularly to share their knowledge and experience while working collaboratively to improve the technology skills of all members of the school community. The common goal of the Technology Learning Community is already built in: Improve the technology know-how of everyone in the school.

It takes careful planning to form TLCs that function as learning opportunities for everyone. However, once the time and energy is put in to create the foundation and structure for this type of learning community, the rewards and benefits become apparent. You might think of this as an "unconference" or a loosely structured conference type of event that emphasizes the informal exchange of information and ideas between participants. This might be an event that is held once a month and includes the whole school, or it could be done with one or two grades at a time. Defining the "when and where" will depend on teachers' desires to have their students participate and where space is available. Choices might include the library, cafeteria, a large classroom, or even a hallway. Ideally, however, you want people centralized so that everyone can see the available topics or options for learning. Here are some steps to help you plan your Technology Learning Community time:

1. Define who will attend (e.g., grade level of students, teachers who want to participate, administrators, and staff).
2. Set a date and time.
3. Reserve the venue. Make sure the space provides means to safely charge technology equipment. Also, make sure that tables are available.
4. Seek proposals. Have students define what technology tool they would like to share and how it can be used to support learning and other educational goals. This is where you assess the quality of the proposal submissions to make determinations about who will be the expert for the TLC event.
5. Announce the TLC date and time. This will serve to heighten anticipation for the event.
6. Structure a schedule (e.g., Will students be able to stay at each station for as long as they like or are these going to be 10–15 minute sessions?).
7. Have fun!

As you plan the event, you want to remember that although the TLC events will happen at predetermined dates and times, the TLC is something that can and should permeate learning environments throughout every day that students are in school. Here are a few things to consider when planning Technology Learning Communities in your school:

›   *Collaborate.* Because it is a learning community, everyone has to learn how to collaborate and share. These are important skills for students to learn for success in life, and this event provides teachers with the opportunity to model these skills with and for students. Also, don't force anyone into sharing; some students may prefer to learn. Try to develop a spirit of exploration. No one is the expert in this setting! There should be a feeling of supporting each other and learning together.

›   *Create trust.* There are three considerations when seeking to create a sense of trust that will lead to a comfortable environment and true learning. First, these TLC events should not be graded or assessed. Beyond helping students manage their own behavior, there should be no judgment, particularly about the quality of sharing. Second, it is important that teachers are willing to be genuinely interested in the technology tools that students are presenting. As a teacher, consider how you might incorporate what you learn from students at the TLC event within the lessons you design for your classroom, or simply ask questions of the students as you actively engage in learning from them. Third, have students set their own goals for learning during the event. It is helpful if they have considered, in advance, the kind of work they are trying to complete in school. This will support them in preparing a plan for finding the right tools or apps to learn about. To scaffold students' focus, it might be helpful to give them a few questions to consider while they participate in the TLC events:

» How can I use this to help me do my schoolwork?
» How can I use this to help me better manage my time?
» What kind of product could I create with this technology tool?

› *Allow enough time.* It is important to provide presenters (both teachers and students) with enough time to demonstrate the technology tool so that the learning opportunity is meaningful. This would include sufficient time to allow the learner to ask questions and even practice using the tool. The event does not have to take up too much time, but make sure that the time you provide is balanced with the scale of the event you are planning.
› *Be inclusive.* Within the TLC, remember that teachers and students are learning alongside each other. There should be both students and teachers presenting, but you might also consider inviting office staff, members of the parent community, and administrators. Also, while you are endeavoring to be inclusive, don't require students to present. It may be that they will get far more benefit as a learner.
› *Learning is the key.* Finally, although this is a fun and engaging student learning opportunity, it is important to make sure that students use their time well. To that end, you might consider using one of the Visible Thinking Routines (Harvard Project Zero) as a means to debrief the experience. For example, have students share

» 3 things they learned,
» 2 questions they still have, and
» 1 way they plan to use the technology skill or tool in their work.

Technology Learning Communities provide teachers with the opportunity to model the same kind of collaboration and professionalism they experience in their own Professional Learning Communities. For students, the TLC events enable them to take on the role of "expert" and contribute to the community in productive and positive ways. Imagine the vibrant exchanges that will push everyone to grow professionally regardless of whether his or her role is student or teacher. There is always new technology and something new to learn!

Finally, it is important to remember that in all of this talk about technology, the focus should be on the student. The student is central to every tool, innovation, process, or skill we discuss. Learning should be responsive to students' needs, not only in terms of readiness, but also in terms of interests. We also have to consider that students today are different from preceding generations. The students in our classroom today have never known a world without cell phone technology and Internet access. So, let's forget technology for a bit and focus on the students.

CHAPTER 3

Who Are Your Students?

In Need of Talent Development

You have probably picked up this book because you seek effective strategies for serving gifted and talented students in your school or classroom, but do we really know who the gifted are? Most of the time we identify students as gifted and talented for the purposes of providing appropriately challenging learning opportunities, and the criteria tend to center around the idea that these students are atypical learners capable of advanced performance. They are qualitatively different from many of their same-age peers in their cognitive abilities, personality traits, experiences, and/or affective characteristics (Clark, 2002; Renzulli, 1978, 1996; Treffinger, Young, Selby, & Shepardson, 2002). It is certainly important to acknowledge that certain students can easily go beyond the norm for a given group of students, but we have to be careful that we do not narrow the focus too much because it could advance the belief that giftedness is static or unchanging and that once a student is identified as gifted, he or she will always display these unique capacities.

DID YOU KNOW?

The characteristics of gifted individuals are not static in nature and no one individual possesses or displays all of these characteristics all of the time (Renzulli, 1986, 2005; Sternberg, 1997; Treffinger et al., 2002). We have known for decades that giftedness varies among individuals; across gender, cultures, and socioeconomic status; and across disciplines and time (Bloom, 1985; Frasier & Passow, 1994; Reis, 2005; Treffinger et al., 2002). Many experts suggest that giftedness and gifted behaviors appear as a result of the dynamic interaction between internal and external factors, and view giftedness as a developmental process that is fluid or less fixed than previously believed (e.g., Dweck, 2006; Mönks & Katzko, 2005; Renzulli, 1996, 2002).

That is why we like to say that giftedness happens in certain people, at certain times, and under certain circumstances (see Figure 5). Only when all three of these factors come together can an individual express his or her talents and abilities. With this in mind, we have to recognize that sometimes it is easy to see a student's gifts and talents as she creates products that far exceed expectation or as he asks the kinds of questions that set him apart from his peers. At these moments in time, their advanced capacities are clearly illustrated. Then there are those students, sometimes called *late bloomers*, whose gifts and talents may remain hidden from view. Oftentimes, these abilities remain hidden because of the lack of opportunity, resources, or that spark of curiosity that leads to advanced performance in a domain.

Then there are the students whose gifts and talents may be emerging, slowly coalescing as the environment provides new opportunities for growth and the demonstration of talent. In these students, we see glimpses of their potential, but we cannot really define what it is that we see or how to best guide the development of that potential. Take, for example, a student like DeShawn. He was a quiet student, who spoke softly, unless provoked. In his interactions with other students, he volunteered information rarely, and during 26 observations there were only a few instances when DeShawn was fully engaged in the classroom activities, like collaborating with students in Norway via videoconferences, messaging, and e-mail. DeShawn was off-task more often than not and his regular classroom teachers questioned why he was participating in the fifth-grade gifted pull-out program. Then one day, students needed to place their elementary school on a topographical map to describe their work to students in Norway.

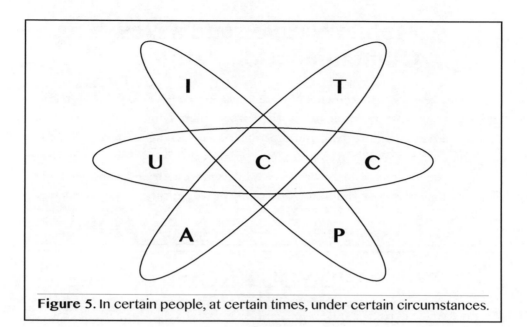

Figure 5. In certain people, at certain times, under certain circumstances.

These gifted fifth graders struggled to determine where their elementary school would be located on a topographical map, a map with no discernable landmarks or roads. As students struggled to place the school on the map, DeShawn's frustration with his classmates was apparent. After watching for a few minutes, DeShawn grabbed the scale drawing of the building he and his classmates were standing in and placed it perfectly on the map. The other students did not trust DeShawn, but after testing and retesting his solution, they finally came to the conclusion that the only right answer was his.

The point here is simply that although not all students are gifted, every student deserves to have his or her potential nurtured so that he or she can express the ability and contribute to the greater good. Some students will excel, reach exceptionally deep levels of understanding, and may even develop solutions to the problems that plague society. The students who excel will be those students who have the capacity, the interest, and the motivation to engage problems and challenges at the highest level and may be gifted. SEM:*Tech* provides the framework for providing advanced-level learning opportunities that challenge *all* students to fulfill their potential and enable gifted students to achieve at a level commensurate with their ability.

That said, we cannot make a plan for developing talent in students without first considering the influence of time and place. The students in our classrooms today are connected via the Internet and mobile technologies in ways that no generation has ever been before.

Mobile Natives and a New Communication Paradigm

Generation Z, also known as Centennials, are considered "mobile-natives" and are even more technologically savvy then their Millennial predecessors. Mobile natives go online daily, and most have access to digital devices linked to the Internet. These children communicate in "likes" and "hearts." This new generation of students increasingly seeks out validation from "friends" and "followers" of which they may have thousands and many of whom they have never actually met.

DID YOU KNOW?

More than half of children 8 to 12 years old have a cell phone (National Consumers League, 2012). As age increases, so too does mobile use. Nearly three-quarters of teens have or have access to a smartphone (Lenhart et al., 2015).

Yet Centennials share a common problem with the former generation of students: They know how to use technology for socializing, but they do not necessarily know how to leverage technology for learning and productivity. It comes as no surprise then, that in a recent research study, the United States ranked 12th out of 31 countries in using digital technology for learning activities like finding websites using hyperlinks and buttons, using charts and graphs to display data, or solving math problems with digital calculators (Organisation for Economic Co-operation and Development [OECD], 2015). As a result of these research findings, the OECD (2015) called on schools to find more effective ways to integrate technology into the classroom and suggested that schools use the kind of pedagogies that require higher order thinking and build deep, conceptual understanding while making the most of technology.

Gifted pedagogy has been focused on higher order thinking and deep conceptual learning since the time of Gen X, a whole two generations ago (Kaplan, 1986; Renzulli, 1976; Renzulli & Reis, 1985; VanTassel-Baska et al., 1988). As a field, we have been demonstrating for more than 40 years that good pedagogy, the kind that develops the talent of all students, is what classrooms need to advance civilization into the future. In recent years, the Common Core State Standards have come on the scene espousing similar goals: a focus on skill development that requires higher order thinking and problem solving. The irony here is that good pedagogy is good pedagogy; technology is not going to change that.

Technology has, however, changed the way we communicate, remember, and produce. For example, the existence of Internet search engines like Google actually changes how and what we remember. According to one researcher, we are more likely to remember things we think are not available online. We are also better at remembering *how* to find something on the Internet than the actual information itself (Sparrow, Liu, & Wegner, 2011). Our attention span is also becoming shorter. In the last decade, our attention span has gone from 12 seconds in the year 2000 to 8 seconds in 2013. Moreover, communications via social media (e.g., Facebook, Instagram, and Twitter) and productivity opportunities on the Internet (e.g., YouTube, Blogspace, Slideshare) have transitioned users from being passive receivers of information to contributing members of a global community.

Because of technology, we are experiencing an era of unprecedented creative productivity. Resnick (2006) suggested that we begin to view the computer more as a paintbrush and less as a technological device. For a moment, think of the digital devices that many of us carry around with us at all times. More than a mere phone, these mobile devices could be viewed as a Swiss Army knife of creative productivity. With this one device, you can take photographs, make comments, record audio or video, edit your creations, and instantly share them with the entire world. And remember, the Internet is becoming not only something we seek, but also something that seeks us. Everyday objects with embedded electronics, software, sensors, and network connectivity (e.g., thermostats, door locks, lights, phones, security systems, etc.) will collect, send, and receive data without human direction. These changes are just the beginning of the interface of technology to humans (e.g., cloud computing, the Internet of Things), humans to technology (the Internet, Web 2.0), and humans to humans (social media).

In the past, we could talk about these shifting trends in communication and productivity as small changes occurring over time. That is no longer the case. There have been, over the last decade, major societal shifts that have broad implications for the future of learning. Therefore, we have to think differently about how we motivate, educate, and engage children, because this generation is unlike any before.

Students at the Center

All too often we deliver curricular content that does not reflect students' interests or what they value. When we are talking about integrating technology into curriculum and instruction, it is important to remember what motivates students to engage in the learning process and that is not the technology itself (Housand & Housand, 2012). Remember, technology is just a part of who these students are. According to experts, to motivate students to engage academically, the curriculum should connect with students' lives, seem real and useful in contexts beyond the classroom, allow for meaningful collaboration, and be sensitive to global concerns. Moreover, the curriculum needs be authentic—focused on real problems and processes, using the conventions of the appropriate discipline, and guided by habits of mind (Hockett, 2009; Kaplan, 1986; Renzulli et al., 2000; Renzulli & Reis, 2014; Tomlinson et al., 2009; VanTassel-Baska, 2011). To get students to engage in that kind of learning and to ensure that they can maintain that engagement over long periods of time, we have to know our students, including what they are interested in outside of school. So, have you asked your students what they are interested in learning about? Have you given them the opportunity to introduce themselves to you—not just who they are as students, but also who they are outside of school?

Within the FutureCasting process (see Chapter 14 for more about FutureCasting), we have an activity in which we invite students to introduce themselves by creating a webpage. The task for students is simple:

> **Student Activity!** Create a website page that tells us who you are as a person. Identify yourself using text, images, and a graphic organization of the page that reflects your personality and communicates who you are as a person.

When we use this with students, we quickly get a sense of who they are and what engages them. Take, for example, the two student pages below. When you look at the first student page (Figure 6), you quickly learn that she likes music, but you can also go deeper and ask:

- › What do you observe about this student?
- › What are her interests?
- › What kind of music does she like?
- › Does she play an instrument? If so, what instrument might she play?
- › What might you be able to infer about her personality given the graphic organization of her webpage?

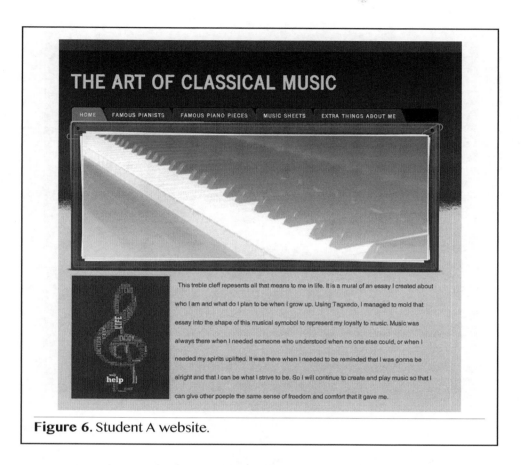

Figure 6. Student A website.

Now look at another student's introductory webpage (Figure 7). Once again, you quickly grasp that she, too, likes music, but look again and ask yourself:

› What are this student's interests?
› Does she have the same interests as the first student?
› What kind of music does this student like?
› How might her interests differ from the first student?
› What might you infer about her personality?

In looking at these pages together, it becomes apparent that a simple webpage reveals an enormous amount about the students. The first student, Student A, was quiet and reserved. She played piano and loved classical music. The second student was very outgoing and loved to socialize. She loved music with solid rhythms and rhyming lyrics like hip-hop and rap. As she developed her website, it quickly became apparent that she was not seeking to be a musician as much as to produce music and help others create music, hence the title of her

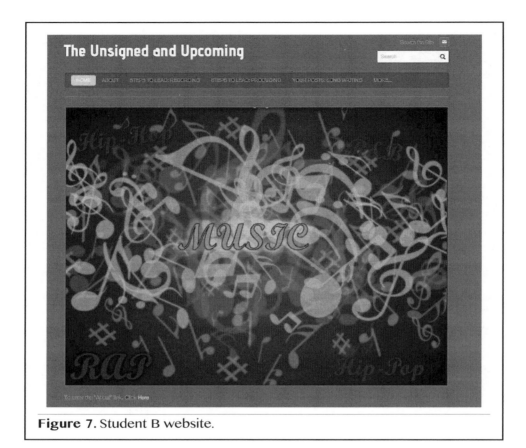

Figure 7. Student B website.

website: "The Unsigned and Upcoming." By simply asking students to introduce themselves with a webpage that includes text, images, and a graphic design that reflects *who* they are, much is communicated and we have set the stage for connecting our curriculum to students' interests, values, and identities.

Interest Inventories

We have to be careful when we seek to ascertain students' interests. One great way to find out what students are interested in is to employ the use of interest inventories. There are numerous inventories on the market, but one of the problems we find is that these inventories are so focused on "school" that they do not really assess the students' interests, but rather topics that are in the curriculum that they might be able to connect to the students. In other words, the inventories start with the idea, "We have a curriculum in place; now which student is interested in what part of that curriculum?" Our goal is to learn as much as we can about the student. Then, we can work to develop the skills and dispositions that will provide students with the transferrable abilities to be successful.

Create an Interest Inventory Online

There are myriad online tools you can use to create what essentially amounts to a survey. Examples include SurveyMonkey, SoGoSurvey, Google Forms, SurveyPlanet, and so forth. The goal for you is to select a tool that is affordable, serves your needs, and that you are willing to spend the time to learn. In general, you will need a tool that allows you to develop, deliver, and collect data.

Things you will want in a survey tool:

1. The ability to add your own questions. Sample questions are provided in the Interest Inventory Examples section starting on page 52.

2. Support for determining the type of question (e.g., multiple choice, short answer text, paragraph text, scaled response, grid, choose from a list, select all that apply, etc.). Typically, this support comes in the form of a list of options that you can select for each question you develop. This way you do not have to program any of the functions of the survey because they are already built in for you (Figure 8).

3. Space for providing instructions or other pure text information for the overall survey, as well as instructions or additional text that might be used in support of specific questions. For example, you want to provide the users with instructions about how to answer the questions and the purpose of your survey. These would be considered general instructions. You might also want to add to a particular question a phrase like, "check all that apply" so that the user knows that while options are provided, he or she is not limited to only choosing one (Figure 9).

4. The ability to order and reorder questions as you develop the survey over time.

5. The ability to preview the survey and test the data collection processes. You want to be able to test how the survey works and how the data is collected and presented on the backside (Figure 10).

6. The ability to skip questions. In some cases you might want to be able to include the ability to go to a specific question based on the users response. For example, you might ask, "Have you ever built a robot?" and provide only two options for the answers (yes or no). If the user says "Yes," you can design the survey to direct the user to additional questions about building a robot. If the user says "No," than it would not make sense to answer more questions about building a robot, so you would design the survey to skip the follow-up questions when the answer to your question was "No" (Figure 11).

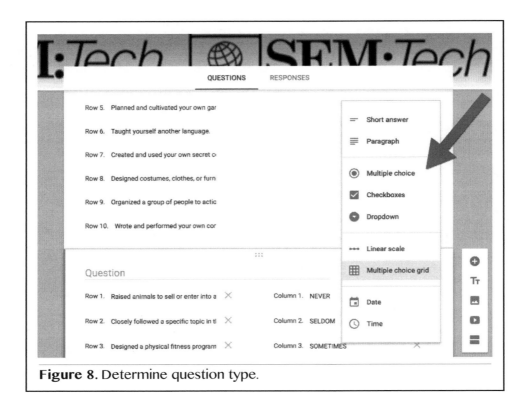

Figure 8. Determine question type.

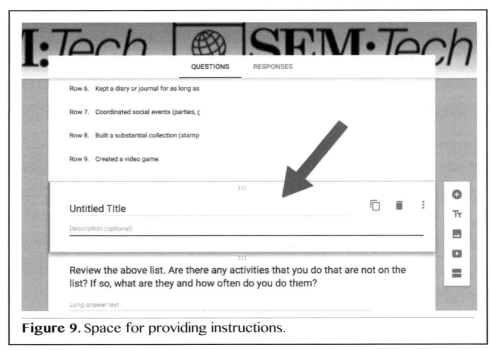

Figure 9. Space for providing instructions.

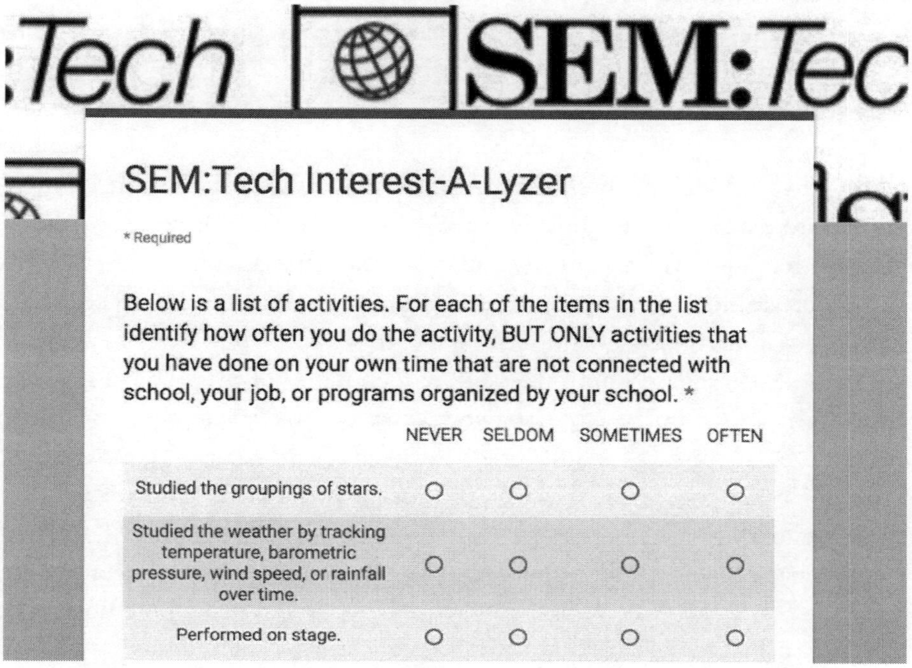

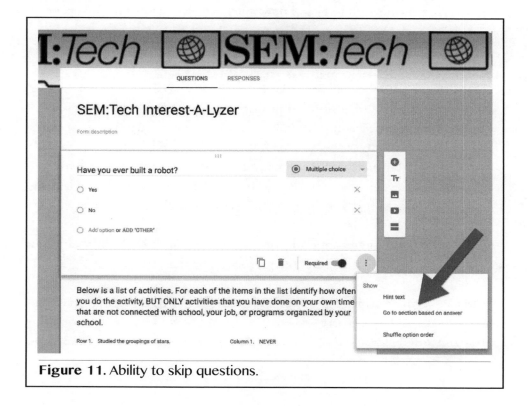

Figure 10. Opportunity to preview.

Figure 11. Ability to skip questions.

7. The ability to share the survey using a URL or direct invitation via e-mail. This is how you direct users to your survey—the less labor-intensive the process, the better (Figure 12).
8. The ability to easily access and download the data you have collected.

How do you decide which survey tool is the right tool for you? First, take some time to read about the tool. There may be instructions provided by the tool developer that allow you to quickly and clearly see the capabilities of the survey tool and determine if it suits your needs. Second, test the tool. Does it seem fairly easy to use? Could others in your school use this tool? Would they be willing to use this tool? There is nothing worse than a clunky tool that requires multiple clicks to achieve a simple goal. Also, who wants to look at an ugly tool? Keep in mind that visual appeal is as important in this day and age as the functionality. As you begin the process of selecting the survey tool that is right for you, consider the following:

› What can you afford? There are free options available online and a simple search for "free online survey tools" will deliver a whole host of options. Just make sure that if you are collecting student data that you have a way to protect that information or have permission from parents for collecting that information with a digital survey.
› What is your skill level and how much time are you willing to spend to learn how to use the tool? Any tool will take a little bit of time to learn, but the less complicated the tool, the easier it will be to use quickly and effectively.
› Does the tool have all of the functionality you need now and might need in the future? It is helpful to prioritize your needs so that when you are making this decision you can focus on what you need most.
› What do you want the data to look like at the end? Does the tool provide data in a format that is easy for you to use and enables you to export to data management and analysis software that you are comfortable using (e.g., Microsoft Excel, Google Sheets, or professional data analysis software like SPSS or SAS)?
› Is the tool visually appealing and easy to navigate for both the person developing the survey and the person taking the survey?

As you begin creating your online survey, there may be times that you experience difficulties. Don't worry—there is a legion of people who have tried this tool or software before you! Whatever difficulty you encounter, your question

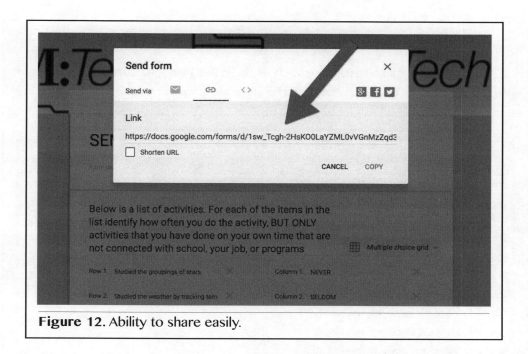

Figure 12. Ability to share easily.

can probably be answered with a simple search online. What if you want to know how to skip three questions when someone answers "No" to your robot question? Simply search for "how to skip questions using (insert your tool name here)." You will get access to blog posts, videos, and even the company's version of an answer. Just remember, if you have the question, it is highly likely that someone before you has had the same question.

It goes without saying that once you create an interest inventory for your students, you will have developed the requisite skills to help your students create their own surveys for the purposes of data gathering, research projects, and polling. Figure 13 includes two examples of interest inventories you could use with your students.

Interest Inventory Example 1

Below is a list of activities. For each of the items in the list, identify how often you do the activity, *but only* activities that you have done on your own time that are not connected with school, your job, or programs organized by your school.

	Never	Seldom	Some-times	Often
Wrote a short story, play, or poem.				
Repaired a computer, machine, game system, or piece of furniture.				
Wrote a blog.				
Produced a vlog.				
Conducted a science experiment.				
Took artistic photographs.				
Created a portfolio of artistic works.				
Organized a team, club, or "gang."				
Started a band or was a member of band.				
Created an app.				
Studied the groupings of stars.				
Studied the weather by tracking temperature, barometric pressure, wind speed, or rainfall over time.				
Performed on stage.				
Started your own business to make money.				
Posted a music video on YouTube.				
Created an original musical mash-up.				
Wrote your own song, opera, or musical.				
Created a movie.				
Posted an original movie (created by you) to YouTube.				
Built or designed a vehicle.				
Built or designed a robot.				
E-mailed a public official or politician.				
Learned to play a musical instrument on your own.				
Learned a craft (weaving, woodworking, sewing, quilting, jewelry making, etc.).				
Planned and cultivated your own garden.				
Taught yourself another language.				
Created and used your own secret code.				
Designed costumes, clothes, or furniture.				

Figure 13. Interest inventory examples.

	Never	Seldom	Some-times	Often
Organized a group of people to action (canned food drive, recycling campaign, home goods for active military personnel, community garden, etc.).				
Wrote and performed your own comedy routines.				
Raised animals to sell or enter into a show or contest.				
Closely followed a specific topic in the news (politics, fashion, literature, foreign conflict, etc.).				
Designed a physical fitness program for yourself (running, yoga, weight lifting, cycling).				
Choreographed a dance routine.				
Made and recorded observations of people or animals on a regular basis.				
Kept a diary or journal for as long as a year at a time.				
Coordinated social events (parties, group outings, trips, vacations, etc.).				
Built a substantial collection (stamps, sharks' teeth, comic books, coins, action figures, etc.).				
Created a video game.				

Review the above list. Are there any activities that you do that are not on the list? If so, what are they and how often do you do them?

_____

_____

_____

_____

Review the above list. Determine which three activities you do most often and highlight them. If you could change what you do most often, would you? If yes, what would you like to spend time doing? If no, why not?

_____

_____

_____

_____

Figure 13. *continued*

Interest Inventory Example 2

Writing Prompts: Remember the Future?

These writing prompts are provided to help you consider your interests and how you like to spend your time. Choose at least two of the writing prompts below and answer the questions. For each prompt you choose, write as if you were creating an entry into a journal: Free flow your thoughts without editing.

1. Pretend that you have been asked to select the keynote speaker for your graduation. Who would you invite? Why? To answer this question, you may want to consider a person you admire or who has inspired you in some way. Make sure to describe what makes him or her special and how he or she might inspire the graduating class.

2. Imagine that you have a means to travel through space and time (for example, a Tardis or a time machine) and you see *yourself* as a 30-year-old person. You want to know more about this person, so you do some research. What were this person's most "creative" accomplishments? How did this person contribute to his or her social circles, community, or society as a whole? What do you think this person might do next?

3. Pretend that you have become a famous blogger with a worldwide following:
    ›   What is the title of your blog?
    ›   What is your blog about?
    ›   Who is your audience?
    ›   Which blog entry had the most favorites? What was the topic and title of the blog entry?
    ›   How does your blog influence people's thinking?

4. Pretend you have been selected for the first human transit space mission to Mars. You are allowed to take five personal possessions to be used in your free time. List the five items you would take. Why did you choose these items? If you could only take one of the five items, which would it be and why is it the one you would choose?

5. Imagine that you have the opportunity to travel through space and time to meet one famous person (living or dead) of your choice. Who would it be and why? What would you ask when you met him or her?

Note. Adapted from *The Interest-A-Lyzer: Adult version* by J. S. Renzulli, 2010, Waco, TX: Prufrock Press. Copyright 2010 by Prufrock Press. Adapted with permission.

Figure 13. *continued*

CHRISTY'S CORNER: HELPING STUDENTS COMMUNICATE THEIR INTERESTS

Christy expressed that her students consistently have a hard time thinking about topics they want to learn about that reflect an interest they have outside of school. In an effort to really get students to think big, she gives each student a large piece of paper. She says that the scale of the paper provides students with the visual understanding that she really wants them to "think big." Some of the questions Christy uses to scaffold students' thinking are:

› What if you could learn whatever you wanted?
› What problems could you solve?
› What do you wonder?
› What question have you always wanted the answer to?
› What do you think you could do if you were given the time?
› How do you spend your time when you are not in school?
› If you could learn anything in the world, what would it be?

Using the questions, and with some superhero music playing in the background for added effect, she asked students to create circle maps of things they were interested in. As soon as they started writing things in their circles, students asked: "Well, is this okay? Can I write this?" One student asked, "Can I write skateboarding?" and Christy said, "Yes, is that what you like to do?" and he said, "Yeah, that is all I like to do." Many students asked a variation of this question, essentially: "You mean it is **really** about what I like and it is okay to like something that is not part of the core curriculum?" To all of those questions, Christy answered, "Yes, there are no wrong answers."

When students started to get stuck, she would help them go deeper by asking questions like, "What questions do you have about skateboarding?" This allowed them to continue articulating exactly what they wanted to learn and gave Christy clear direction for framing Type I experiences and supporting students' Type III productivity.

After students completed their circle maps, they hung them on the wall around the perimeter of the minitheater, an open space outside the classroom. Then students conducted a "museum walk," where they had the opportunity to review the ideas of their classmates. Each student walked around with his or her clipboard or an iPad writing app, looking at and taking notes on what other people were interested in. This really served to expand their thinking further, as they were able to build off the ideas of their classmates to think about their own ideas in different ways or to take their original ideas in different directions.

PART II

Technology Enhancements for the Enrichment Triad Model

CHAPTER 4

Type I—
Curiosity and
Exposure

"I have no special talent. I am only passionately curious."
—Albert Einstein

Type I experiences expose students to a variety of topics, areas of potential interest, fields of study, occupations, people, places, and events. These exposure experiences are not the kind of learning encounters students might see in more traditional educational settings. Instead, these exposure experiences take on a sense of adventure and wonderment as the world beyond the classroom walls is revealed to students in a way that delights yet still helps them develop meaning for their own lives. Type I experiences are intentionally designed with three primary objectives:

1. Enrich the lives of students by expanding the scope of their experience.
2. Stimulate new interests that might lead to more episodes of curiosity or intensive follow-up like that of a Type III experience.
3. Provide direction for making meaningful decisions about the kinds of skill, content, and processes (Type II experiences) that should be selected for a particular student or group of students.

Curiosity and Delight

Type I experiences can take on many forms. Naturally occurring Type I experiences might happen on a family vacation as a child sees the mountains, the ocean, or the Grand Canyon for the first time. Questions abound at the foreignness of something they have only ever seen on TV or in pictures; these questions are the purest form of curiosity. How did the mountains get here? Why does the ocean smell that way? Why doesn't it look like that in the pictures? All of these questions have the potential to lead to deeper levels of curiosity. Type I experiences are not relegated to extreme events like a family vacation. The same kind of experiences can be planned and delivered in educational settings, with similar outcomes—curiosity, delight, and the awareness that there is always more to learn in life.

At the heart of a Type I experience is the element of curiosity. Human beings are naturally curious. We seek out answers to our questions about the world around us. For many youngsters, this quest for truth and understanding results in a seemingly insatiable curiosity that often plagues anyone who is willing to listen and respond to incessant questions of *why* and *how come?* No longer is a question something deemed to be addressed at some future time, nor are all of the answers to those questions the acumen of teachers. With laptop computers, tablets, and smartphones, technology-rich environments provide ready access to vast quantities of information. The answer to their questions may well exist in knowledge beyond what the teacher possesses, but curiosity about the answers persists.

Think of curiosity as an episode that happens in three stages. The first stage of curiosity is the trigger. This is where some kind of stimulus leads to a question or need for information. Recall the family vacation scenario: The moment the student rolled down the window of the car and got a whiff of the salt air and maybe some seaweed that had come ashore, the question was, "Why does the ocean smell like that?" The smells are a trigger to a moment of genuine uncertainty—one could imagine a million different reasons why it smells, but the answer to the question is genuinely unknown. The trigger is followed by a reaction, like seeking out the answer to the question. Once that question is answered, this episode of curiosity is resolved. Learning is dependent upon whether the episode of curiosity was satisfied or not. If the curiosity is not satisfied, learning in that instance does not occur and the impetus for the next episode of curiosity is negated (Arnone, Small, Chauncey, & McKenna, 2011). Think of it this way: The instant that moment of curiosity is resolved, one of two things can happen: (1) the student is satisfied, suggesting that he or she may not have been intensely interested, and the cycle of curiosity, and thus learning, ends; or (2) the answer to the question leads to another question. This new question becomes the trigger in the next episode of curiosity. When curiosity is fed, it can continue for minutes, hours, weeks, or even a lifetime.

DID YOU KNOW?

Although intelligence is the single most powerful predictor of an individual's academic success, effort combined with intellectual curiosity rivals that of intelligence alone. Having a "hungry mind" may be underestimated when it comes to students' academic achievement (von Stumm, Hell, & Camorro-Premuzic, 2011).

Information-level learning can meaningfully scaffold deeper and more complex meaning-making, thus supporting and sustaining curiosity, which can be a powerful motivator. As teachers, we want to create these episodes for our students. If only we had the budget to take all of our students to the Grand Canyon. Right? This is where technology steps in as a powerful tool to open a window onto the world. Students who may never have traveled out of the county or province in which they were born now have unprecedented access to all levels and domains of knowledge and opportunities to view parts of the world that only the most expertly trained individuals dare to explore. Imagine spelunking in the alien world of Luray Caverns in Virginia's Shenandoah Valley or following an astronaut on an untethered space walk outside the International Space Station. Virtual experiences cannot replace the intensity and richness of firsthand experiences (at least not yet) but they do provide glimpses of the possibilities the world has to offer.

The access students have to new information goes beyond observing. Now students can participate and do so in a global society. They can learn the languages and cultures of people from across the globe or across the state. Technology affords curious gifted students with almost limitless opportunities for exploration and the development of their interests. The sheer amount of information and resources can be overwhelming. Therefore, teachers have to help direct students toward potentially worthwhile and meaningful experiences in a way that leads to meaningful curiosity for students.

DID YOU KNOW?

The more curious we are, the more likely we are to enjoy strong relationships and life happiness. Curious people actually live longer, too (Kashdan & Steger, 2007; Swan & Carmelli, 1996).

Our objective is not simply to inform, but rather to provoke curiosity about the dynamic nature of a field and incite the desire to pursue further research or seek deeper levels of knowledge. We want students to delight in learning so that they "feel compelled to become an investigator in areas where some curiosity or concern has been motivated" (Renzulli, 1976, p. 323). We want students to have an experience that moves them.

Naturally occurring Type I experiences have merit. Certainly students have found passion areas without the support or direction of teachers, but true Type I experiences are purposefully designed with clear objectives, yet are also loosely structured to ensure that freedom, joy, and true exploration are maintained as part of the overall event. A great Type I experience does not happen by accident, but instead is the result of careful planning and preparation. Only educators possess the knowledge and expertise to engineer these nuanced experiences for students.

True Type I experiences are teacher-initiated for the whole class, small group, or for an individual student. Type I experiences are dynamic events that are planned in advance and engage students. The SEM:*Tech* Type I experiences have a distinctive three-part structure, so let's break it down.

Creating Dynamic Experience

Experience, whether it springs from a product, process, project, or performance, is an encounter made possible by and understood through the senses. An effective experience stays with us, it elicits feelings, and it puts us in touch with our emotions. Understanding the factors involved in producing an experience that changes how we think, feel, or behave is what makes the design of a Type I interesting and engaging. To make an experience memorable and to incite curiosity, look to form these three stages:

› *Stage 1: Heighten anticipation.* This can be considered as the moment leading up to the event. It is the moment ripe with possibility. Previous experience might come into play as students hope for something, but for what, they may not know. There is likely some uncertainty in this phase. A sense of adventure in the unknown sparkles through the air.

› *Stage 2: Stimulate interest.* This is the main moment of exposure. It is an occurrence that may bring all of that anticipation into focus on a single point in space and time. Something develops during this event, but being able to clearly define it may be impossible. At this point, the sense of adventure created in the anticipation phase has not diminished, merely changed into something more easily grasped by the mind.

› *Stage 3: Deepen understanding.* This is not an academic endeavor of merely answering questions about the observable aspects of the experience. Instead, this is a phase of exploration that helps students define what it is that they felt, thought, heard, saw, touched, smelled, or tasted during the event. The debrief is *not* an academic assessment, but rather an opportunity for students to make meaning of the event and connect the myriad sensations to the reality of who they are and what they value, to place the event into their own realm of understanding, or to bring light to the importance of a shared moment.

When you are able to effectively implement these three stages, you create the opportunity to go beyond, the opportunity to go deeper into the content or help students form the need to learn new skills and processes. Think of it this way: If after a Type I experience a student or students realize they need to know more, are inspired to ask more, produce more, share more, engage more, learn more, and ultimately achieve more, you have created the opportunity for them to go deeper. Being prepared for this moment is difficult, but being flexible enough to adapt and respond to this moment is the essence of artful teaching. This opportunity is the bridge to more intensive follow-up learning by individuals or groups of students (a.k.a. Type III) or it can provide direction for selecting and planning processes that will continue the episodes of curiosity and learning (a.k.a. Type II).

Initially, Type I experiences may be challenging to create, but remember, if you keep students' interests in mind, you will start to see the potential for Type I experiences in myriad places, people, and sources. After a while, you will be able to imagine almost anything as a Type I experience, or at least the "event" portion of a Type I experience. It is important to remember that the real secret to a Type I experience is helping students connect with the experience. The debrief, for example, provides the opportunity for students to ask "how come?", ponder "why?", or simply consider "What does this mean to me?" It is vitally important that we debrief the event as it provides the bridge to going deeper or, in this case, opportunities to go beyond.

The adage, "The sum of the parts is greater than the whole," could not be more true. Meaningful, memorable, emotionally engaging, unusual, and unexpected experiences influence the way students perceive learning and feel about the Type I experience as a transition to deeper exploration. So as you begin the planning process, ask yourself: Are you willing and able to change with your students? Are you ready and equipped to create meaningful experiences that keep them hooked? See Figure 14 for the Type I Planner template.

A successful Type I experience is not just an opportunity for the students. It is an opportunity for teachers. The entire process of planning, delivering, and responding to the Type I experience is ripe with information about how to proceed with future experiences. A Type I should not be a one-time event; rather, there should be numerous and varied events over the course of an academic year. Before, during, and after the Type I experience, it is important to listen to your students. What are they sharing and what are they saying about the experience? Pay careful attention to what students reflect back to you because that information will help you replicate and optimize future Type I experiences as well as plan pertinent enrichment clusters. This is how to engineer and further develop Type I experiences for your students:

1. Listen to your students—whether you use information from one of the many interest inventories or simply ask them what they do outside of school. What engages them when adults aren't looking, when they are left to their own devices?

2. Seek to learn about your students as their journey with the experience unfolds. What questions do they ask and what information do they seek? In what situations do they talk about the experience? What and who influences their thinking about the experience?

3. Engage students based on their expectations. What was their "aha" moment? What aspects of the experience provided value? When were they most engaged?

4. Adapt your processes, strategies, technology tools, and time investment to improve the first three steps.

Technology's Role in the Type I Experience

Just because you can use technology doesn't mean you have to use technology. Certainly, searching online can make the process more efficient, particularly when you are looking for something specific (e.g., recycling at the nearby university). If you have access to guest speakers who can take the time off of work or are willing to find time in their busy schedule, that is great! Technology is a tool,

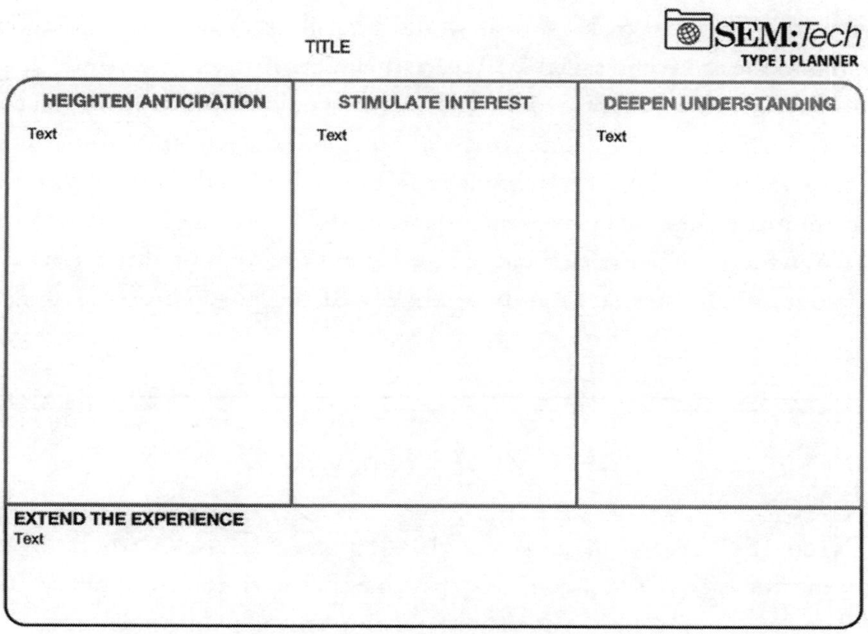

Figure 14. Type I planner.

and just because it is available, does not mean that it is always the best option. Ask yourself:

› Is the use of technology supporting the learning process for students?
› Is the use of technology making instruction better, easier, or more efficient?
› Is the use of technology providing students with the opportunity to learn or develop specific technology skills?

The answer to at least one of these questions should be "yes." If the answers to these questions are "no," then we have to ask ourselves: Why have we chosen to use the technology? Are we using technology for the sake of using technology? Is it merely an add-on so that we can say we used technology? It is important to remember that good pedagogy is the most important thing to consider when working with students. The technology cannot make a bad lesson good, but it can help to make a good lesson easier, more efficient, and more in keeping with how students function—with a piece of technology always at the ready.

You might think about it this way: In the past, showing a video to students was a big event. We had to reserve the TV cart, roll the cart into the classroom on our very short break, make sure the DVD player was hooked up properly, and test the DVD to make sure it would actually play. As soon as students walked into the room and saw the TV cart, their anticipation was already heightened—"We get to see a movie today!" Then, you would play the movie that could be anywhere between 15 minutes to a half hour, and the students would remain engaged the entire time. The technology in this case (i.e., the DVD player and TV cart) made the movie an event in and of itself. For the kids, it was more about "watching a movie" than being excited about the content of the movie. The technology took center stage and overshadowed the purpose of watching the movie.

DID YOU KNOW?

Tweens (8–12 years old) and teens (13–18 years old) have 4:36 to 6:40 hours of screen time each day, not counting the time they spend in front of screens at school or doing homework. The majority of this time is spent watching TV and online videos (Common Sense Media, 2016).

Students today spend an enormous amount of time in front of screens watching videos and playing games. Videos specifically and technology generally are no longer themselves an event for these students. Our role in the Type I experience has become to help students connect the event to their own lives. In the example of the teacher showing a video, we have to help students see how the video might be relevant to their interests, their identities, and their personal aspirations. We also have to consider what kind of video will keep a modern student engaged. Students' attention spans are short and the pace that they like to get information is fast and compact. Consider using videos that employ jump cuts, a film-editing technique that gives the impression of jumping forward in time. Also, humor is always a plus. The most important thing to remember: Just because it is interesting to you does not mean that it will be interesting to the students. Take, for example, the 2008 Emmy-winning seven-part miniseries *John Adams*. If you love history, this series demonstrates the pivotal role John Adams played in the American Revolution with true cinematic beauty and dramatic style. It was also a true history lesson and in order to sit through this lengthy lesson, you either have to love history or have the maturity to want to learn—traits our students do not necessarily possess. So, just as we ask students to consider their audience in the creation of Type III products, so, too, we ask you to consider your audience for a Type I experience—the students.

DID YOU KNOW?

Students engage more with shorter videos. The optimal video length is 6 minutes or shorter. After 6 minutes, engagement in a video drops dramatically. In one study, when students were presented with a 12-minute video, they only watched, on average, 3 minutes of the video. However, when students were given a 6-minute video, they would typically watch until the end (Guo, 2013).

As the role of technology in students' lives evolves, we have to consider how the use of technology evolves in the Type I experience. Technology provides a window to the world, but it does not necessarily provide an equivalent experience. Take, for example, viewing the Eiffel Tower. This is not an opportunity that we can likely plan as a field trip because it would be expensive, logistically challenging, and the educational relevance might be difficult to justify. Technology provides the opportunity for students to see the Eiffel Tower in thousands of uploaded images, in real time using EarthCam (http://www.earthcam.com/world/france/paris/?cam=eiffeltower_hd), and even in a virtual tour (http://www.3dmekanlar.com/en/eiffel-tower.html). Google Maps provides amazing opportunities to see views of Paris from the tower and views from streets below. Even more immersive, Google Cardboard allows you to virtually stand at the base of the Eiffel Tower and turn in any direction to see the surrounding area. It is truly amazing to visually experience standing on the street in front of the Eiffel Tower, but missing from all of these experiences are the sounds of the French language, cars honking on the road, leaves blowing in the trees, or the clanking of the elevator as it ascends with passengers to the top. Gone is the experience of waiting in line and observing international culture and language as you wait alongside people from around the globe. Also missing is that shared experience in line of being slightly bored but very excited to be going to the top. We are not suggesting that everyone see the Eiffel Tower (it is shorter than you might expect anyway). The point here is that technology is a powerful tool, but it does not and should not replace experiences like going to see a theater production, visiting museums, attending readings at a library, or experiencing guest speakers in person. Technology *does* allow students to have experiences that they might not have otherwise gotten the opportunity to experience, but it is still imperfect, so it is important to balance face-to-face experiences with technology-supported Type I experiences. Before you can begin creating Type I experiences, we first have to identify sources of information on a variety of topics, disciplines, issues, occupations, hobbies, persons, places, and events. The source of all information is people.

Building a Community of Experts

Who are the experts in your community? In the community of the school, that could be students with intense interests or passions for specific topics who have become the resident "experts." It might also be the teachers, who may have the most advanced knowledge and expertise on a given topic. Or there may be staff or administrators who have skills they use outside of work to support their hobbies. There are any number of potential experts within the school, so imagine how many experts will be available when you extend your search beyond the school walls. This could include parents of students in the school, members of the regional community, or any number of experts from across the globe! With technology, building a community of experts allows you to cast a wide net or narrowly focus your search to one specific topic or person.

CHRISTY'S CORNER: BUILDING A COMMUNITY OF EXPERTS

Christy started building her community of experts by soliciting the parents of students in the school. A great way to do this is to simply send out an e-mail request. Include within the e-mail a link to a brief survey that gathers information about parents' interests, hobbies, and careers as well as contact information and whether or not they would like to share their knowledge with students in the school. Christy has used this technique with great success, garnering help from a local university professor who makes movies, a professional computer programmer, and more! She found that once parents had the opportunity to share their knowledge and expertise with the students, word spread and there was no shortage of people willing to share their time and energy. Of the experience, Christy said:

> I started by soliciting parent and community resources that I thought were valuable based on student interests. I asked parents if they had a talent, skill, or passion that they would be willing to share. Once I asked, it just started snowballing!

Christy went beyond the parent community. For example, arts and the environment kept coming up on students' interest surveys. She kept this in mind. One Sunday, she was out and about and came across a store called Re-eco Design. The store provides products for the eco-conscious consumer. The Re-eco team consists of four artists who specialize in upcycling or creating art from reclaimed and recycled materials. Christy went to the owner and asked, "Would you be willing to do an enrichment cluster on upcycling with my students?" He said "yes" and Christy found herself asking all around town. At the local grocery store, she asked, "Do you have a community service program about recycling?" Christy also used Google for local sources, where she found information about the recycling program at the local university. Anyone who might be able to provide students with expert knowledge in their area of interest found themselves at the other end of the question, "Would you be willing to share your expert knowledge with my students?" The key here is that Christy asked. Over and over she asked. The worst anyone could say was "no," but as Christy found, more often than not, people were happily willing to share their expertise with students, whether through a presentation, enrichment cluster activities, via Skype, or a field trip opportunity.

With just a little effort and the willingness to take a risk—by asking—Christy attained a new level of responsiveness to her students. Now, she is doing a much better job of matching her students' interests to the talent pool of the community.

CHAPTER 5

Type I— Engaging Students

Heighten Anticipation

As you begin the process of creating a Type I, it is important to consider the journey that students will experience. What is the story you are trying to tell? What do you want students to get excited about? The attractions at Disney World spring to mind when thinking about how to craft a Type I. What sets Disney parks apart from other amusement parks is the story that is told with each and every ride. For example, at Disney World one does not simply ride a rollercoaster; instead, each phase of the experience is enveloped in a story that often starts before you even get to the line. The structures leading up to the attraction, the elements one is confronted with in the line, and being buckled into the seat are all part of the attraction. One is involved in a story throughout the entire experience. Likewise, a Type I should involve the learner in a thoughtful sequence of stages that enables the learner to get excited and curious about what will happen next. Students should be engulfed in a story or an experience that is unlike regular curricular experiences.

Recall, there are three stages in a well-crafted Type I experience:
› *Stage 1: Heighten anticipation.* The moments leading up to the event that create uncertainty.
› *Stage 2: Stimulate interest.* The main moment of exposure that engages students and brings their attention into focus.

> › *Stage 3: Deepen understanding.* A debrief that helps students understand what they felt, thought, heard, saw, touched, smelled, or tasted during the event.

Teachers have long understood the importance of setting the stage for a lesson or hooking students at the beginning of a lesson. In *Mastery Teaching*, Hunter (1982) outlined the importance of anticipatory sets or short activities to focus student attention before the actual lesson. However, Hunter's lessons are often very prescriptive in their design and implementation. However, Stage 1: *Heighten Anticipation* is meant to be a very brief activity or series of questions to pique students' curiosity or spark their imagination and to provide a purpose for the students to keep in mind as they move deeper into the Type I experience.

In the *Incubation Model of Teaching: Getting Beyond the Aha!*, Torrance and Safter (1990) emphasized the importance of heightening anticipation before an activity begins. This is akin to stretching before exercising and is an attempt to prepare the mind for thinking.

The purpose of this stage is not to deliver or teach content, but is instead meant to heighten the desire to know and do more. Although there is no one way to accomplish this, we suggest that you consider one of the following ways for heightening anticipation:

1. *Point to ponder.* Begin with an intriguing idea or thought.
2. *Tickle the imagination.* Begin with an intriguing or puzzling image.
3. *Provide examples and nonexamples.* Share something that is an example and something that is definitely not an example.

Point to Ponder

Beginning with an intriguing thought or idea provides an accessible entry point into the lesson. This is often accomplished through the use of quotations. Consider the frequency with which a book, journal article, or even a movie begins with a quotation. This serves to provide a frame of reference from where to begin. Quotations can provide both clarification as well as a puzzle to solve. Consider beginning your Type I experience this way. When selecting a quotation, find one that provides students with something that is open to interpretation. For example, consider this quote from Mark Twain that was retrieved from Goodreads:

> There is no such thing as a new idea. It is impossible. We simply take a lot of old ideas and put them into a sort of mental kaleidoscope. We give them a turn and they make new and curious

combinations. We keep on turning and making new combinations indefinitely, but they are the same old pieces of colored glass that have been in use through all the ages.

There are multiple perspectives from which this quote can be discussed and a variety of topics that it could serve to introduce. Students might choose to view this from the point of view of original thought or creativity. It might lead to a discussion of copyright or intellectual property, or it could serve to demonstrate that the more things change, the more that they stay the same. Alternatively, it could serve as a lead-in to discussion of the process of iteration. The key point here is that it provides students with something new to consider and think deeply about to start their discussion and investigation. A quotation should serve as an invitation to begin wondering about things and asking questions.

Although gathering quotations was once an act of clipping articles or jotting down notes and placing them in a folder, access to the Internet has significantly increased our ability to find exactly the right quote for almost every situation. Gone are the days of scouring through *Bartlett's Familiar Quotations*. To help you in your quest for the perfect quote to serve as your point to ponder, we suggest that you consider the following resources:

› *BrainyQuote* (http://www.brainyquote.com) is one of the oldest quotation sites on the Internet and claims to be the largest. There is a broad collection of quotations featuring prominent historical figures as well as current newsmakers. Quotations are arranged by author and by topic. Additionally, a search feature makes finding a specific quote even easier. BrainyQuote also features a collection of quotes with inspiring nature images.

› *Goodreads* (https://www.goodreads.com/quotes) is primarily a social network for book readers, but the quotes section provides a comprehensive collection of thought-provoking quotations pulled from the pages of books featured on the site. Quotations are arranged by author as well as by recent additions and most popular quotes. The collection is also categorized into 1,000 different subjects that can be either searched or browsed through.

› *The Quotations Page* (http://www.quotationspage.com) was established in 1994 and contains more than 28,000 quotations from 3,400 authors. Like the previous sources, you may explore by author or subject, or you may choose to search their collection.

> › *Bartleby* (http://www.bartleby.com/quotations) presents a collection of classic books in an online format. Here you can peruse through historical collections of quotations, including *Bartlett's Familiar Quotations* published in 1919 and *Hoyt's New Cyclopedia of Practical Quotations* from 1922.
>
> › *Wikiquote* (https://en.wikiquote.org) is a project from Wikimedia Commons, the collective behind Wikipedia. This resource has the same look and feel as Wikipedia, and it also allows users to contribute to and edit the collection. Featuring more than 26,000 articles, Wikiquote contains quotations from literary works, films, television shows, and other notable people.
>
> › Although many sites devoted specifically to quotations exist, you might also turn to *Pinterest* (https://www.pinterest.com/categories/quotes) to see what others are collecting and talking about. This is a place to start for all quotations, but you can also search within Pinterest for quotations on particular topics or by a certain author. Because Pinterest tends to be more visual in its formatting, most of the quotations you will find here are already part of some intriguing image or visual. From here, you can easily share a thought-provoking quote with a visually appealing image.

Finally, do not forget about simply using a Google search to look for quotations on the topic you are introducing. We suggest that you combine your topic with the word "quote" or "quotation" for the best results. However, in our many searches for quotations, we are typically led to one of the sources that we have already covered. When searching Google for quotations, we encourage you to also examine the options available in Google Images (https://images.google.com). Here you will find a huge collection of quotations that have been posted online as images that typically contain a photo of the speaker or a visually interesting combination of fonts and images to further heighten the anticipation of your students.

Tickle the Imagination

Although quotations may serve well as a point to ponder, we all recall the saying that a picture is worth a thousand words. The use of an intriguing or puzzling image can serve to tickle the imagination of your students as they begin a Type I experience. By tickle, we mean to delight, entertain, or excite agreeably. The idea is to help students start to imagine what might be coming up in their Type I experience.

›   The *Library of Congress* (https://www.loc.gov/law/find/collections.php) offers more than 250 different online collections of some of their extensive catalog of holdings. Here you can view photographs, maps, letters, diaries, and newspapers throughout history. From this collection, you might choose to provide a historical perspective of a modern exploration so that students might begin considering how things have changed or remained the same over time.

›   The *National Archives* (http://www.archives.gov) provides another substantial collection of digital images and artifacts to explore. The most efficient way to navigate this extensive resource is through the search feature. However, the National Archives also provide a useful collection of teachers' resources and activities (http://www.archives.gov/education). Perhaps the most intriguing resource from this site is DocsTeach (http://docsteach.org). Here thousands of primary source documents related to the history of the United States are collected and organized by historical era. This includes a range of images including photographs, documents, maps, and letters. In addition to the collection of documents, DocsTeach features a collection of activities (http://docsteach.org/activities) that have students utilizing primary source documents to develop historical thinking by completing tasks such as finding a sequence, focusing on details, mapping history, and weighing the evidence. Although these activities are definitely engaging, they do extend well beyond the idea of tickling the imagination of your students. That being said, choice activities could be utilized as either Type I experience or Type II training exercises for interested students.

›   *LIFE Magazine* has long served as a source for interesting and historical photographs that were presented to gifted students throughout the past several decades. Many of you may recall being in a gifted classroom when your teacher unveiled a *LIFE* magazine and removed it from its plastic cover, or you may even have your very own collection of *LIFE* magazines that you have shared with your students. The LIFE Picture Collection (http://www.gettyimages.com/collections/lifepicture) and the LIFE photo archive hosted by Google (http://images.google.com/hosted/life) offer an extensive collection of images that were featured in the print edition of *LIFE* as well as an enormous catalog of previously unpublished photographs. The LIFE Picture Collection from Getty Images contains close to one million images documenting the American experience through politics, culture, celebrity, and the arts.

› Similar to *LIFE* magazine, *National Geographic Magazine* has a long-standing place in the classroom. For more than 125 years, *National Geographic* photographs have served to transport the reader to far away places and to imagine the wonders of our world. National Geographic Creative (http://www.natgeocreative.com/ngs/) opens the vault to more than 10 million images in its extensive bank of photographs from around the world. Images are searchable by keyword, photo ID, and photographer. A large part of this collection is even able to be used royalty free should you or your students decide to repurpose the images commercially.

› A growing number of libraries are hosting digital collections of their holdings. In 2016, the *New York Public Library* (http://www.nypl.org/research/collections/digital-collections/public-domain) released more than 180,000 items into the public domain to be freely shared and reused. The collection includes thousands of stereoscopic photographs, maps, postcards, sheet music, lithographs, and photographs dating back to the 11th century. Similarly, *The British Library* (https://www.flickr.com/photos/britishlibrary/albums) launched a photo group on Flickr highlighting many of the aspects of their collection.

› One final collection that we would like to highlight is the *Project Apollo Archive* (https://www.flickr.com/photos/projectapolloarchive/albums). Although you are undoubtedly familiar with many of the iconic images captured during the NASA Apollo space missions of the 1960s and 1970s, perhaps you have wondered why you see only a few of the images, or thought that even if we went as far as the moon, why didn't anyone bother to take more photos? The Project Apollo Archive makes available thousands of images taken from those early missions.

Provide Examples and Nonexamples

When learning new concepts, it is can be very helpful to provide students with both examples and nonexamples. Examples serve to help the students understand what something is. However, by having students examine nonexamples, they are able to deepen their understanding and better identify what something is not. Viewers of the PBS television series *Sesame Street* may recall a reoccurring segment called "One of these things" in which viewers are asked to determine which one of the four items was not like the others. To frame the examples and nonexamples, we have created a Google Drawing (see Figure 15) that allows you to insert four images into a grid for easy display (http://bit.ly/

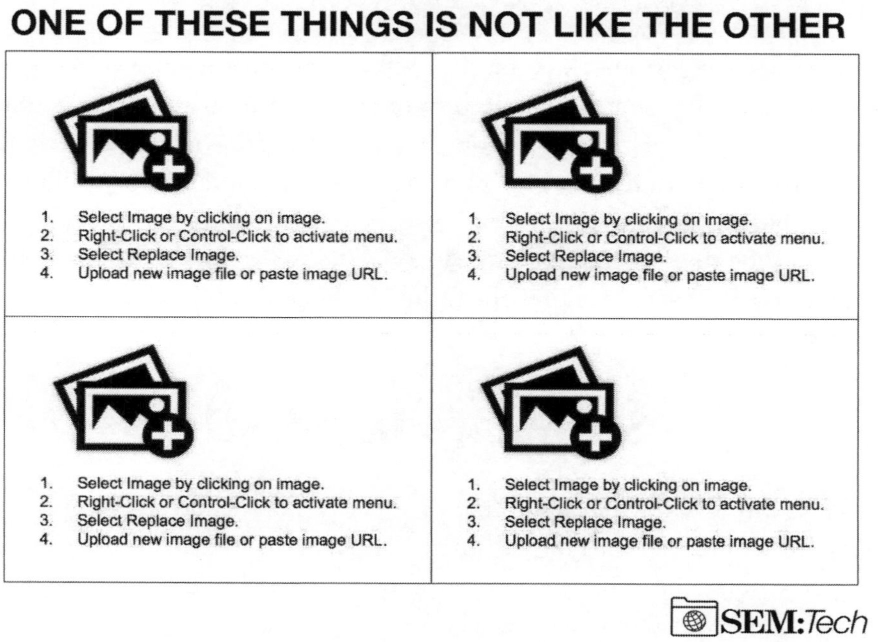

ONE OF THESE THINGS IS NOT LIKE THE OTHER

1. Select Image by clicking on image.
2. Right-Click or Control-Click to activate menu.
3. Select Replace Image.
4. Upload new image file or paste image URL.

1. Select Image by clicking on image.
2. Right-Click or Control-Click to activate menu.
3. Select Replace Image.
4. Upload new image file or paste image URL.

1. Select Image by clicking on image.
2. Right-Click or Control-Click to activate menu.
3. Select Replace Image.
4. Upload new image file or paste image URL.

1. Select Image by clicking on image.
2. Right-Click or Control-Click to activate menu.
3. Select Replace Image.
4. Upload new image file or paste image URL.

SEM:*Tech*

Figure 15. One of these things is not like the other.

sem-tech-other). There are numerous templates that are referenced throughout the book. Instructions for accessing these templates on the internet are available in Appendix B.

Explore the image galleries described in the section above, or search for appropriate images using a Google Image Search (https://images.google.com) or any of the ever growing free online image collections. For example, Pixabay (https://pixabay.com) offers nearly 600,000 free photos and images that are free of copyrights through Creative Commons Zero. This means that you can copy, modify, distribute, and use the photos for free in any way that you wish—even commercially. Flickr (https://www.flickr.com) hosts millions of uploaded photos, many of which are published using a Creative Commons license. Like most things on the Internet, Flickr features a powerful search tool that allows you to enter keywords and find exactly what you are looking for. Flickr also allows you to browse through collections of interesting or curious images. All of the images are tagged or labeled with keywords, and viewers can explore photo categories that are currently trending and the most popular categories over time (https://www.flickr.com/photos/tags). Flickr also allows you to view photos based on the location where they were taken using the map feature (https://www.flickr.com/

map) and by the type of camera with which they were taken (https://www.flickr.com/cameras).

When selecting images, look for things that are both obviously and not obviously connected. By creating a collection of images that share common characteristics, you will be able facilitate conversations that delve into the relationship between seemingly unrelated images to heighten the anticipation of your students as they begin their Type I experience. To view an example of how this might work, be sure to examine the sample activity discussed later in the book, One of These Selfies Is Not Like the Other (see Figure 31, p. 124).

Stimulate Interest

When the Schoolwide Enrichment Model was first conceived, the Internet was still in its infancy with only a smattering of individuals and organizations having access. At that point, finding resources online required a great deal of time and patience, and to make matters even more challenging, we were connecting at dial-up speeds that are thankfully a thing of the past.

Originally, Type I experiences were dependent on a great number of nontechnology-related resources and a very dedicated enrichment specialist to gather them together. Often this involved ordering media materials like films, audio recordings, filmstrips, or books from an assortment of lending libraries. Those of you of a certain age can vividly recall the excitement you felt as a student when coming into class and seeing that the TV cart had been rolled in or a film projector set up. Many others of us know the amount of time and energy that was involved to ensure that such an experience was possible. What was once a "special event" that required hours, if not days, of planning has been streamlined into a series of clicks or quick searches on the Internet.

Although it may be difficult to believe, it was not until 2005 that YouTube came into existence. Prior to this time, the idea of viewing streaming video online was something that did not exist. In 2015, YouTube touted more than 1 billion users who watch hundreds of millions of hours of video each day. Although quality content has become increasingly accessible thanks to the Internet, it also has become much easier to become mired in the seemingly endless amount of irrelevant information.

In Stage 2 of a Type I experience, we will present technology resources that are designed to *stimulate interest* in the minds and hearts of our students. Think of this stage as providing a stimulus for your students to rouse mental energy and entice them to desire to move to action to solve a problem or investigate the topic further. The main goal is not to teach students all that there is to know on the topic, but to instill in them something to be curious enough about to want to further their own learning and investigation either independently or in small groups.

To stimulate interest in a given subject, we suggest using a variety of engaging technology resources. In this section, we will explore some possible sources for finding such stimulating materials. These include videos, digital primary sources, images and photographs, games and simulations, virtual field trips, and other websites.

Collect Sources

When planning for Stage 2 of a Type I experience, you must carefully and thoughtfully select quality resources that will not only inform and educate, but also appeal to the interests and curious nature of your students. Type I experiences may provide brand new information on a previously known topic, or they might introduce a brand new topic that is previously unknown to the students but related to expressed areas of interest. When selecting a stimulus for this stage, it should be:

> *Based on students' interest.* Remember that Type I experiences are not necessarily part of the regular curriculum. There should be a connection between the expressed interests of your students and the Type I experiences that you are planning.

> *Curiosity inducing.* The stimulus provided should raise questions or concerns in the minds of the students to such a level that they feel compelled to continue the learning. Often the best Type I experiences feature stimuli that are intriguing and even puzzling.

> *Purposeful.* The content delivered should serve to instruct students at least at their current grade level if not above. Also, even thought you are collecting a source that has a purpose, it can still be entertaining and fun. Indeed, we feel that the best resources not only meet your learning objective, but also serve to delight. As you may note, many of our suggested resources are often witty and lean to the humorous side of life.

> *Appropriate*—as a teacher you should make your best judgment about whether or not the stimulus is suitable for your students. Although we have taken caution in selecting and recommending resources for this section, keep in mind that not all of the content may be appropriate for every student. You should pay close attention and be sure to carefully

review any resource before sharing with your students. Only you know what will be the best for your students.

Sources for Type I

Guest speakers. When the Schoolwide Enrichment Model was first designed, one of the hallmarks of a superlative implementation was the use of guest speakers for delivery of Type I experiences. For those of you who have hosted a guest speaker in your class or at school, you know that it can be a very worthwhile experience for the students, particularly when the speaker directly aligns with the interests of the students. You probably also know that locating a suitable guest speaker can often be very time consuming. Having a guest speaker used to mean having someone physically visit the school to talk with your students. However, thanks to the ubiquitous nature of video technology like Skype, Google Hangouts, and Facetime, we have the capability of bringing experts into our classrooms on a regular basis.

Experts are often very willing to share their knowledge and talk with a curious group of students. However, taking time off from work to travel to your classroom may not be a possibility. We have found that a great number of people are more than willing to take a break during their day to videoconference with students if they are asked. When looking for a guest speaker, we have developed the following tips for success.

Think big! When thinking about potential guest speakers on a topic, identify nationally recognized experts on the subject. Thanks to the Internet and social media, experts are more accessible than ever before. Chances are that the leading experts in any given subject area have a website, Twitter account, Facebook page, or, at the very least, an e-mail address that you can readily access. Ask yourself and your students, "If you could talk with anyone about the topic that you are passionate about, then who would it be?" Locate the contact information for that person online, friend him or her on Facebook, and definitely follow him or her on Twitter. Once you have identified your dream list of experts, then it is time to start contacting them.

"Nos are free." We know. We can feel your hesitation. For whatever reason, teachers are often afraid of asking someone to help them. But, in the words of Melissa Bilash, founder and codirector of The Grayson School (http://thegraysonschool.org), "Nos are free." Bilash's advice should remind you that to contact a guest speaker and ask him or her to talk to your students does not cost you anything. The worst that he or she could say is "no," but just imagine if he or she says "yes."

While developing a unit on the Titanic for a summer camp for gifted students at East Carolina University, Anica Weeks and Melani Blewett took this advice to heart and sought out the biggest Titanic expert that they could think of, Dr. Robert Ballard, oceanographer and discoverer of the Titanic's final resting place. Anica and Melani contacted Dr. Ballard via e-mail, thinking that they would not hear back from him. Instead, they exchanged several e-mails with him in which he answered several of their questions, and while he did say "no" to doing a video conference with the class, they did have an exciting story to share with their students.

Do your homework. As you are preparing to contact an expert, you should find out all that you can about his or her professional background and what makes him or her an expert. Look for possible personal connections to the expert. Is there something that you might be able to say that would compel him or her to say yes to your invitation? Although flattery will not necessarily get you everywhere, it might get you in the door. Opening your invitation by valuing his or her expertise and professional contributions to his or her field will increase the chances that your e-mail will be read.

State your purpose. When contacting a potential guest speaker, take time to succinctly state your purpose. When confronted with a very lengthy e-mail from an unknown sender, a natural reaction is to hit the delete button. Instead, try to limit your request to a few sentences. Be sure to include information about the age range and number of your students, but most importantly, highlight the students' level of interest in the topic. Chances are, the expert that you are contacting probably recalls what it was like to be a student at the same age as your students, and he or she may even remember having an intense interest in a subject at an early age. You might even ask him or her at what point he or she became interested in the subject area, just to jog his or her memory a little bit.

In stating your purpose, you should also outline how long you would like for him or her to speak with your students. Keep in mind that longer is not necessarily better, especially if you are planning to do a videoconference. An hour-long Skype session can become a tedious experience for everyone. Instead, ask for 15–20 minutes of the expert's time. This keeps the level of commitment to a minimum for the expert, and if things are going well, then it is relatively easy for him or her to extend the time to 30 minutes or more.

Always ask a follow-up. When contacting a potential guest speaker, acknowledge that his or her time is valuable and recognize that he or she has a busy schedule. Many times an expert would really love to speak with your students, but may not have time. You should always inquire about other possible experts who you might contact. For example, you might ask, "If you are not available to videoconference, can you recommend someone else who might be available?" Frequently, there are a number of other colleagues, graduate students, or experts in closely related fields to whom the person you are contacting may have ready access. These individuals might be able to help you if your initial contact person was unable to do so.

Remember etiquette. Throughout your request, you should employ proper etiquette. Be sure to thank the expert for his or her time in reading and responding to your e-mail request. Remember that "please" is a magic word. A well-crafted e-mail request can make all the difference in someone saying yes or no. Aim to make your request both personal and professional.

Don't forget your local community. Although it is wonderful to dream big when it comes to guest speakers, it can be just as rewarding to work with someone on a more local level. Consider local businesses and industries, colleges or universities, and museums. There is a wealth of knowledge and expertise in every community. Quite often, local experts are even available to visit your classroom or school in person. Remember to utilize the same approach when contacting them to be a possible guest speaker as you would a nationally recognized expert within the field. Even though they are local, it does not necessarily mean that they will be able to take the time to visit in person, so extend the same opportunity for a videoconference to your local experts. In the end, valuing their time and expertise may help them to say yes.

Recommendations for videoconferences. Bringing a guest speaker into your classroom can be a very rewarding experience for your students, as it gives them personal access to an expert that they might not have in any other setting. With some careful planning and considerations, you can help to ensure that this is a positive experience not only for your students but also for the presenter.

1. *Choose a platform.* There are a number of free options available. You might begin by asking your guest speaker what he or she would be most comfortable using. We have had success using Skype, Google Hangouts, and Facetime when videoconferencing. Determine which platform will work best for you and the speaker and which tool will work the best in your school setting. If you are looking for tips for getting started or setting this up, you might refer to Skype in the Classroom (https://education.microsoft.com/skypeintheclassroom) for some suggestions.

2. *Establish a timeline.* Being flexible with your schedule may mean the difference between having a big name guest speaker and not having one. However, we fully recognize that many school schedules are not able to

be altered. As soon as possible, work with your guest speaker to create a timeline or schedule. Be sure to include how long the videoconference will be in total. Establish how long the speaker will present, as well as how much time will be allowed for questions from the students.

3. *Test the connection.* When you are creating a schedule, also make every effort to set up a very brief test run to ensure that you can easily connect with the speaker when it is time. Taking a minute or two to test the connection ahead of time can make the entire experience run more smoothly.

4. *Make a backup plan.* Remember that you are dealing with technology, and anything can happen. In the event that you are not able to connect with your guest speaker through the preferred method, establish a backup plan. For example, if for some reason you cannot connect on Skype, what should you try next to contact them? As a backup, you could always resort to a phone conversation on speaker phone. Although it may not be ideal, it is an acceptable alternative to not having the experience at all. Remember, scheduling a guest speaker can be a challenge, and you want to do everything that you can to honor the time that he or she has donated to you and your students.

5. *Prepare your students.* Work with your students to prepare them for the experience. You should encourage them to develop some questions to ask ahead of time. However, you do not necessarily want to resort to students simply reading from a list of prepared questions. Ideally, the videoconference should be more interactive in nature, but we have seen on numerous occasions that students can become very awkward when posing questions in this setting.

6. *Set up the classroom.* This step is very important for an optimal experience. Consider how the room is set up. Will the video of the guest speaker be projected on a screen? Where will the students sit? Where is the camera positioned? Can the presenter see all of the students? This may require some reorganization of your classroom. You want to ensure that the speaker can see and hear all of the students. You will also need to consider the microphone set up in your classroom. Will students need to approach the computer to be heard when asking a question? Setting up a test run with a colleague will allow you to work through many of these details.

7. *Follow up with a thank you note.* After the guest speaker has finished, be sure to send a thank you e-mail later that same day. A quick thank you

helps to provide some closure on the experience, and it lets your guest expert know that he or she was appreciated and did well. Have students write their own thank you notes and collect them to send to your speaker. Encourage them to include how the guest influenced their thinking and what they plan to do with the new information that they learned. A handwritten thank you note creates a lasting impression that will far outweigh almost any e-mail that you might send. At the end of it all, it should be your goal that the experience not only be a meaningful one for your students, but that it also was rewarding to your expert so he or she might consider doing it again.

YouTube video channels. With billions of hours of videos available, it is hard to know where to look first. We have collected some of our favorite sources of videos on YouTube that could possibly serve as a stimulus for Stage 2 of a Type I experience. In selecting these YouTube channels, we have attempted to only choose those sources that seem to have a good track record of providing quality content and have a strong potential for continuing to produce new videos for the foreseeable future.

›   *YouTube EDU* (https://www.youtube.com/education) centralizes educational content from hundreds of different content creators, including individual users, colleges and universities, businesses and organizations, and other content creators. YouTube EDU allows one to browse through a wide range of categories and themes that might be of interest. The collection of videos is organized into three main channels: Primary and Secondary Education, University, and Lifelong Learning. If you are not exactly sure what type of video resource you are looking for, this is a great place to start. Think of it as browsing the stacks at a university library.

›   *VlogBrothers* (https://www.youtube.com/user/vlogbrothers) is the creation of John Green, author of *The Fault in Our Stars* and *Looking for Alaska*, and his brother Hank Green. They describe their video collaboration as "Raising nerdy to the power of awesome." Essentially this vlog is a video conversation between the two brothers, with John Green posting a video on Tuesdays and Hank Green posting on Fridays. In these conversations, they manage to not only inform the viewers on a wide range of topics, but also entertain. The conversations are exactly the type of curious ramblings that many of our gifted students regularly engage in, only elevated to a worldwide stage. Although the videos may not be the best fit for your Type I experience, other YouTube projects created by the VlogBrothers might be precisely what you are looking for.

› *Crash Course* (https://www.youtube.com/user/crashcourse) is a collection of courses taught by John and Hank Green, in addition to other collaborators, covering a variety of traditional subjects covered at the high school level including U.S. and world history, biology, chemistry, psychology, and literature. Each video lesson typically lasts between 10 and 15 minutes and provides an entertaining overview of a specific topic that could easily introduce advanced content to interested students.

› *Crash Course Kids* (https://www.youtube.com/user/crashcoursekids) focuses on elementary science topics including life science, physical science, engineering, Earth science, space, and physical science. Each Crash Course Kids video is hosted by Sabrina Cruz, lasts about 5 minutes, and features lively animations that delve into a "big" question. The videos quickly and effectively deliver content that could serve as an excellent starting point for elementary students to start an investigation into a topic of an interest.

› *National Public Radio* (NPR; https://www.youtube.com/user/npr) delivers breaking national and world news alongside programs that address the top stories in business, politics, health, science, technology, music, arts, and culture. If you are an NPR listener, you probably know the power of their intriguing and in-depth stories. You may have even had a "driveway moment"—that moment where you are unable or unwilling to leave your car after arriving at your destination because you are so riveted by the story that you are listening to. Although the NPR website (http://www.npr.org) allows you to go back and listen to a program or story, the NPR YouTube Channel offers a collection of engaging video stories that extend the experience beyond listening to the radio to seeing the stories come alive. NPR features many different video projects and one of the more interesting is NPR's Skunk Bear (https://www.youtube.com/user/NPRskunkbear), which investigates the secrets of the universe and wonders of nature with "sweet" science videos. Much like the VlogBrothers, Skunk Bear utilizes quick-witted humor and a heavy dose of puns to entertain and educate.

› *THNKR* (https://www.youtube.com/user/thnkrtv) presents four original video series that are designed to challenge your thinking and "change" your mind. BOOKD explores game-changing books through the insights and opinions of engaging personalities. EPIPHANY invites impassioned thought leaders across all disciplines to reveal the innovative, the improbable, and the unexpected from within their domain. PODIUM embraces the art of oration and conversation, and explores various genres of speechmaking and rhetoric. Finally, PRODIGIES showcases the youngest and brightest and the stories behind them as they challenge themselves to reach new heights.

› The *Royal Society for the Encouragement of Arts, Manufactures and Commerce* (RSA; https://www.youtube.com/user/theRSAorg) is on a mission to enrich society through ideas and actions. RSA is probably best known for its RSA Animate videos featuring quick draw animations created by Cognitive Media and featuring audio of theorists and psychologists such as Sir Ken Robinson, Carol Dweck, and Daniel Pink. The animation creates a compelling viewing experience, as abstract concepts are often explained in a visual manner that works to increase comprehension and attention. The RSA Shorts series is another collection that effectively utilizes animation to translate audio from lectures into videos that are entertaining and educational. The audio for each of these series comes from RSA events, many of which are available for viewing in their entirety. The RSA Spotlight series selectively edits much longer lectures to 10 minutes of key talking points and big ideas that could serve perfectly as a Type I experience. Highly interested students might then choose to view the longer recording as they choose to continue to explore the topic. Finally, the website for the RSA (http://thersa.org) offers many additional educational resources worthy of exploration for Type I experiences.

› *Numberphile* (https://www.youtube.com/user/numberphile) was created by Brady Haran and features videos about numbers that offer insight into the mystery and beauty of mathematics. Numberphile takes abstract mathematical concepts and transforms them into memorable viewing experiences. For example, "Mile of Pi" (https://youtu.be/0r3cE KZiLmg) displays a million digits of pi printed on one piece of paper 1.05 miles long. After viewing this, one will have a new appreciation for just what a marvel pi is. Meanwhile, videos such as "The Problem in *Good Will Hunting*" (https://youtu.be/iW_LkYiuTKE) show that seemingly complex problems can easily be solved if you only understand the concept.

› *Vi Hart* (https://www.youtube.com/user/Vihart) takes doodling in math class to an art form by utilizing quick draw animation to create videos that show that math is far more than just adding numbers. Instead, she creates videos that tell the story behind a multitude of mathematical concepts and theorems. Instead of students simply memorizing the Pythagorean theorem, by viewing "What Was Up With Pythagoras?" (https://youtu.be/X1E7I7_r3Cw), they can unveil a fascinating history of Pythagoras, including his apparently irrational fear of beans. Similar to many of the other video collections highlighted in this section, Vi Hart presents information in a way that is filled with clever banter and highly engaging for talented students.

› *Sick Science* (https://www.youtube.com/sickscience) is created by Steve Spangler and delivers short videos of "beyond cool experiments that you can do at home." Sick Science demonstrates the experiments, but the videos intentionally do not explain why the phenomena happens. Instead the viewer is invited to hypothesize why and how the result has occurred. Spangler also has a companion website (http://www.stevespanglerscience.com) and is perhaps best known for the Mentos and Diet Coke geyser experiment that went viral.

› *The Brain Scoop* (https://www.youtube.com/user/thebrainscoop) features Emily Graslie, the Chief Curiosity Correspondent of The Field Museum in Chicago. This video series highlights many of the amazing things that are part of the museum's zoological collection. Video playlists include topics such as fossils and geology, mammals, sharks and other fish, and insects and invertebrates. Other playlist highlights include Ask Emily! where she answers viewers' questions, and Versus, where she explores the differences between moths versus butterflies or crocodiles versus alligators. New episodes are uploaded to YouTube every Wednesday.

› *Big Think* (https://www.youtube.com/user/bigthink) provides a large collection of educational content featuring experts ranging from Bill Clinton to Bill Nye. Big Think explores big ideas and core skills that define knowledge in the 21st century. The collection features both short-form videos in the 5–10 minute range as well as longer lecture-style videos in the 45–60 minute range.

› *Talks at Google* (https://www.youtube.com/user/AtGoogleTalks) was started in 2006 and has brought thousands of speakers to various Google locations since that time to deliver lectures to the Google employees. In 2015, more than 400 talks were a part of this series. Typically the sessions last 40 to 50 minutes and might be the type of resource to share with students who are highly interested in a particular topic of study.

A great number of museums such as the *American Museum of Natural History* (https://www.youtube.com/user/AMNHorg), the *Museum of Modern Art* (https://www.youtube.com/user/MoMAvideos), and the *Smithsonian* (https://www.youtube.com/user/smithsonianchannel) present video highlights of their collections and a wide range of short-form videos that could serve well in stimulating students' interest in a topic. We recommend searching YouTube by museum to uncover some hidden treasures.

Organizations like the *National Science Foundation* (https://www.youtube.com/user/VideosatNSF) also host YouTube channels that serve as an outreach of their research and work. The NSF includes a multitude of playlists covering topics such as brain research, computer science, and physics.

PBS Digital Studios. Since 1970, the Public Broadcast Service (PBS) has produced television programming that is not only educational but also entertaining and informative. The PBS Digital Studios (https://www.youtube.com/user/pbsdigitalstudios/channels) aims to bring that same level of production to its YouTube channel by creating original Internet programming for people who are curious and never want to stop learning. Although PBS Digital Studios provides an ever-growing list of shows, we would like to highlight five that might be of particular interest to you and your students and prove useful for constructing an engaging Type I experience.

› *It's Okay to Be Smart* (https://www.youtube.com/user/itsokaytobesmart) is hosted by Joe Hanson and focused around science topics such as biology, space, and physics. Other special series include curious explorations like "100% Awesome (and True) Shark Science!" and "Why Your Body Is Shaped That Way." According to the About page, "We officially live in the future, and everyone should know that it's okay to be smart!"

› *Blank on Blank* (https://www.youtube.com/user/blankonblank) takes vintage and previously unheard interview audio recordings with cultural icons and transforms them into animated shorts that tend to spotlight 20th-century popular culture. Videos include highlights such as John Coltrane on "Giant Steps," Ayn Rand on "Love and Happiness," and Maurice Sendak on "Being a Kid."

› *The Art Assignment* (https://www.youtube.com/user/theartassignment) is hosted by Sarah Green, who travels around the U.S. and interviews working artists who describe their creative process and current projects. The artists then offer art tasks for the viewer to complete based upon their work. Viewers are encouraged to share their creations on social media using the hashtag #theartassignment; that way one can see what others have created in response to the prompt.

> *Physics Girl* (https://www.youtube.com/user/physicswoman) is Dianna Cowern, who presents "physics videos for every atom and eve" that tackle puzzling science concepts in a way that is both intriguing and easy to understand but without oversimplification. Physics Girl addresses intriguing questions such as "Why do mirrors flip horizontally (but not vertically)?" and "Why is the universe flat?" and also presents a collection of experiments you can try.

> *BrainCraft* (https://www.youtube.com/user/braincraftvideo) explores psychology, neuroscience, human behavior, and other topics related to brains. Written and hosted by Vanessa Hill, each episode covers a single topic of interest such as "Amazing Effects of Sleep (and Lack of It)," "The Bizarre Ways Your Name Affects Your Behavior," and "Do Dogs Really Miss Us?" The host presents these ideas and then connects the topics to psychology and brain research.

> *Gross Science* (https://www.youtube.com/user/grossscienceshow) covers the icky side of science that both repels some students with disgust and attracts others with delight. If your students like science that it is slimy, smelly, or creepy, then this is the YouTube Channel for them. Exploring questions like, "What Really Causes Cavities?" and "How Far Do Sneezes and Vomit Travel?", creator Anna Rothchild teaches memorable science content while exploring the grossness that fills the world around and inside of us.

Khan Academy. What began as a series of tutorial videos for Salman Khan's cousin in 2004 has evolved into a worldwide nonprofit education organization that aims to deliver a free, world-class education for anyone, anywhere. Although Khan Academy (https://www.khanacademy.org) is perhaps best known for the math tutorials that Salman Khan originally created, those videos are not necessarily engaging enough to serve to stimulate students' interest. However, Khan Academy has created a multitude of partnerships with other video content creators and organizations to deliver a wide range of video collections and activities that would provide an appropriate stimulus for students to develop an area of interest.

To locate and view all Partner Content, one needs to navigate to https://www.khanacademy.org/partner-content (see Figure 16). Here all of the Khan Academy Partner content can be browsed by topic and provider. We would like to highlight a few of the partners that we feel could be of particular interest to your students.

The partner content does tend to present information in a format that could easily be investigated over a series of days or even weeks. However, for the purpose of a Type I experience, you should choose one particular segment or video to entice students' interest and then allow them the opportunity to explore the resources if they choose.

› *All-Star Orchestra* (https://www.khanacademy.org/partner-content/all-star-orchestra) presents video lessons and activities designed to introduce students to the basics of music notation and rhythm, as well as how to begin reading music. In "Instruments of the Orchestra" (https://www.khanacademy.org/partner-content/all-star-orchestra/instruments-of-the-orchestra), principal players from famous symphony orchestras teach about and play all of the various instruments of a full orchestra. For students who may have already developed an appreciation of orchestral music, Conductor Gerard Schwarz delivers numerous in-depth explanations of "Masterpieces Old and New" (https://www.khanacademy.org/partner-content/all-star-orchestra/masterpieces-old-and-new) ranging from Beethoven's "Symphony No. 5" to Philip Glass's "Harmonium Mountain."

› *Pixar in a Box* (https://www.khanacademy.org/partner-content/pixar) is a collaboration between Pixar Animation and Khan Academy that is sponsored by Disney. This collection of video resources, lessons, and activities takes students behind the scenes at Pixar Animation Studios and explores the math and science behind computer animation. Using examples from their movies, Pixar animators demonstrate the use of parabolic arcs in computer modeling and how such mathematical concepts as subdivision are needed to construct their three-dimensional figures. If your students have ever wondered when they would ever use math in the future, this series from Pixar provides some memorable and thought-provoking examples.

› *Big History Project* (https://www.khanacademy.org/partner-content/big-history-project) takes learners through 14 million years of history and poses big questions about our universe, our planet, and life in general. The lessons present information from multiple perspectives and across disciplines. The content is divided into 10 different units of study and presents an intriguing journey through time emphasizing discovery and connections.

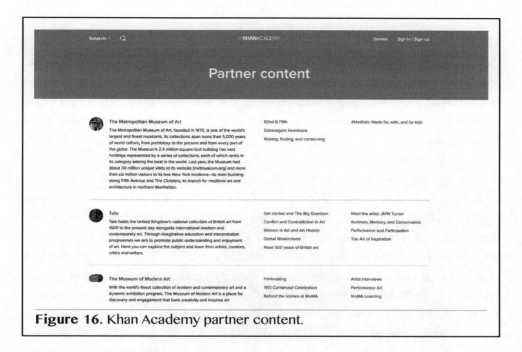

Figure 16. Khan Academy partner content.

› *Wi-Phi* (https://www.khanacademy.org/partner-content/wi-phi) intends to introduce learners to philosophy and offers courses on the history of philosophy, value theory, critical thinking, metaphysics, and epistemology. The lessons provide an entertaining, interesting, and accessible introduction to the topics.

TED and TED-Ed. If we had to recommend only one source for stimulating video content, then that would have to be TED (http://www.ted.com). TED began in 1984 as a conference where Technology, Entertainment, and Design converged and has now become a worldwide phenomena covering almost every topic imaginable. Since 2006, video recordings of the annual conference as well as local TEDx events have been posted to the TED website as well as YouTube. TED has elevated the lecture to an art form by focusing on powerful stories and brevity. Rather than lengthy PowerPoint-driven talks stretched out over an hour, TED Talks are condensed to a highly stylized structure that conveys meaning and purpose in 18 minutes or less. TED features thousands of thought-provoking talks that can naturally serve to stimulate students' interests.

With an ever-growing collection of TED Talks available, TED has attempted to make it as easy as possible to find just the talk that might inspire you and your students to do great things. Perhaps the most useful way to browse what is available is to use the TED Topics page (https://www.ted.com/topics). Here you could begin to match your students' interests with an appropriate video. You might also utilize the TED Playlists (https://www.ted.com/playlists) to provide suggestions for students who want the opportunity to go beyond the current Type I experience and learn more. TED also has created the TED Studies page (https://www.ted.com/read/ted-studies), which curates TED talks into an experience that more resembles an online course. This comes complete with learning outcomes, an introductory essay, relevant TED talks, and a summary analysis of the content.

As an extension of its TED Talks, which really have a target audience of adults, TED sought to extend its influence by creating TED Ed (http://ed.ted.com), which features lessons worth sharing. These animated video lessons created by teachers cover a wide range of academic subjects as well as areas of interest that are beyond the regular curriculum. Videos tend to be in the 4–5 minute range and are engaging, entertaining, and informative. To go along with each video, TED Ed has created a lesson in which students are presented with a series of multiple choice and open-ended questions to check their knowledge and understanding in the Think Section. Next, they are invited to "dig deeper" and explore some additional resources. Finally, each lesson contains a "discussion" section where students are encouraged to respond to a prompt or to pose their own questions. Perhaps the best feature of TED Ed is that the creators have opened this platform up to teachers to customize any of their lessons for their own students. Later in this chapter, we will examine how you can use TED Ed to create your own lessons using any YouTube video to fully customize an interactive Type I experience.

Content curated by others. We have reviewed some of what we feel are the best YouTube channels for finding videos for stimulating interest in your students as part of a Type I experience. We do not want to overlook the fact that literally billions of hours of video content exist on YouTube. We have chosen to focus on what we consider to be quality content produced by individuals and groups with consistency and frequency. That being said, there are a number of individuals who focus on *curating* video content that can serve as excellent sources for stimulating student interests.

› *The Kid Should See This* (http://thekidshouldseethis.com) was started by Rion Nakaya in 2011 for her own children. She saw that the Internet was filled with a plethora of amazing content that was not necessarily designed for kids but was actually perfect for them. Described as "smart videos for curious minds of all ages," The Kid Should See This (TKSST) posts 8–12 videos each week. The site currently contains more than

2,300 videos in topics including science, technology, space, animals, nature, food, music, and art. The selection criterion for inclusion on the site is driven by wonder, enthusiasm, and "wow!" moments. The TKSST rule is, "Don't dumb it down!" Nakaya believes that we should not underestimate what children can learn or what they might be interested in.

› *Curiosities and Puzzlements* (http://puzzlements.co) is curated by Ian Byrd, who blogs at http://byrdseed.com. This companion site offers a free weekly e-mail newsletter of five links to videos and other intriguing Internet resources every Friday.

Google Cardboard. Since the early days of the personal computer in the 1980s, the idea of virtual reality has been something that seems just over the technological horizon. Since that time, there have been many devices that have tried and failed to bring virtual reality to the mainstream, but sadly, the dream of virtual reality remained just a dream.

In 2016, all of that seemed to change when, after years of prototyping and development, the Oculus Rift (https://www.oculus.com) was finally available for sale to the public. Although the virtual reality headset is quite expensive at its initial release of $599, and the device still requires a very powerful Windows PC to run its applications, the Oculus Rift is nevertheless a giant leap forward into a virtual future. Meanwhile, other virtual reality devices such as the Samsung Gear VR and Sony's PlayStation VR promise that the virtual horizon is nearly upon us. Yet, these devices still manage to keep their distance from use in the classroom due to their costs and lack of educational applications.

To remedy this situation and to bring virtual reality to the masses, Google introduced its Cardboard device. Google Cardboard (https://www.google.com/get/cardboard) is a cardboard viewer similar to a ViewMaster that uses your smartphone to bring an immersive experience to you for a very low cost. A wide range of Google Cardboard devices have been produced by a growing number of manufacturers (https://www.google.com/get/cardboard/get-cardboard). A typical cost for a Cardboard viewer is about $15. However, you should keep in mind that the devices are made of cardboard and are not necessarily built to last. We recommend investing a bit more and getting a device that is made of plastic and will withstand long-term use by you and your students. Our personal favorite is the Mattel View-Master VR (https://store.google.com/product/mattel_view_master_starter_pack), which retails for $29.99. This device has the look and feel of a futuristic View-Master and safely holds your iPhone or Android phone.

The official Google Cardboard app provides your first glimpse into the power and potential of virtual reality with a variety of immersive demos. Similar to stereoscopic images or View-Master reels, the viewer is witness to a variety of images that appear to be three-dimensional. However, the images are not static. Instead, as the viewer turns his head, the device reacts to display what is in that direction. Thus, Google Cardboard provides a 360-degree vantage point of the scene, including looking up and down. At this point, more than 1,000 apps have been developed for use with Google Cardboard. This is not limited to just still images, as there is a growing collection of 360-degree videos available on YouTube (https://www.youtube.com/360). As you watch the video, you are able to look in any direction to see what is beside or even behind you.

In November of 2015, the *New York Times* released the NYT VR app (http://www.nytimes.com/newsgraphics/2015/nytvr), which features short journalistic immersive films. Many of the Google Cardboard apps (including this one) are designed to be used with headphones, and as the viewer moves, not only does the image change, but the direction that the sound is coming from also changes.

Although the majority of the apps being developed at this point would fall into the gaming or entertainment category, Google is working to ensure that Cardboard is also finding its way into classrooms. Google Expeditions (https://www.google.com/edu/expeditions) was created to allow teachers to take their classes on immersive virtual field trips using a class set of Cardboard devices. At this point, more than 100 journeys have been designed using images from Google Street View. The teacher uses a tablet device to guide the tour, and up to 50 students use their Cardboard devices to experience the field trip. You can set a marker or point of interest for your students to examine, and on your tablet screen an icon marks where every student is looking. The Expedition Program also includes content information about each of the scenes to share with your students as you are guiding them.

The types of experiences provided by Google Cardboard represent the potential of technology to take students to places that they would not ordinarily have the opportunity to visit. Although it will never replace the experience of actually being there, Cardboard can help to bring much more of the world into the classroom; it can serve as a device for vicarious experience.

CHAPTER 6

Type I— Connecting to Student Understanding

Deepening Understanding

As we open this chapter, we would like for you to recall the experience of taking your students on a field trip. In this moment, don't think of all of the hours and days of planning. Don't think of the experience itself. Instead, we want you to focus on the bus ride back to school. In our own experiences, our students were often so excited to talk about what they had seen and heard. Beyond this, field trips tend to offer sensory experiences that tap into all of our senses and create memories. Our students wanted to share their experiences with each other and discuss what they learned in the process. Unfortunately, the bus seldom offers a great place to have a whole-class discussion. And far too often, the excitement of the day has completely exhausted the students so that by the time everyone gets back to school, the buzz of learning has begun to wear off. Not to mention, you are likely rushing to get them back to the classroom and prepared for dismissal, which does not allow for time to debrief with the students and help them to deepen their understanding.

Similarly, you may have had the experience of having a guest speaker visit your class or school. There is a natural tendency to fill the entire class period with hearing from the speaker, but far too often little or no time is left for debriefing with the students once the speaker is done.

Leaving time for closure as part of a lesson is quite common. As teachers, we often feel the pressure to pack our lessons with more and more content, but we overlook the importance of allowing those morsels of intellect to digest properly. Far too often, we create the equivalent of a competitive eating competition— delivering as much content as quickly as possible, rather than taking the time to enjoy the experience bite by bite and, more importantly, allowing proper digestion of the experience.

In Vygotsky's (1978) theory of social constructivism, he describes the learning process as a social and collaborative activity: "By giving our students practice in talking with others, we give them frames for thinking on their own" (p. 19). It is through the act of intellectual discussions that learning experiences become personalized and memorable. Vygotsky (1978) also believed that "the child begins to perceive the world not only through his eyes but also through his speech" (p. 32). By only viewing an experience, the learning is passive. By having students discuss with one another, you as the teacher can help to contextualize the experience. Without debriefing with your students, much of the time and effort spent organizing a Type I experience may have been wasted.

Although gifted students may possess above-average intellect, the ability to critically reflect on an experience may not be a skill that they have yet developed. As teachers, we are in the position to scaffold the learning for our students. Vygotsky's Zone of Proximal Development allows us to help our students access content that is above their current level in a way that allows them to stretch and grow. It is precisely this way of thinking and learning that is at the heart of Stage 3 of the SEM: *Tech* Type I experience.

We have collected a series of proposed activities to help you as a teacher develop critical thinking and self-reflection in your students. You should not assume that students have necessarily developed these skills on their own. Neither should you view any of these activities as an assignment to be graded. In fact, many students may not honestly or deeply reflect if they feel that their responses are going to be assessed as right or wrong.

Instead, we envision the following activities to be an important starting point for discussions between students and with the facilitator of a Type I or with you as a teacher. These conversations may take place in person, virtually, or even as part of a discussion board. We believe that these discussions help create a bridge for students that allows them to connect the learning to their own experience. This is where the learning becomes personal and, as understanding is deepened, growth occurs.

It all starts with a question, but the tricky part is, "Which one?" In working with beginning teachers, we have witnessed that they often believe that they will think of the perfect question to spur students' interest in the moment of teaching.

However, hundreds of hours spent observing in classrooms has revealed that this happens very rarely without some careful planning and forethought. Likewise, as teachers we have all heard on numerous occasions that we should be asking higher order thinking questions á la Bloom's taxonomy, but if we are really honest with ourselves, then we know that it does not happen nearly as often as we would like. Asking good questions of your students is a skill that requires not only planning but also plenty of practice.

What follows is a series of activities that can be completed individually, in small groups, or as a whole class. We have created a series of 10 digital templates using Google Drive. These templates may be printed out for your students if you are in a situation where every student does not have access to a digital device, or you may create a digital copy of the template and allow students to complete the form online and submit it to you using Google Drive. Instructions for accessing and copying the templates as well as a full listing of the SEM:*Tech* templates can be found in Appendix B. For your convenience, you may also access the SEM:*Tech* templates at http://sem-tech.org/templates.

Google Drive Templates

A-E-I-O-U. A-E-I-O-U (http://bit.ly/sem-tech-aeiou) works as a general debrief that would work well as a part of almost any Type I experience. Students are asked to respond to a five individual questions that deal with what the students learned, how they felt, what they found interesting and surprising, and perhaps most importantly, what they want to learn more about (see Figure 17).

A — List 3 **ADJECTIVES** that describe what you learned.
E — Name an **EMOTION** that describes how the experience made you feel.
I — Describe something that you found **INTERESTING.**
O — Tell about something that made you say **"Oh!"**
U — What is a question that **YOU** want to learn more about?

As part of the debriefing, we have found it useful to have students discuss the similarities and differences in their responses. This offers some great insight into your students' thinking when discussing the emotions of the experience. So often, we focus only on the content and cognitive process and forget to address the affective and emotional responses of our students. By delving into this, we can get at the heart of the subject and better identify not only what students are interested in, but what they are passionate about.

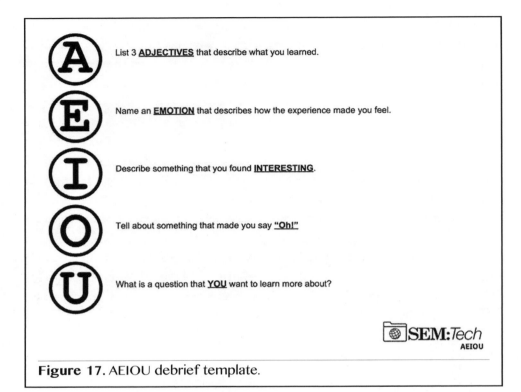

Figure 17. AEIOU debrief template.

Compass Points. This is a thinking routine adapted from Project Zero's Visible Thinking. We have made some subtle changes to create a better fit with Type I experiences, and we have constructed an interactive Google Drawing template (see Figure 18) for you to use with your students (http://bit.ly/sem-tech-compasspoints). Compass Points is a useful tool when students are considering how they might use information learned in a Type I experience to further their investigation on the topic. This prompt may not work for every Type I experience, and it should only be used with students who wish to further explore the topic or possibly develop a Type III product.

Students should use the compass points form to address four prompts. The four prompts are made up of two sets of continuums running from East to West and from North to South. Have students start on the horizontal axis and respond to how they are feeling about the topic under investigation.

> **East** = I am **EXCITED** about . . .
> **West** = I am **WORRIED** about . . .

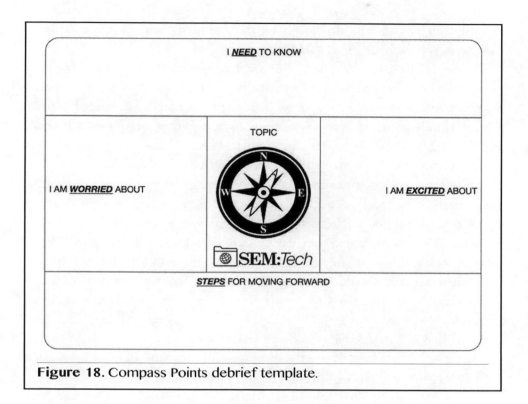

Figure 18. Compass Points debrief template.

By expressing what they are excited about versus what they are worried about, we can begin to explore their emotional tension and interest level in the subject. By asking students what is worrying them, we give them an opportunity to acknowledge what is not perfect and help them to realize that it is natural to be both excited and worried at the same time. Some students might think of this worry related to what they will do next, how they will get started, or even how they can make a difference. Some students will look at this from a personal perspective, while others may view these emotional responses from a more systematic or universal approach. As with any of these debriefing activities, there are no right or wrong answers.

Next, students should complete the vertical axis, starting with **North** or "I **NEED** to know . . ." and then ending with **South** or "**STEPS** for moving forward." The "I need to know" prompt serves as a starting point for the students for information that might be a part of additional Type I experiences, or even a launching point for Type II training focusing on the methodological skills needed to conduct their investigations. Finally, the students are constructing their initial draft of a management plan for getting started on a Type III investigation. Again, Compass Points may not be an activity that you would want all of your students to complete. Instead, it is meant only for those students who have expressed an interest in continuing their investigation on the topic.

Connect, Extend, Wonder. This debriefing activity (see Figure 19) is designed to help students connect their prior knowledge with any new learning or experience that they may have had. We have adapted the idea from the Visible Thinking (http://www.visiblethinkingpz.org) routine: Connect, Extend, and Challenge. The Google Drawing template (http://bit.ly/sem-tech-cec) was created for use by individual students. A benefit of this particular debrief tool is that it honors what students already know and encourages them to identify questions that they still wonder about or concepts that are still difficult for them to understand, particularly related to the Type I experience. Rather than focusing on questions that are comprehension-based and meant to measure a basic understanding, this debriefing guide is meant to personally connect to your students' interests. You should encourage your students to begin to examine some of the unanswered questions or mysteries of a topic that may be tangential in nature.

At the core of this activity are three questions or prompts.
1. CONNECT: How are the ideas and information presented *connected* to what you already knew?
2. EXTEND: What new ideas did you get that *extended* or pushed your thinking in new directions?
3. WONDER: What *wonderings*, puzzles, or questions do you now have?

We have also included a section for students to identify their Next Steps in exploring the topic in this Type I experience. Note that some students may choose to not continue their investigation. However, this activity is meant to extend the invitation to those students who are interested.

CSI: Color, Symbol, and Image. The CSI prompt asks that students reflect on their experience in a nonverbal manner using only visual information and metaphors (see http://bit.ly/sem-tech-csi). Students are first asked to select a color that best represents their feelings regarding the experience and information provided. By first clicking on the black triangle, students are then able to select the paint bucket icon from the tool bar to change the fill color.

Next, students should select a symbol or icon that reflects how they are feeling about their experience. Image placeholders (see Figure 20) have been provided in this document and feature the directions for changing the image in the template.

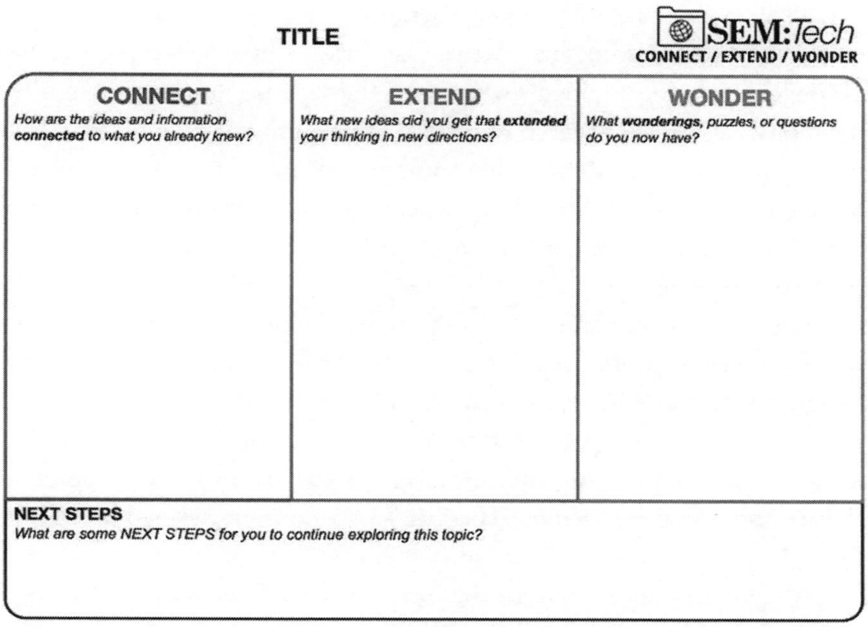

TITLE

SEM:*Tech*
CONNECT / EXTEND / WONDER

CONNECT	EXTEND	WONDER
How are the ideas and information **connected** *to what you already knew?*	*What new ideas did you get that* **extended** *your thinking in new directions?*	*What* **wonderings**, *puzzles, or questions do you now have?*

NEXT STEPS
What are some NEXT STEPS for you to continue exploring this topic?

Figure 19. Connect, Extend, Wonder debrief template.

1. Select Image by clicking on image.
2. Right-Click or Control-Click to activate menu.
3. Select Replace Image.
4. Insert image to Upload or by pasting URL

Figure 20. Image placeholders.

Although students might wish to do an image search, we suggest that you try using The Noun Project (https://thenounproject.com). This is a collection of more than 150,000 icons that cover a vast array of potential topics. The icons are all simple black-and-white drawings, and they are organized into a multitude of collections. Best of all, a search tool will allow you to quickly find exactly what you are looking for on the site. Students might also choose to use an emoji for the symbol section. The idea is for them to select some type of symbol that expresses their thinking. Alternately, students may wish to create their own symbol and insert it into the form.

Although we are all familiar with the saying "a picture is worth a thousand words," this image section of CSI puts this to the test. An image is meant to be a photograph and should represent a visual metaphor of the students' thinking. An image search may be conducted using any tool that you would like to recommend. You may choose to limit students to certain image collections or even create additional constraints. The image collections described in Stage 1 are excellent resources to utilize. Also, some students might appreciate the challenge of taking their own photograph for the image section. See Figure 21 for the CSI Debrief Template.

Frayer Model. Although the Frayer Model (http://bit.ly/sem-tech-frayer) was originally designed to promote vocabulary building, this graphic organizer can easily be elevated to provide a structure for students to explain their conceptual understanding of a given topic. The organizer is divided into four quadrants with one central section. In the center, ask the students to enter the topic of the Type I experience. In the top left quadrant, students are asked to define the topic. Here they might provide a general description or overview of the topic. In the top right quadrant, students should list facts or characteristics regarding the Type I experience. When completing this for the first time with your students, you may want to emphasize the distinction between these two boxes. In the lower half of the graphic organizer, students are asked to provide some examples and some nonexamples. By indicating what something is as well as what something is not, then students are able to develop a deeper understanding of the topic. As with all of the debriefing tools in this section, not every tool will work with every Type I experience. See Figure 22 for the Frayer Model Debrief Template.

I Used to Think, But Now I Think . . . Sometimes the best debriefings start with the easiest of prompts. Adapted from a Visible Thinking routine, "I Used to Think, But Now I Think . . ." (http://bit.ly/sem-tech-used-to-think) asks students to reflect on what they used to think about a topic before they had a Type I experience on the topic. This allows students to identify any preconceived

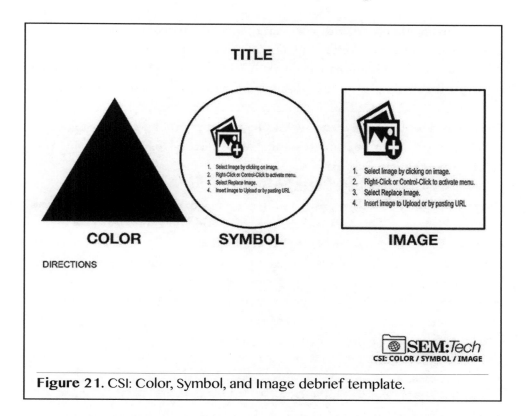

Figure 21. CSI: Color, Symbol, and Image debrief template.

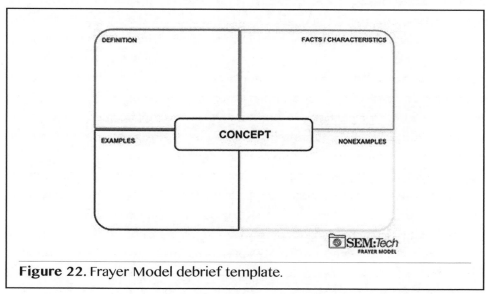

Figure 22. Frayer Model debrief template.

103

notions or prior knowledge. By connecting what was previously thought to what the students currently think, they are able to reflect on the learning that has taken place. Although this may seem like a very simple prompt, it has the potential to lead to thought-provoking discussions with your students. This prompt is particularly useful with Type I experiences that have shifted students' perspectives about a topic or provided new information that may have clarified students' misconceptions or limited understanding of a topic. See Figure 23 for the I Used to Think . . . Debrief Template.

Hexagonal Thinking. The purpose of the Hexagonal Thinking Map (http://bit.ly/sem-tech-hexagon) is for students to begin exploring the connections between their ideas and concepts of a Type I experience. This Google Drawing contains a dozen hexagons distributed across the page. Ask your students to change the text in each hexagon to reflect something that they learned or found interesting about the Type I experience. Each of the hexagons is a separate image and can be moved anywhere on the page. Ask your students to find the connections between each of their thoughts by positioning hexagons adjacent to each other that are related. Hexagons that are touching each other must be related in some way. Each hexagon may be related to as few as one or as many as six hexagons.

Although this activity could be completed individually, the discussions could be much more engaging and meaningful for students if they were working as pairs or trios. Because the Google Drawing is collaborative, multiple students can work simultaneously if they each have their own device. Additional hexagons can easily be added by copying an existing hexagon and pasting it onto the page. This is a debriefing activity that could be used with almost any Type I experience and will serve to help students see the interconnectedness of a topic. See Figure 24 for the Hexagonal Thinking Debrief Template.

Question Starts. A common behavioral characteristic of gifted learners is question asking. This search for answers is heightened when a student is particularly interested in or passionate about a topic. Unfortunately, this high level of curiosity is often squelched. For those students who seem to be incessant in their question asking, the Questions Starts (http://bit.ly/sem-tech-question-starts) strategy will help them to focus on quality questions rather than the quantity of questions. Additionally, the prompts presented are also beneficial to students who are not sure exactly where to start in their question asking.

Invite students to brainstorm a list of at least 12 questions about the topic, concept, or object that has been presented as part of the Type I experience. Students may use these question-starts to help them think of interesting

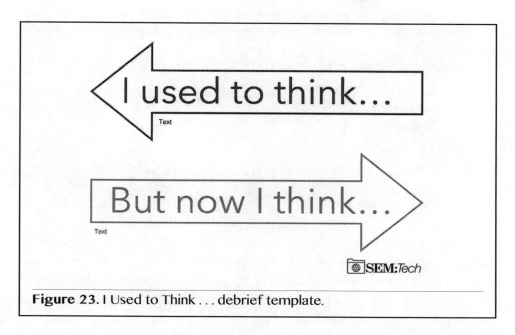

Figure 23. I Used to Think . . . debrief template.

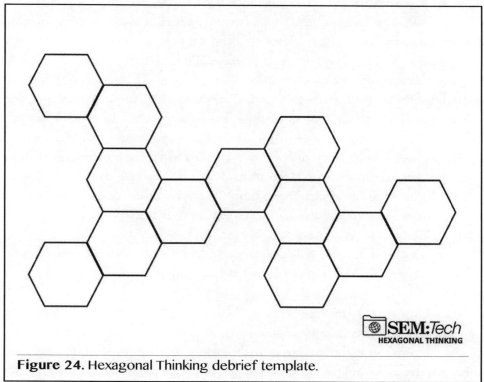

Figure 24. Hexagonal Thinking debrief template.

questions, but they should not feel limited by what is presented here. Consider the following:

- › Why . . . ?
- › How would it be different if . . . ?
- › What are the reasons . . . ?
- › Suppose that . . . ?
- › What if . . . ?
- › What if we knew . . . ?
- › What is the purpose of . . . ?
- › What would change if . . . ?

After the students have constructed a list of at least a dozen questions, have them review the brainstormed list and highlight the questions that seem most interesting. Then, select one or more of the starred questions to discuss with someone else for a few moments. During this time, the students may realize that they have similar questions, or they might realize that there are a variety of different perspectives presented. Finally, have the students reflect on what new ideas have emerged as a result of this activity. As a part of this reflection, look for opportunities to extend the students' thinking into a Type II or Type III activity. See Figure 25 for the Question Starts Debrief Template.

The Cartesian Debrief. Using a two-dimensional Cartesian coordinate for debriefing (http://bit.ly/sem-tech-cartesian) provides a unique opportunity for students to think about aspects of their Type I experience in *relation* to each other. As the teacher, you can define dimensions you would like for them to consider or you can let them define the dimensions that are most meaningful to them. For example, we've seen students explore relationships like:

- › Rational to Emotional in relation to Actions to Ideas
- › Informative to Uninformative in relation to Biased to Impartial
- › Strengths to Weaknesses in relation to Opportunities to Threats
- › Relevant to Inapplicable in relation to Modern and Antiquated
- › Concrete to Abstract in relation to Inspiring to Boring

The Cartesian Debrief (see Figure 26) is one of the easiest to differentiate. For primary students, simply separate the axes into two separate lines. This allows them to think about degrees without forcing them to consider relationships directly. For younger students, you might define dimensions like:

- › Fun to Not Fun on one line and Right and Wrong on another line
- › Good to Bad on one line and New to Past on another line
- › True to Untrue on one line and Funny to Sad on another line

106

QUESTION STARTS

Brainstorm a list of at least 12 questions about the topic, concept or object. Use these question-starts to help you think of interesting questions:

Why...?

How would it be different if...?

What are the reasons...?

Suppose that...?

What if...?

What if we knew...?

What is the purpose of...?

What would change if...?

Review the brainstormed list and HIGHLIGHT the questions that seem most interesting. Then, select one or more of the starred questions to discuss.

REFLECT: What new ideas do you have about the topic, concept or object that you did not have before?

Figure 25. Question Starts debrief template.

The important thing to remember here is that this is not an academic exercise, but rather an opportunity for students to think about how the Type I experience relates to their personal values and interests. It is okay if they say the Type I was boring or not fun. This gives you information about the students' interests and helps you understand the kind of experiences that are engaging for them.

Finally, you may want to include questions to help scaffold students' thinking, particularly the first time students engage in the Cartesian Debrief. Take, for example, the Informative/Uninformative and Biased/Impartial example. You can identify the axes' characteristics; one axis is assessing the content in relation

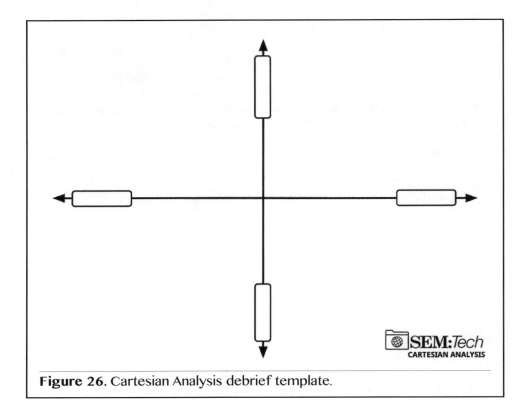

Figure 26. Cartesian Analysis debrief template.

to the students' background knowledge and the other axis is assessing the information provided based on the students' ability to critically examine the information. Table 2 is an example of how you might scaffold the debriefing process.

The Bull's-Eye. During a Type I experience, students may have a multitude of ideas, thoughts, and perspectives regarding the topic. The Bull's-Eye (http://bit.ly/sem-tech-bullseye) helps students to visualize what is central to their thinking and what is tangential. Based on the Visible Thinking routine, Generate, Sort, Connect, and Elaborate, this strategy is combined with a graphic organizer to aid in transitioning abstract ideas into a concrete representation of thought. During the debriefing, students should begin by generating a list of ideas or initial thoughts. Ten small circles or bubbles are provided to start this process. Students are able to select each and then replace the text in each circle. The text and circles can be resized and color-coded as each user sees fit. Next, the students should sort their ideas and place them onto the bull's-eye. Central ideas are placed near the center and more tangential ideas are toward the outside of the figure. The circles can easily be reorganized on the page by clicking and dragging each one separately. Students may choose to overlap the circles to show their close relationship with one another. After the circles have been placed, ask

TABLE 2
SCAFFOLDING FOR CARTESIAN DEBRIEF

Consider the following questions as you complete your Cartesian Debrief.

CONTENT		PARTIALITY	
Informative	**Uninformative**	**Biased**	**Impartial**
How was the information new to me? Did I learn something new that I did not know before? How did I grow as a result of the information?	Have I heard this information before? What did I already understand about the topic before? Was I surprised by any of the information provided?	How did the information presented change my thinking? Was the presenter trying to persuade me to a particular way of thinking? What opinions did the presenter express?	Was the information provided based on fact? How do I know? What evidence did the presenter provide to support his or her opinion? Does the presenter have a strong understanding of the topic?

students to connect related concepts with lines using the drawing tool. Students might also choose to change the color of the thought circles to indicate a relationship between ideas or concepts. After this step, it would be a beneficial time to have the students explain how and why they made their choices. Finally, ask the students if they would like to elaborate on their thoughts by adding any new ideas that might significantly expand their thinking. During this step, look for opportunities to extend the students' thinking and interest in the topic to Type II or Type III activities. We have presented a Google Drawings organizer for you and your students to use. However this could just as easily be accomplished with chart paper and sticky notes. You should always choose what is going to be best for you and your students and focus on the thinking and learning in a task rather than on the technology. See Figure 27 for the Bull's-Eye Debrief Template.

(Why x Five). Undoubtedly, you have experienced a precocious toddler who incessantly asks the question, "Why?" in an attempt to make sense of the world around her. Often this insatiable curiosity is squashed out of her at an early age with a resounding, "Because, I said so!" However, for many of our gifted and talented students, this line of inquiry continues throughout their early school years. Although there is a tendency to simply be annoyed, did you ever stop to think that there is something that we can learn from these inquisitive minds? As suggested by Michelle Macdonald in her 2016 blog post, "How Asking 'Why' 5 Times Can Change Your Life" (http://www.entrepreneur.com/article/253820), asking "Why?" multiple times helps one get to the root of the problem. Similarly,

109

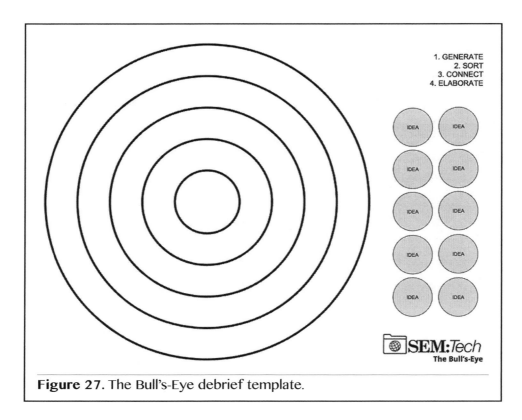

Figure 27. The Bull's-Eye debrief template.

setting up a situation where students are asking "Why?" multiple times helps them get past their first idea and dig deeper.

Although this debriefing strategy may not work with every Type I experience, we do feel that it could be a helpful way for inquisitive students struggling with an issue that been has raised to get to the root of a problem and springboard into a potential Type III project. Using the template (http://bit.ly/sem-tech-why), students are invited to ask "why" and then to think of a "because" response five separate times. With each "why," the student should delve to a deeper level in a way that is akin to peeling away the layers of an onion. After five rounds, a deeper problem is revealed, and the student is asked the question, "How could this problem be solved?" Although this debriefing activity could be completed by an individual student, students working in small groups could benefit from the rich conversations resulting from each of the resulting "because" statements. See Figure 28 for the (Why x Five) Debrief Template.

SEM:*Tech*

WHY? X FIVE

WHY #1

Because

WHY #2

Because

WHY #3

Because

WHY #4

Because

WHY #5

Because

How could you solve this problem?

Figure 28. (Why x Five) debrief template.

Other Tech Options

Beyond the use of the Google Drawing templates we have created, lies a whole host of other technology-related options for debriefing a Type I experience with your students. In this section, we will highlight some viable options for helping students unpack their experiences and deepen their understanding.

Blog posts and discussion boards. Depending on the delivery method of a Type I, the experience may not be synchronous with a group of students. Many opportunities exist to construct a range of Type I experiences that could be enjoyed by individual students at various times. One way to effectively manage student discussions is to have them reflect on the Type I experience on a blog or discussion board.

During a typical in-class discussion or debrief, there is a clear preference given to those students who are more verbal and able to confidently interject their ideas into a conversation. As a teacher or facilitator of such a group, you have probably noticed that there is often an individual or small group of students who tend to dominate the conversation. By incorporating a blog or discussion board, all of the students have an equal opportunity to have their voices be heard (or rather, read). Also, this allows students some time to reflect on their thinking and compose their thoughts in a thoughtful manner. Some students may find it difficult to get a word in edgewise, but when everyone is expected to post their thoughts, then it creates a different environment. In class, discussions might extend from your students' postings. Keep in mind that this is quite different than asking students to write a reflection that only you, the teacher, will read. Instead, students' ideas are positioned for a much broader audience. Also, by creating this type of online forum, the discussion is not limited to only the class period. Instead, the conversation can continue well beyond the time and space that was initially allotted for debriefing.

3 words, 2 questions, and 1 metaphor. Sometimes students need a place to start their thinking and a technique to focus their ideas about a given experience. In this activity, adapted from a Visible Thinking routine, students are invited to respond in three very different ways.

First, students come up with three words regarding the Type I experience. These three words might represent how they felt, ideas that came to mind, or concepts that came to mind or that they heard specifically mentioned or used in the experience. This part is intentionally left open-ended with the one restriction that it is only three words. In using this strategy, you might find that some students will come up with a three-word phrase or even strategically hyphenate words to get in more content. Regardless of a student's ability level, he or she will be able to identify three words. You will begin to see varying levels of understanding and thinking in this stage.

If you were to create a survey using Google Forms (http://www.google.com/forms), you could take the words that were submitted and copy and paste them into a word cloud generator like Wordle (http://wordle.net) or Tagxedo (http://www.tagxedo.com) to analyze the frequency of the words. In a word cloud, words that appear more frequently will appear larger and words used less frequently will appear smaller.

Second, ask the students to create two questions regarding the Type I experience. These questions might be about the content that was presented. Some students might choose to imagine that they are asking the speaker in a video a question. Others may pose questions of a more philosophical nature. It is in the types and levels of questions that the students ask that you can begin to see how interested they might be in the topic. Also, by allowing everyone to create questions, you will be able to see a broad range of perspectives in your students' understanding. In this stage, you also will be able to see the complexity in your students' thinking based on the quality of the questions that are being asked.

Finally, students are asked to compose one metaphor based on the Type I experience. Here you will be able to see students make connections between what has been presented to other aspects of their prior knowledge and to the world as a whole. By asking students to think metaphorically, then you are able to gain further insight into your students. It is quite often during this stage that teachers report seeing students in a new light.

This debriefing activity also serves well in a before and after setting. In this manner, teachers and students are able to gain insight to what is already known about a topic or how students feel about the subject featured in the Type I experience. By utilizing the 3-2-1 activity before the experience, teachers and facilitators gain insight into any preconceived notions or misinformation that might be present. As with all of the debriefing guides presented in this section, it is important to remember that this is not intended to be an assessment, nor are there any right or wrong answers.

Headlines and hashtags. In some instances, there is an advantage in having students distill their thoughts and feelings about a Type I experience down to its essence. One classic debriefing strategy is to have students create a headline for a front-page newspaper article. Using this strategy, students are required to communicate a main idea or point of interest in an intriguing and succinct way. Although this is still a very worthwhile activity, today's students might be more responsive to the activity if it is instead framed as a tweet. Twitter was founded on the idea that instead of lengthy posts and discussions, users could communicate thought through short comments that were limited to 140 characters. Since its creation in 2006, Twitter has grown to well more than 300 million users. Although the use of 140 characters at first seems like a confinement, users have quickly learned how to creatively work inside of the box through the use of inventive spelling, acronyms, abbreviations, and hashtags.

You could make use of Twitter for a Type I debrief, asking students to use the same hashtag to mark your discussion and allow you then to search for their tweets using Twitter's search box. However, if you are hesitant to utilize Twitter, you could easily create a private chat room using TodaysMeet (https://todaysmeet.com). Created for education, TodaysMeet allows you to create a free discussion room for your students. You can decide how long you would like for your room to be available online, ranging from one hour to one month. To invite students to your TodaysMeet discussion room, you must simply provide them with the room name. Participants do not need to create an account and they do not need an e-mail address. Each post is limited to 140 characters. By utilizing this tool, you can empower students to speak and share without having to wait their turn. You will also have a record of the transcript that you can refer back to.

Another option for these types of discussions with even more features is Padlet (https://padlet.com). Imagine an online version of sticky notes, and you will have a pretty good idea of what Padlet is. Although sticky notes allow you to write or draw ideas on them, Padlet expands this to allow users to not only enter text, but also upload files, take pictures using the camera on their device, record audio or video, and even insert hyperlinks to web resources. Posts can be reordered and organized on the page just as sticky notes would be on paper. When creating a Padlet, the layout is automatically set to freeform, which allows posts to be put anywhere and resized freely. We have found that in the idea generation stage this can often be confusing for users as they are inadvertently stacking their posts on top of one another. Our recommendation is to go into the settings and adjust the layout to either grid or stream. This will keep the posts separated from one another and allow all of the posts to easily be seen.

Nontech Options

Although the central focus of this book is the integration of technology into the learning environment, sometimes it is advisable to forget the technology. It is crucial to not allow your quest to utilize technology get in the way of the learning. Although we have presented a number of ways that technology could possibly enhance this stage of the Type I experience, we also see that there are multitudes of ways in which students' understanding can be deepened by not using technology. Each of the previous strategies and activities could be adapted and completed without the use of the Google Drawing templates. One compelling reason to not use the digital versions would be a lack of devices in your classroom. You must determine along with your students what means of debriefing and deepening understanding is going to be the most useful and meaningful. As we conclude our discussion of Deepening Understanding (Stage 3), we want to outline one additional strategy for debriefing that may work best without the use of technology.

The five questions. In their book, *Open to Outcome: A Practical Guide for Facilitating & Teaching Experiential Reflection*, Jacobson and Ruddy (2004) outline a framework of five questions that serve to guide the debriefing of an experience. The questions are based on the experiential learning cycle outlined by Kolb (1984) and Pfeiffer and Jones (1985) that is a central focus of the 4-H model of experiential learning.

Question 1: Did you notice . . . ? With the first question, students are describing what it is that they have experienced as part of the Type I. Jacobson and Ruddy (2004) asked us to note that this is closed-ended question. By asking a completely open-ended question, the topic can begin too broad and actually discourage responses in a group setting. We often may not be able to put into words what was just experienced. It is up to the teacher or facilitator to make an observation and to begin directing the debrief. By starting with a question that can be answered with a yes or no, you are able to provide an initial direction for the conversation and a natural way to ease into the debrief. The opening question is an invitation to the students to begin telling their story and sharing their experience.

Question 2: Why did that happen? With the second question, students are asked to interpret the experience. Note that this is an open-ended question. Here, the students are speculating about the cause-and-effect relationship of the experience. Use this question to help students connect this experience with their prior knowledge. Students should be encouraged to delve into the reasoning behind what they have observed.

Question 3: Does this happen in life? By shifting back to a yes or no question, students are able to begin making connections to other experiences that they may have had or to other content areas. As with the first question, by offering a closed question, the facilitator is able to shift the students' thinking and help them make connections to their own lives. Undoubtedly, students will want to explore these new connections within the discussion as it becomes more personal.

Question 4: Why does that happen? Shifting back to an open-ended prompt, Question 4 has the students continuing their generalization thinking. Here students are able to begin drawing conclusions about how these types of events take place in everyday life. As a result, students are able to make deeper connections between the Type I experience and themselves. Depending on the Type I and the content presented, students might identify existing issues or problems to be solved that are specific to the content of the Type I or even related to their own areas of interest in some way.

Question 5: How can you use this? The final question asks the students to look for ways that they might be able to apply what they have gained from the Type I experience to their own lives or to a deeper investigation of the content and material. This final question provides an open invitation for students to continue their study and investigation into a topic. As with any Type I experience, the students' line of inquiry and curiosity should not be extinguished because the lesson is over. Instead, the intent of every Type I Experience should be to add intellectual fuel to the fire of curiosity and interest.

CHAPTER 7

Type I— Student Experiences

Examples of student experiences may help to illustrate the ways that technology can support the development of Type I experiences. Here, we provide examples that are based on two potential student interests: traveling to Mars and taking selfies. With these expressed interests in mind, we develop Type I experiences in the hopes that we can encourage the interest in other students and further develop the fledgling interests in those students who identified these topics on their Interest-a-Lyzer.

These examples illustrate the full arc of a Type I experience, from heightening anticipation to creating the opportunities for going deeper into the content. Hopefully, these examples will support your efforts to provide powerful and engaging Type I experiences for your students.

Mission Possible

It probably comes as no surprise that many of the technologies that have been developed for space travel have improved our lives on Earth! For example, light-emitting diodes (LEDs) designed to grow plants on spacecrafts ease human muscle and joint pain on Earth. The National Aeronautics and Space Administration's (NASA) work on robotics and shock-absorbing materials is supporting the development of better human prostheses. Goodyear Tire and Rubber Company developed a material 5 times stronger than steel for NASA parachutes, which led to safer and longer lasting radial tires. These represent just a few of the technologies designed to support space exploration that benefit humans on Earth (NASA, 2008). Therefore, inspiring students with space travel is just one bridge to rich core content and the possibilities that lie beyond.

Sending astronauts to Mars is a top long-term priority of NASA's human spaceflight program. Its goal is to send humans to Mars by 2040. Engineers, researchers, scientists, historians, politicians, journalists, technicians, administrators, managers, accountants, craftspeople, artists, astronauts, and teachers represent just a few of the players who are integral to the success of a future crewed mission to Mars. NASA is not the only organization seeking human space flight to Mars, but it certainly has the most comprehensive plan and thoughtful consideration for returning astronauts to Earth.

Another group, Mars One, seeks to send humans on a one-way mission to Mars, to land the first colonists on the surface of the red planet. Their premise: The future of the human race cannot be confined to Earth. The approach this group is considering is very controversial, but rife with opportunities to consider the moral, ethical, logistical, emotional, cultural, societal, and political implications.

The notion of visiting another planet holds inherent interest for many students. Using a Type I approach alongside a topic that engages students' interest creates a pathway for deeper learning.

Stage 1: Heighten Anticipation

Students have seen so much about space travel—the historical Space Shuttle flights, the crewed International Space Station, SpaceX rocket tests, and so on—that they may not realize the true distance to Mars. To heighten anticipation and to quantify that distance, show students the video by David Paliwoda and Jesse Williams (http://www.distancetomars.com). This video provides a concrete visualization of the distance and allows students to understand how much farther Mars is from Earth than the moon. Be sure to point out to students that the International Space Station is in low Earth orbit! It is difficult to see at first, and this enables them to understand that the trips we make now are very short flights. Other things you might consider doing to heighten anticipation:

› Share the first minute of NASA's Orion flight test launch video (https://www.youtube.com/watch?v=UEuOpxOrA_0).

› Share the number of satellites orbiting Mars and the number of functioning rovers (https://en.wikipedia.org/wiki/List_of_artificial_objects_on_Mars).

Remember, heightening anticipation is creating a moment to build excitement, so this should be brief and *more is not better*. Really consider what might get your students excited and go with that. Time spent heightening anticipation for this example should be 5 minutes or less.

Stage 2: Stimulate Interest

In 2013, Mars One conducted a worldwide search for applicants to take the one-way flight to Mars. They received 202,586 applications, and by February of 2015, that list had been narrowed to 100. The 100 faces of the Mars One project (https://youtu.be/xxS7dCMBvSI) are introduced in a highly produced, very dramatic 2 1/2-minute video that plays like a blockbuster hit movie trailer.

Remember, the goal here is to stimulate interest in a way that engages students and opens the door to possibilities. The last thing we want to do is narrow students' thinking by sharing with them that the Mars One project is fraught with controversy and the likelihood of achieving its goal in the next 10 years is virtually impossible. Instead, we want to invite students to consider the potential and identify the problems to be solved—the problems of an unknown future. We want to make sure that students are considering beyond this moment and asking: What if? Other things you might consider doing to stimulate interest:

› Invite a guest speaker who has experience, knowledge, or understanding of space flight or space travel.
› Take a field trip to a museum with exhibits on Mars or space exploration.
› Do a series of themed Book Hooks on Mars. Here are just a few examples:
  » *The Martian Chronicles* by Ray Bradbury
  » *You Are the First Kid on Mars* by Patrick O'Brien
  » *Mission: Mars* by Pascal Lee
  » *Looking Down* by Steve Jenkins

› Show a movie clip of the popular Hollywood production *The Martian*.

Stage 3: Deepen Understanding

Now that you have shown students the Mars One video, it is time to help them consider what they just saw. To accomplish this, we are going to apply one of the Visible Thinking Routines developed by Harvard's Project Zero (http://visiblethinkingpz.org). Specifically, we have chosen to use their Compass Points routine, a core routine for examining propositions. The four points of the compass are represented as four considerations about the proposition of going to

Mars (see Figure 29; see also Compass Points Template, Chapter 5, Figure 18): Excited (E), Worrisome (W), Need to know (N), and Stance or Suggestion for moving forward (S). Each of these four considerations are then scaffolded with questions to help support students' thinking:

E — What excites you about the idea of a one-way trip to Mars?

W — What do you find worrisome about the idea of a one-way trip to Mars?

N — What else do you need to know about a one-way trip to Mars?

S — What is your current stance on the prospect of a one-way trip to Mars?

Using the Harvard Project Zero's Visible Thinking Routine allows students to consider the many implications of a one-way trip to Mars. If students get excited about the idea, it creates a bridge to deeper learning. If they decide they are definitely against sending people on a one-way trip, then you refocus them on NASA's approach designed to send humans to Mars and return them home safely.

Remember, it is important to listen to students and their excitement level for the process. If there is no joy or enthusiasm, then Mars may not be the right choice as a catalyst for deeper learning. However, when a Type I is successful, there are likely a few students who want to know more.

Opportunity to go beyond. Mars has entry points into so many different domains, providing opportunities to engage in processes that are meaningful for learning. The opportunities to go deeper at this point should still be designed to entice students to want to learn more. This is a delicate point in the process. Students have been introduced to the possibilities, asked to consider their own perspective on that proposition, and now they need more information. It is important, however, to avoid moving into a classical lesson too quickly. So consider some of these learning opportunities that provide fun, but informative follow-up, should a student's interest merit the need:

Apps

› *NASA App* (http://www.nasa.gov/centers/ames/iphone/index.html): The NASA app is for smartphones and tablets. It provides a collection of the latest NASA content. Mission information, videos, images, satellite tracking, and more are contained in this easy-to-use app.

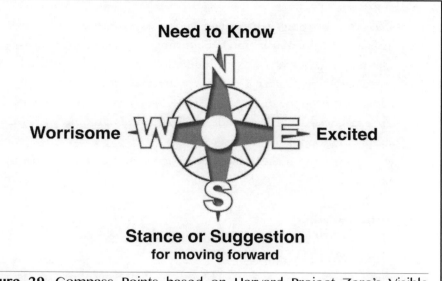

Figure 29. Compass Points based on Harvard Project Zero's Visible Thinking Routine.

› *NASA 3DV* (http://www.nasa.gov/content/new-nasa-app-shares-excitement-for-deep-space-missions): We love this app for tablets and smartphones because it allows the user to look in any direction, up, down, left, or right. This app provides a 360-degree visual experience in every direction. Students can see three-dimensional views of the Orion spacecraft, the Space Launch System, crawler transporters, and more.

› *Spacecraft 3D* (http://www.jpl.nasa.gov/apps): NASA's Jet Propulsion Lab's Spacecraft 3D is an augmented reality app for tablets and smartphones that gives students the ability to experience four different models. The 3D models allow students to see Mars Odyssey, Mars Reconnaissance Orbiter, Curiosity, and MAVEN, right on their desk!

› *Mars Globe* (http://midnightmartian.com/MarsGlobe): Do you want to explore the surface of Mars? This Apple app allows students to take a tour of the Mars surface. The virtual globe uses high resolution satellite images and topographic lighting so you can view the surface from above.

› *Eyes on the Solar System* (http://eyes.nasa.gov): NASA's Jet Propulsion Lab has developed a way for students to explore the cosmos from their computer. This app allows students to control space and time with this visualization tool, including comparing the size of the International Space Station to a yellow school bus.

Videos

› *Will future spacecraft fit in our pockets* (https://youtu.be/Y7IsyjFROHE): This TED-Ed video explores the future of spacecraft. Scientists suggest that micro spacecraft, which would fit into your pocket, could be sent to scout habitable planets and describe astronomical phenomena.

› *Mars: Crash Course Astronomy #15* (https://youtu.be/I-88YWx71gE): This fast-paced video provides a tremendous amount of information about Mars in a short time. Research-based knowledge combined with jump cuts make this video a dense and engaging informational experience.

Nonfiction Reading

› *How We'll Live on Mars* by Stephen L. Petranek
› *Mission: Mars* by Pascal Lee
› *The Mighty Mars Rovers: The Incredible Adventures of Spirit and Opportunity* by Elizabeth Rusch
› *Mars Up Close: Inside the Curiosity Mission* by Marc Kaufman

Selfies

Today's youth have become quite obsessed with taking selfies. If we think about this from a psychological development standpoint, then it is not necessarily surprising that as children develop into adolescents they begin exploring their own identities and their sense of self. Although previous generations may have spent hours in front of a mirror, the accessibility of technology serves to heighten the experience. Equipped with digital devices featuring forward-facing cameras, one can not only see one's self on the screen, but also capture an image of whatever he or she is doing, edit the image, apply filters, and instantly share it with the world. It is this social aspect that allows us to feel accepted, approved, and liked by our peers and by the world.

The topic of selfies is one that may be of great interest to a wide range of students. To tap into this concept and to demonstrate that it is not one that was recently created, we have assembled a range of resources and experiences that can demonstrate how selfies could extend through each of the three types of experiences of SEM:*Tech*. To best demonstrate what this might look like in your classroom, we have created a Blendspace for the topic: http://bit.ly/sem-tech-selfie-blendspace. See Figure 30 for the Blendspace sample.

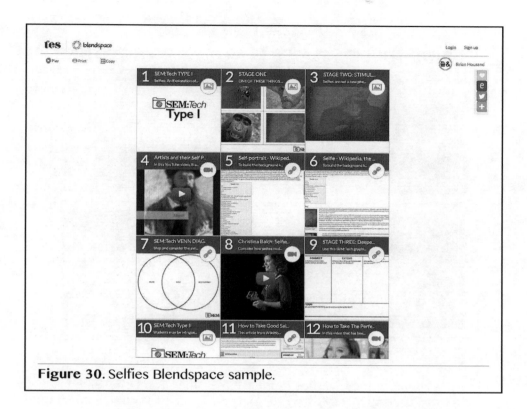

Figure 30. Selfies Blendspace sample.

For the Type I experience, we first want to establish what a selfie is and what it is not. In addition, we want students to consider the relationship that exists between selfies and self-portraits. In the Type I experience, we will guide students through each of the three stages.

Stage 1: Heighten Anticipation

The illustration in Figure 31 demonstrates how this strategy could be used with your students as a means of heightening anticipation for a Type I experience about the history of self-portraits and selfies. This collection of four images was intentionally selected to have a great deal in common while also being unique. There are subtle differences between each of the images with the express purpose of spawning debate and discussion about which image is not like the others. For example, the Van Gogh painting is not a photograph, but a self-portrait. The images of NASA's Curiosity rover and the macaque are not images that were taken by a person. Does that make them selfies? Students might be interested to learn that on December 22, 2014, the United States Copyright Office stated that the works created by nonhumans are not subject to copyright, including photographs taken by monkeys. The fourth image is a photograph taken in 1839

Figure 31. One of these selfies is not like the other. Top Left: Selfie taken by NASA's Curiosity Mars Rover (2016). Top Right: Self-Portrait with Straw Hat (1887) by Vincent Van Gogh. Bottom Left: Self-portrait by the depicted *Macaca nigra* female. Bottom Right: The first photographic portrait ever made was a self-portrait by Robert Cornelius in 1839.

by Robert Cornelius and is considered to be the first photographic portrait ever made. Interestingly, it was a self-portrait by Cornelius. The collection of images can be accessed at http://bit.ly/sem-tech-other-selfie.

Rather than providing examples and nonexamples with obvious differences, one can increase the complexity to deepen students' understanding and broaden their perspectives of the concept being presented. This is intentionally a messy problem.

Have the students examine the four images and consider the following:

1. What do they have in common?
2. What are the differences between them?
3. Is there one that is significantly different from the other three? Why?

Make your case for why your response is correct.

Stage 2: Stimulate Interest

In Stage 2, aim to take students from a heightened sense of anticipation to a state of stimulated interest by providing some background information and new information. For example, selfies are not a new phenomenon. Since the introduction of photography, people have been taking pictures of themselves. Robert Cornelius, an American pioneer in photography, produced a daguerreotype of himself in 1839, which is also one of the first photographs of a person. Because the process was slow, he was able to uncover the lens, run into the shot for a minute or more, and then replace the lens cap. He recorded on the back "The first light Picture ever taken. 1839." Next, explore and present some of the history of selfies as described in this Wikipedia article (https://en.wikipedia.org/wiki/Selfie). By this point, students may begin to see the connections between selfies and self-portraits.

In the video "Artists and their Self Portraits" (https://youtu.be/73aD0682yBE), Blake Prim, an elementary art teacher, assembles 40 self-portraits by some of the greatest artists of all time. This video demonstrates the long history and artistic merits of self-portraits. Have students consider how and if self-portraits are significantly different than selfies. As a follow-up, gather appropriate information from or refer to the Wikipedia entry on self-portrait (https://en.wikipedia.org/wiki/Self-portrait).

Next, you might have students clarify the similarities and differences of a selfie and a self-portrait using a Venn diagram. We have designed a Google Drawing (http://bit.ly/sem-tech-venn-selfie) to help facilitate this process. Students can make a copy of the Google Drawing by going to the "File" menu and selecting "Make a copy." A copy will be added to their Google Drive folder. This copy can then be shared with you or with other students for collaboration.

After discussing the similarities and differences between selfies and self-portraits, watch the 3-minute TED Talk from Christina Balch (https://youtu.be/iyBprFsu900) entitled "Selfies and seeing ourselves—one artist's look in the mirror." Here, we can see how Balch uses the form of selfies to alter what we choose to celebrate. Instead of highlighting the most flattering images, Balch chooses to focus on what she looks like when she first wakes up in the morning. Have students consider how selfies could be used to explore who they are as a person and how they are a reflection of their identity.

Stage 3: Deepening Understanding

Now that students have some new information and perspective about selfies, it is time to deepen their understanding and help them to consider some possible technology infused projects that they might investigate. We have selected the SEM:*Tech* Connect, Extend, Wonder graphic organizer to facilitate this stage (http://bit.ly/sem-tech-cec).

CONNECT: How are the ideas and information presented connected to what you already knew?
EXTEND: What new ideas did you get that extended your thinking in new directions?
WONDER: What wonderings, puzzles, or questions do you now have?

As with the other Google Drawings, students are able to make a copy of the graphic organizer by going to the "File" menu and selecting "Make a copy." Be sure to take time to discuss with your students how they completed the form. As with any SEM:*Tech* debrief, the purpose is not to have the students simply completing a form. Instead, their understanding is deepened through the discussion that they have with you and their peers. As a part of this debrief, it is important to have the students consider their next steps by posing the question, "What could you do to continue exploring this topic?"

CHRISTY'S CORNER: A TYPE I

Christy finds that there is a lot of scaffolding that goes into making the Type I exposure experience something that leads students to want to go deeper. To support students in really embracing the learning opportunity that a Type I experience has to offer, she first starts by heightening anticipation for her planned Type I exposure experience. In one case, Christy heightened anticipation by inviting a former student to share a video game he had created using Scratch, a programming language developed by the MIT Media Lab. Once the young man showed students the game and talked about some of the processes he used to create the game, students got the opportunity to play the game! Playing the game got students excited to learn more about coding.

Christy had already planned to have an enrichment cluster on coding as a way to stimulate interest in computer programming. For 8 weeks, her former student returned to school to work with students as they created their own programs using Scratch (https://scratch.mit.edu).

Less than 10% of the school population is identified as gifted in Christy's school, and she felt it was important to provide this learning opportunity to more students than just her formally identified gifted population. Therefore, Christy provided the enrichment cluster opportunity to any student in the fifth grade who was interested in creating a video game or learning about coding. We asked Christy why she only wanted fifth graders to participate that year and her response was that she wanted to start small: "I would rather do a little bit well and scale up than to start too big and fail."

One aspect of implementing this kind of instructional approach surprised Christy. The fourth Friday of the enrichment cluster, Christy missed a session:

> I came back and I couldn't catch up. They were so far ahead of what I could do. I could say to students, "Hey, that looks great" or "Nice job," but I wasn't really helping them. They helped each other. I had to let go, but I found that it was very empowering for students to surpass their teacher.

After that experience, Christy characterized it as one of the great strengths of the SEM approach to instruction. Christy was able to take on the role of facilitator and allow students to become the experts. The enrichment cluster was a success! Fifteen students participated and by the end, each had developed his or her own coded creation and shared it in the community available on the Scratch website. One student's passion for designing code was ignited, leading to further investigation.

The combination of seeing a former student's product and learning about coding enabled students to see that they could learn about something "real," something that professionals do.

Steps to Create Your Type I

We have given you several examples of Type I learning opportunities and even provided resources that you can use as your own Type I starters. Now it is your turn to develop a Type I. We will guide you through the process. Simply follow these steps:

1. Review the students' interest inventories. Look for trends or patterns in their interests.

2. List potential topics for Type I. Remember to focus on topics that are not typically covered in the core curriculum areas. Avoid thinking in terms of procedures, as you are not listing activities, just ideas for providing students with exposure to numerous and varied experiences. Think unusual topics, interesting people, current events, cool jobs, and unique opportunities.

3. Generate a long list of ideas. This should be a long list because you want to have a lot of ideas to choose from.

4. From the list, select a topic for a Type I experience that you feel might interest your students.

5. Once you have selected a topic, imagine an exciting event that you might provide for students. This will probably require online research. The event to Stimulate Interest could be a short and engaging video, a field trip, guest speaker, demonstration, artistic performance, news article, etc. Don't forget to look into opportunities for guest speakers to appear via Skype.

Remember, when developing a Type I, it should expand students' scope of experience, be an engaging event (e.g., a guest speaker, field trip), and spark interest. To accomplish this, make sure you:

1. Heighten Anticipation
2. Stimulate Interest
3. Deepen Understanding

When you are done, share your Type I with your colleagues because, as Leonard Nimoy noted, "The more we share, the more we have."

CHAPTER 8

Type II—
Technology
Processes

Type II processes are the strategies, skills, and dispositions that can be characterized as the "knowledge-how" components of learning in a digital age. Type II processes are necessary for students to become effective consumers of information and producers of new knowledge. It is important for all students to develop thinking and problem-solving capacity like that in the Type II processes.

How does Type II instruction differ from other pedagogical and curricular approaches? To illustrate the difference, we often ask the question: What is the non-negotiable content that students need to learn? Typically we get responses like "decoding," "math facts," or the "scientific method." When we think about this question and begin to dig deeper into what the question is asking, it starts to be a simpler question: What do students need to memorize to be successful in life? Certainly one could argue that memorizing math facts and letters is important, but following closely behind that notion is the thought that students should learn to read. Yes, they must learn to read, but now there has been a fundamental shift in thought: Reading or being able to read constitutes a set of skills that result in the process of reading. Similarly, the scientific method is a set of skills that together create a process of inquiry. This is the essential beauty of Type II processes as a pedagogical approach to instruction: Type II focuses on developing the thinking and problem-solving processes rather than memorizing information that could easily be found with a Google search.

Another way that Type II instruction differs from other curricular approaches is the way in which it relates to the standards, particularly skills-based standards like that of the Common Core State Standards (CCSS). It is important to note that there is a lot of controversy around the CCSS. In our minds, the problem with the CCSS is not the standards themselves, but rather how they are implemented in schools. What often happens in the design of curricular materials is someone picks up the standards and says, "We are going to design a lesson around these three standards." The impetus for learning in this case becomes the standards themselves rather than *real* learning and solving *real* problems. Within the Type II processes, the learning is based on students' needs rather than on the standards. As students need new information or to develop new skills to find solutions to their problem or pursue their own curiosity, they naturally develop the skills of learning along the way, whereas when the lesson is designed around the standards, students develop the skills but without a frame of reference that allows them to apply those skills in meaningful ways. The learning is abstracted because the students solve one theoretical problem after another, but they don't really get to apply their learning to their own experience of the world. They apply it to the curriculum designer's contrived experience.

Type II processes provide instructional methods and materials designed to support the development of children as thinking and feeling beings. They are curious, want to share what they understand, and are continuously growing. To support the development of a child's mind, Type II processes teach cognitive skills, affective skills, learning how-to-learn skills, advanced research skills, and communication skills (see Table 3).

In the SEM:*Tech*, we have developed a Taxonomy of Type II Processes for the Digital Age (see Table 4). This Taxonomy is an extension of the original Taxonomy of Type II Enrichment Process Skills (see Appendix A). The original Taxonomy of Type II Enrichment Process Skills, first published in 1985, was well ahead of its time. Many of the skills associated with college and career readiness or being successful in the 21st century are the same skills listed in that original work. Now, almost 40 years later, we attempt to do two things in the SEM:*Tech* Taxonomy. First, we make a shift away from the notion that these types of skills are for enrichment purposes alone. Instead, we see these skills as fundamental to success in learning and life, particularly as we prepare students for an ill-defined future where they may be working in jobs that do not currently exist. The SEM:*Tech* Processes Taxonomy for the Digital Age presents skills that are fundamental rights of all learners. These skills will enrich and enliven the curriculum, but more importantly, these processes shift the focus away from achievement on standardized tests (e.g., content memorization, application of skills to contrived or theoretical situations) to success in the work of being a student and the work of life.

TABLE 3

TYPE II PROCESSES FOR LEARNING

The Child	Development Supported by Type II
Thinking	Cognitive skills
Feeling	Affective skills
Growing/Seeking	How-to-learn skills
Sharing	Communication skills
Questioning/Curious	Advanced research skills

The second thing we try to accomplish in this extension taxonomy is to focus on the skills for consuming and producing knowledge in a digital age. In traditional educational settings, the focus was on the skills associated with consuming information. For example, standardized tests of the last decade have measured subject-specific knowledge, and "school success skills" were essentially reading comprehension and getting the "right" answer to math problems. Even now, with new forms of standardized tests that require students to show their work, students have to learn the "right" processes to be successful. Real problems don't have "right" answers. Real problems have current best solutions, and these solutions are only the best until someone comes along and does it better. We cannot teach children to seek "right" answers, rather we must teach children to seek solutions—the best solution attainable given their current understanding, access to resources, and limits of technological advancement. Therefore, we make the distinction between consuming information and producing new knowledge. As we prepare students to become contributing members of society, they will have to be both consumers and producers, particularly if we want them to solve the world's most pressing problems and advance society into the future

Given that we are talking about a digital society with an unknown future, the extension is simplified from the original version and some domains have been added. For example, effective communication via digital media requires individuals to be able to express themselves verbally through written and oral communication, which is not new. Written and oral communication is not enough. Students must also be able to communicate in graphics (e.g., data visualization) and code (e.g., computer programing) to be successful in the rapidly advancing technology-driven world in which we live.

Like the original Taxonomy of Type II Enrichment Process Skills, these are not intended to present a complete list of every thinking and feeling process. Also, while we set out to provide lists separated by consuming information versus producing new knowledge, the processes presented here are not mutually

TABLE 4
SEM:TECH—A TAXONOMY OF TYPE II PROCESSES FOR THE DIGITAL AGE

Processes and Skills for Consuming Information Using Technology		
Understanding basic technology	• Using technology devices (e.g. computer, tablet, phone, etc.) • Creating, editing, and modifying digital files • Troubleshooting hardware and software problems	• Saving data • Accessing the Internet • Independently assessing web-based information
Becoming self-aware	• Analyzing strengths and weaknesses • Self-reflecting	• Clarifying values • Developing coping behaviors
Listening, observing, and perceiving	• Focusing attention • Identifying themes, main points, and concepts • Asking questions • Following directions	• Active listening • Separating relevant from irrelevant information • Making inferences and predictions
Searching for information	• Identifying types and sources of information • Triangulating sources • Assessing sources • Using information retrieval systems (e.g., library and search engines)	• Understanding the specialized types of reference information (tables, charts, directories, timelines, infographics) • Understanding nontext reference information (videos, images, graphs)

Evaluating information	• Highlighting
	• Bookmarking
	• Identifying:
	  ◦ Content
	  ◦ Elements
	  ◦ Trends and patterns
	  ◦ Relationships
	  ◦ Organizing principle
	  ◦ Propaganda and bias
		• Assessing quality
		• Reflecting
		• Understanding whole/part relationships
		• Identifying the "big picture," patterns, themes, sequences

Processes and Skills for Productivity Using Technology		
Self-regulation	• Planning • Monitoring progress • Self-directing • Self-consequating • Reflecting	• Persevering • Prioritizing • Maintaining comfort with ambiguity
Curating	• Discovering • Gathering • Presenting • Determining relevance • Categorizing	• Contextualizing • Refining style • Understanding whole/part relationships
Conducting research	• Synthesizing extant research • Gathering data • Organizing data • Coding and classifying data	• Analyzing data • Drawing conclusions • Making generalizations • Reporting results

TABLE 4, *continued*

Processes and Skills for Productivity Using Technology, *continued*		
Generating ideas	• Fluency • Flexibility • Originality • Elaboration	• Forced relationships • Comparison • Attribute listing • Association
Modifying	• Substitution • Combination • Adaptation	• Magnification • Elaboration • Reversal
Iterating	• Rapid prototyping • Evolving ideas • Testing and redesign	• Risk taking • Failing
Critical thinking	• Conditional reasoning • Classification • Validity testing • Reliability testing • Translation	• Interpretation • Extrapolation • Patterning sequencing • Inductive/deductive reasoning
Problem solving	• Problem finding • Problem focusing	• Solution finding • Idea finding
Decision making	• Identifying desired goal states • Identifying obstacles and constraints	• Identifying alternatives • Understanding cause and effect
Collaborating	• Understanding others • Working in groups • Peer relationships	• Dealing with conflict • Coping behaviors

Communicating effectively	• Identifying audience
	• Editing and selecting content
	• Developing technique
	• Developing style
	• Storytelling
	• Written communication:
	  • Using proper grammar
	  • Developing paragraphs
	  • Developing four basic writing forms (exposition, argumentation, description, and narration)
	• Oral communication:
	  • Vocal delivery
	  • Developing presence (gestures, eye contact, expression)
		• Visual communication:
		  • Website development
		  • Video production (recording, editing, lighting, sound, visual design)
		  • Creating multimedia images
		  • Taking photographs
		  • Creating presentation slides
		  • Creating infographics
		  • Graphic design (color, space, composition, typography)
		• Digital communication:
		  • Coding
		  • Animating
		  • Illustrating

exclusive. As you work to help students learn these skills, it quickly becomes clear that they are difficult to separate because there are many instances when the processes interact with one another. When students are learning these processes as part of authentic problem solving, the need for applying several processes simultaneously is obvious. Remember, problem solving is cyclical and ongoing; so, too, is the application of these processes. Because this is the case, these skills should not be taught in an item-by-item fashion, but rather as integrated parts of a larger whole.

The Schoolwide Enrichment Model (Renzulli & Reis, 1985) is not the only model proposing a processes and skills approach for student learning, but it may be the first. As technology becomes increasingly integrated into our daily lives, others have proposed similar approaches to learning in a digital age. For example, The International Society for Technology in Education (ISTE, 2016) provides a set of standards to prepare students for the future. Similarly, the Partnership for 21st Century Learning (P21, 2009) has proposed a framework of skills and knowledge students need to succeed.

When we compare the original Taxonomy of Type II Skills with modern standards for skill development in technology, we see several similarities (see Table 5). For example the ISTE standards for students focus on cross-curricular skills that help students become successful participants in a globalized society. The ISTE standards for students focus on students being active agents in the learning process to take on the roles of contributing members of society. In much the same way that the Enrichment Triad Model (Renzulli, 1977) seeks to have students thinking, feeling, and doing like practicing professionals, the ISTE standards require students to take on active learner roles. The ISTE learner roles are:

1. Empowered Learner
2. Digital Citizen
3. Knowledge Constructor
4. Innovative Designer
5. Computational Thinker
6. Creative Communicator
7. Global Collaborator

Likewise, P21 proposes a framework of knowledge and skills that enable students in today's classrooms to succeed in work, life, and citizenship. Like the Taxonomy of Type II Processes, the framework includes life and career skills, learning and innovation skills, as well as information, media, and technology skills.

TABLE 5

COMPARISON OF SEM:TECH TYPE II TAXONOMY, ISTE STANDARDS, AND P21 FRAMEWORK

SEM:*Tech* Type II Processes	P21 Framework for 21st Century Learning (2009)	ISTE Standards for Students (2016)
Learning How-to-Learn Skills		
Conducting research		Computational Thinker: b. Collect data or identify relevant data sets, use digital tools to analyze them, and represent data in various ways to facilitate problem-solving and decision-making.
Evaluating information	Critical Thinking & Problem Solving: ♦ Use systems thinking.	Computational Thinker: c. Break problems into component parts, extract key information, and develop descriptive models to understand complex systems or facilitate problem solving.
Critical thinking	Critical Thinking & Problem Solving: ♦ Reason effectively.	Knowledge Constructor: d. Build knowledge by actively exploring real-world issues and problems, developing ideas and theories and pursuing answers and solutions.
Innovation Skills		
Modifying	Creativity & Innovation: ♦ Think creatively.	Creative Communicator: b. Create original works or responsibly repurpose or remix digital resources into new creations.
Iterating	Creativity & Innovation: ♦ Implement innovation.	Innovative Designer: a. Know and use a deliberate design process for generating ideas, testing theories, creating innovative artifacts or solving authentic problems. c. Develop, test and refine prototypes as part of a cyclical design process.
Problem solving	Critical Thinking & Problem Solving: ♦ Solve problems.	Innovative Designer: a. Know and use a deliberate design process for generating ideas, testing theories, creating innovative artifacts or solving authentic problems. Computational Thinker: a. Formulate problem definitions suited for technology-assisted methods such as data analysis, abstract models and algorithmic thinking. c. Break problems into component parts, extract key information, and develop descriptive models to understand complex systems or facilitate problem solving.
Decision making	Critical Thinking & Problem Solving: ♦ Make judgments and decisions.	Innovative Designer: b. Select and use digital tools to plan and manage a design process that considers design constraints and calculated risks.

TABLE 5, *continued*

SEM:*Tech* Type II Processes	P21 Framework for 21st Century Learning (2009)	ISTE Standards for Students (2016)
		Self-Regulatory Skills
Becoming self-aware		Digital Citizen: a. Cultivate and manage their digital identity and reputation and are aware of the permanence of their action in the digital world.
Self-regulation	Initiative & Self-Direction: • Manage goals and time. Work independently. • Be self-directed in learning. Productivity & Accountability: • Produce results. • Manage projects.	Empowered Learner: a. Articulate and set personal learning goals, develop strategies leveraging technology to achieve them and reflect on the learning process itself to improve learning outcomes. c. Use technology to seek feedback that informs and improves their practice and to demonstrate their learning in a variety of ways.
Generating Ideas	Flexibility & Adaptability: • Adapt to change. • Be flexible.	Innovative Designer: d. Exhibit a tolerance for ambiguity, perseverance and the capacity to work with open-ended problems.
		Communication and Collaboration Skills
Communicating effectively	Communicate clearly • Interact effectively with others.	Creative Communicator: a. Choose the appropriate platforms and tools for meeting the desired objectives of their creation or communication. c. Communicate complex ideas clearly and effectively by creating or using a variety of digital objects such as visualizations, models or simulations. d. Publish or present content that customizes the message and medium for their intended audiences.

TABLE 5, *continued*

SEM:*Tech* Type II Processes	P21 Framework for 21st Century Learning (2009)	ISTE Standards for Students (2016)
	Communication and Collaboration Skills, *continued*	
Collaborating	Creativity & Innovation: ♦ Work creatively with others. Communication & Collaboration: ♦ Collaborate with others. Social & Cross-Cultural Skills: ♦ Interact effectively with others. ♦ Work effectively in diverse team. Leadership & Responsibility: ♦ Guide and lead others. ♦ Be responsible to others.	Global Collaborator: a. Use digital tools to connect with learners from a variety of backgrounds and cultures, engaging with them in ways that broaden mutual understanding and learning. b. Use collaborative technologies to work with others, including peers, experts or community members, to examine issues and problems from multiple viewpoints. c. Contribute constructively to project teams, assuming various roles and responsibilities to work effectively toward a common goal. d. Explore local and global issues and use collaborative technologies to work with others to investigate solutions.
	Information and Media Literacy Skills	
Searching for information	Information Literacy: ♦ Access and evaluate information. ♦ Use and manage information. Media Literacy: ♦ Analyze media.	Digital Citizen: c. Demonstrate an understanding of and respect for the rights and obligations of using and sharing intellectual property. Knowledge Constructor: a. Plan and employ effective research strategies to locate information and other resources for their intellectual or creative pursuits.

137

TABLE 5, *continued*

SEM:*Tech* Type II Processes	P21 Framework for 21st Century Learning (2009)	ISTE Standards for Students (2016)
		Information and Media Literacy Skills, *continued*
Evaluating information	Information Literacy: ◆ Access and evaluate information. ◆ Use and manage information. Media Literacy: ◆ Analyze media.	Knowledge Constructor: b. Evaluate the accuracy, perspective, credibility and relevance of information, media, data or other resources.
Curating	Information Literacy: ◆ Use and manage information. Media Literacy: ◆ Analyze media. ◆ Create media products.	Knowledge Constructor: c. Curate information from digital resources using a variety of tools and methods to create collections of artifacts that demonstrate meaningful connections or conclusions.
		Technology Skills
Understanding basic technology	Information, Communications, & Technology Literacy: ◆ Apply technology effectively.	Empowered Learner: d. Understand the fundamental concepts of technology operations, demonstrate the ability to choose, use and troubleshoot current technologies and are able to transfer their knowledge to explore emerging technologies. Digital Citizen: d. Manage their personal data to maintain digital privacy and security and are aware of date-collection technology used to track their navigation online Knowledge Constructor: d. Build networks and customize their learning environments in ways that support the learning process.

With the emphasis on processes and skills becoming more common in the vernacular of education, we have a tremendous opportunity to engage students in learning that reflects their interests and honors their preferred expression styles. Now students can focus on creating products for an authentic audience, an audience that exists beyond the school walls. Students can practice using the conventions and tools of a profession as they seek to solve real problems (i.e., problems with no "right" answer). The nature of this kind of approach means that the learning transcends time and discipline, allowing students to develop skills and knowledge that are transferrable.

CHAPTER 9

Type II—
Technology
Skills

Basic Technology Skills

Before we can get started with the Type II processes in technology, there are some very basic technology skills that must be in place. These skills are the foundational skills that all students need to function in a technology-rich world. In the same way that reading, writing, and basic arithmetic were the skills necessary for successful living in the 20th century, technology basics have become necessary for successful living in the 21st century. Generally, these skills are:

1. Basic hardware and software skills
   a. Use a computer, tablet, smartphone, etc.
   b. Create, edit, and modify documents, presentations, and spreadsheets
   c. Back up data

2. Digital citizenship skills (Common Sense Media, 2015)
   a. Internet safety
   b. Privacy and security
   c. Relationship and communication
   d. Avoiding cyberbullying and digital drama
   e. Digital footprint and reputation
   f. Self-image and identity
   g. Information literacy
   h. Creative credit and copyright

3. Self-learning skills
    a. Effective Internet search
    b. Help menu search
    c. Utilize user information forums online to make minor fixes (e.g., when computer freezes, network connection is lost, etc.)

Students must develop the skills that will enable them to effectively use technology, but addressing *all* of these skills is beyond the scope of this book. There are numerous outlets that provide curriculum related to teaching these skills and we provide information about advancing many of these skills later in the book. Moreover, many of the Type II processes and Type I experiences in the SEM:*Tech* embed opportunities to teach these skills when you find some or many of the basic technology skills are missing from our students' toolboxes.

Therefore, we have to make determinations about the skills our students already possess through preassessment.

You may recall that we had students create a webpage to introduce themselves (see Chapter 3). The activity presented us with an opportunity to preassess students' skills. Further embedded within the activity were opportunities to teach and model more advanced skills. Having students create a webpage revealed whether or not students were able to:

› turn on the computer and log onto the Internet;
› effectively key a search term that enabled them to find the correct application on the Internet;
› navigate to find the login page;
› log in to the class site on their own given the requisite login information;
› navigate within the webpage creation site;
› utilize the tools available within webpage creation application (e.g., insert text, images, video; change the font, backgrounds, color schemes, and graphic organization);
› employ self-regulation strategies to find answers to questions;
› navigate between websites to search for images; and
› find public domain images, those images that are not protected by copyright.

Some of these skills are very basic and we would hope that students have already mastered them (e.g., turn on the computer and log in, open a search engine, navigate to a webpage on the Internet). We cannot, however, assume that students already possess these skills because early skill development in technology depends on access to computers and technology at home and in the classroom. Access varies widely across students based on family culture, socioeconomic status, and teachers' use of technology in the classroom.

Other skills listed above are more advanced (e.g., find public domain images, employ self-regulation strategies to find answers to questions). For these more advanced processes, students may benefit from having the skills reviewed, modeled, or explicitly taught. For some students, these skills may be grasped rapidly and almost intuitively, while for others, multiple practice opportunities will be required for mastery of even the most basic skills. Addressing this variability from an instructional perspective becomes easier as students collaborate with peers and work toward outcomes that are aligned with their personal interests.

Teaching technology skills is not the goal of the SEM: *Tech*. Instead the goal is to provide experiences that set the stage for developing technology skills that are seamlessly embedded within instruction to develop talent. That said, just as being able to decode words is foundational to being able to read, there are some foundational skills necessary for developing more advanced technology skills and dispositions. Therefore, we provide a preassessment checklist in Table 6. Consider these skills a starting point. This technology checklist is not meant to be comprehensive. It is merely designed to help us ensure we do not make assumptions about students' capabilities before we jump into preplanned Type II experiences. It is a precautionary first step in ensuring that students will meaningfully benefit from the skill development provided within Type II learning.

Digital Citizenship

We believe unequivocally that students need to develop the skills to participate in a global society safely and professionally. With the advent of computers, the Internet, and mobile devices, participation in society is no longer limited to region, state, or nation—participation in society occurs on a global stage and in a digital landscape. Gifted students must develop the skills and dispositions to make the world a better place by actively contributing to and benefiting from participation in society and becoming leaders who are wise, responsible, and compassionate.

As schools move to one computer or tablet for each student, it becomes increasingly important that students learn not only how to use these devices, but also how to use them appropriately. Digital citizenship, sometimes known as digital wellness or digital ethics, can be characterized as the norms of appropriate and responsible technology use. Digital citizenship helps define social mores for a society where technology is fully integrated. There are numerous approaches to

TABLE 6
BASIC TECHNOLOGY SKILLS CHECKLIST

Yes	Not Yet	Basic Computer Skills
		Identify parts of a computer system:
❑	❑	Monitor or screen
❑	❑	Keyboard, trackpad, mouse
❑	❑	Printer
❑	❑	Peripherals (e.g., surge protector, back-up storage, router, speakers)
		Demonstrate correct use of technology interface components:
❑	❑	Keyboard (10-finger typing with proper finger placement)
❑	❑	Mouse/trackpad (left click, right click, double click, click and drag, highlight text)
❑	❑	Touch screen
❑	❑	Printer (paper refill)
		Basic computer actions:
❑	❑	Turn computer on
❑	❑	Log in
❑	❑	Find and open applications
❑	❑	Switch between open programs
❑	❑	Create new files
❑	❑	Open and close existing files
❑	❑	Save files
❑	❑	Resize windows
Yes	**Not Yet**	**Word Processing Skills**
		Composition:
❑	❑	Type sentences and paragraphs at the keyboard
❑	❑	Use the keyboard fluently and accurately
❑	❑	Revise
❑	❑	Check spelling
		Functional actions:
❑	❑	Copy and paste
❑	❑	Insert letters
❑	❑	Delete letters
❑	❑	Replace letters
❑	❑	Format text (e.g., select, font size, bold, italics, justification)
❑	❑	Undo last text entry
❑	❑	Print file
❑	❑	Name and save file for later retrieval
Yes	**Not Yet**	**Internet Skills**
		Functional actions:
❑	❑	Open a web browser
❑	❑	Type a basic search into a text box
❑	❑	Open a new web browser tab
❑	❑	Click on links
		Navigation:
❑	❑	Find relevant search results
❑	❑	Navigate to a specific webpage
❑	❑	Switch between tabs

developing digital citizenry in our students. For example, Riddle (2015), in the book *Digital Citizenship in Schools*, organized the concept of digital citizenship into a framework of nine elements that inform ethical practices for technology use in school, at home, and in any community setting. His approach to organizing activities for students is called REPs: Respect, Educate, and Protect. The strength of his approach is that it provides a structure for developing, implementing, and assessing a schoolwide digital citizenship plan.

Another program for developing digital citizenship in students is the *K–12 Digital Literacy and Citizenship Curriculum* by Common Sense Media (2015). Educators at the Harvard Graduate School of Education developed this cross-curricular approach with a scope and sequence for kindergarten through 12th grade. This curriculum aligns with the Common Core State Standards, reflects the ISTE Standards for students, and is free. Although the two approaches to digital citizenship are different, they do have multiple similarities (see Table 7).

DID YOU KNOW?

A recent Stanford University study found that girls as young as 8 who spend a lot of time multitasking on digital devices tend to have lower self-confidence and social skills (Pea et al., 2012).

Type II for Advancing Basic Technology Skills

One of the challenges we face in educational settings today is the fact that technology is always changing and advancing. The idea of keeping up with technology, much less planning skills instruction, may seem overwhelming, but it is important to remember that having a learning disposition is the key to successfully learning alongside your students as new technologies come online, as you wade through the vastness of the Internet, and as you develop lessons that will engage your students.

TABLE 7
A COMPARISON OF DIGITAL CITIZENSHIP APPROACHES

Digital Citizenship in Schools (Riddle, 2015)	K-12 Digital Literacy and Citizenship Curriculum (Common Sense Media, 2015)
Digital Literacy: Learning how to learn and the processes of teaching specific to using technology effectively.	**Information Literacy:** Identifying, finding, evaluating, and using information effectively.
Digital Etiquette: Appropriate behavior and standards of conduct within a digital society. **Digital Communication:** The exchange of information in digital environments such as cell phone conversations, e-mail exchanges, participation on social media, etc.	**Relationships and Communication:** Using intrapersonal and interpersonal skills to build positive online communication and communities.
Digital Law: Understanding and being responsible for one's actions within digital environments.	**Creative Credit and Copyright:** Responsibilities and rights as creators and consumers as it relates to plagiarism, piracy, copyright, and fair use.
Digital Rights and Responsibilities: The basic rights extended to everyone in a digital society and the responsibilities that correspond with upholding those rights.	**Cyberbullying:** Exploring positive and negative actions that can have an effect on peers and the broader community. Building supportive online communities.
Digital Security: Protections that help to guarantee safety from adverse sources in a digital environment.	**Privacy and Security:** Managing online information and keeping it secure while avoiding online scams and schemes.
Digital Health and Wellness: Awareness about the inherent dangers, both physical and psychological, that exist when using technology.	**Digital Footprint and Reputation:** Understanding the permanency of digital content and avoiding overrevealing. **Self-Image and Identity:** Exploring digital lives through the comparison of online identity versus offline identity. **Internet Safety:** Understanding opportunities for collaboration with people worldwide while staying safe.
Digital Access: The equitable access to technology that enables full participation in a digital society.	
Digital Commerce: The ethical and legal concerns associated with buying and selling goods online.	

Searching the Internet

How many times have you gone online today? Did you check the weather this morning? Did you receive a push notification with the latest breaking news? Have you had a question and searched the Internet for the answer?

Notice that we did not ask *if* you had gone online, but rather *how many times*. It is becoming increasingly difficult for many to function without constant access to the world of information available on the Internet, but we don't just use the Internet to seek information. We use the Internet to learn, understand different points of view, gain access to a global society, and stay connected to family and friends. Broadband Internet is becoming more widely available, and slowly but surely the cost of connecting devices to the Internet is decreasing.

DID YOU KNOW?

Of teens ages 13–17, 92% go online daily (Lenhart et al., 2015), but only 31% of 12–15-year-olds can identify the advertisements in Google's search results (Ofcom, 2015).

With increased access and decreased cost, participation and information available on the Internet will continue to rise. Therefore, we MUST teach children *how to* search the Internet effectively, understand the information in the results they find, determine the best sources of information, identify advertisements in the search results, distinguish between fact and opinion, and save time by targeting their search effectively.

Search engines. As a teacher, your first inclination when considering an activity that requires students to go onto the Internet is probably: How do I keep students safe in online environments?

You might first consider how you teach children to keep themselves safe in the physical world: You explicitly teach them not to get into a car with strangers or that they must look both ways before crossing the street. In the same way, you have to explicitly teach students the skills of online safety using the Internet safety components of a digital citizenship curriculum. Once those skills have been addressed, it is time to go searching on the web.

Sometimes we forget that Google is only one of numerous options available for searching the Internet (see Table 8). There are hundreds of search engines

TABLE 8
POPULAR SEARCH ENGINES

Name	General Description	Web Address
Google	General; most recognized; top search engine globally	https://www.google.com
Yahoo!	General search engine; third largest in U.S.	https://www.yahoo.com
Search	Aggregator; prioritizes Google ads and results from CBS Content Network	https://www.search.com
Ask.com	Natural language (increases ease of use for learning search processes)	http://www.ask.com
AOL Search	General; provides a safe search filter	http://search.aol.com/aol/webhome
WOW	Aggregator; focused on entertainment and lifestyle; provides a safe search filter	http://www.wow.com
WebCrawler	Aggregator	https://www.webcrawler.com
MyWebSearch	General; powered by Google	http://home.mywebsearch.com/index.jhtml
InfoSpace	Aggregator	http://infospace.com
Info.com	Aggregator; results include social media results as sidebar	http://www.info.com
DuckDuckGo	Emphasizes protecting privacy and avoiding personalizing search results	https://duckduckgo.com
Dogpile	Aggregator that "fetches" results from multiple search engines	http://www.dogpile.com
Alhea	General	http://www.alhea.com

available for searching the Internet, and each search engine tries to distinguish itself with unique characteristics. With so many search engines to choose from, it might be worthwhile to consider some of the differences between them. For example, America OnLine (AOL) Search and WOW both provide a simple SafeSearch filter feature that excludes adult sites from search results. Seems like a great idea for educational settings, but no filter is 100% accurate, so a filter is only one step in protecting our kids. The WOW search engine focuses its searches on breaking news, top videos, and trending topics. Other search engines like WebCrawler and Dogpile search multiple other search engines to compile a more comprehensive search. For example, WebCrawler returns results from both Google and Yahoo! and seeks to position itself as a single source to search the web. Dogpile, on the other hand, has a friendly interface and makes searching the web easy. This might be useful for students just starting to learn how to search for information on the Internet.

Many search engines use cookies to track your activity on the Internet. By tracking your activities and collecting your personal data, these search engines can provide advertising based on your personal information and targeted toward your interests. These search engines also seek to provide search results that are targeted. This creates a bit of a conundrum. Students using these search engines to conduct research are provided increasingly narrow responses to their search queries; for the purposes of learning, this can inhibit a student's ability to thoroughly review a topic, seek answers from connected but different domains of knowledge, and learn the skills of targeting their results with quality search phrases. One search engine, DuckDuckGo, prides itself on *not* tracking its users or collecting personal information. This is great for maintaining student privacy and extending opportunities for learning from multiple domains.

DID YOU KNOW?

Google and Bing are the world's most popular search engines (first and second respectively; Net Market Share, 2015). Together, these search engines index 4.73 billion webpages (worldwidewebsize.com, 2015), which is only a small portion of the entire content of the Internet.

Choosing a search engine really depends on your priorities. Once you have chosen the search engine to suit your needs, it will be important to develop skills for effectively finding information on the Internet.

Tips for effective searches. Although there are many search engines to choose from, Google will likely remain the most popular search engine for the foreseeable future. Google currently holds nearly 70% of the global market share for desktop search engines (Net Market Share, 2015) and has some advanced search features that set it apart from its competition. Most people default to a Google search, and start with simple keyword searches, adding words to narrow their results as they continue to search. This is the basic first step in searching online, regardless of which search engine you use. The challenge is that a simple keyword search can lead to overwhelming results. Take, for example, a search for *enrichment*. This search will generate close to 42 million results in half a second.

No one has time to look through 42 million websites to find the information they seek. Therefore, the search needs to be narrowed, which can be accomplished by adding words to the original search. Now the search keywords are *enrichment pedagogy*, resulting in roughly 400,000 results, and some familiar websites are appearing on the first page of the results (e.g., The Neag School of Education at the University of Connecticut). This still does not lead to the intended target—enrichment opportunities for an entire school—so more words are added to the search for *schoolwide enrichment pedagogy*. There are still around 400,000 results, but these results are far more focused and the Schoolwide Enrichment Model dominates the results.

That was an easy search, and the likelihood of finding a good match for the query was pretty high given the search criteria. This is how most people search. Often, the results are not so helpful, but there are a variety of ways to improve your search results.

Word choice is very important. *Enrichment*, for example, is a term that is very specific to education, and the search was conducted with the full knowledge that the term would likely appear on the kinds of pages being sought, thereby increasing the likelihood of finding a good match for the query. Students have to choose words carefully. For example, if someone wants to know what to do when he or she has a cold, and therefore searches for the words *cold* or *snotty nose*, then the results will be varied and few, if any, will lead to the answer he or she seeks. A better search query would be *treatment for a cold*, which returns results about treating the common cold.

It is important to understand that when you define or select multiple words for your search, the search engine will do one of two things. Typically, the search engine will treat your search as a string of words that are automatically linked together as the search engine adds the conjunctions AND or OR between each of the words in your search. Google's search engine defaults to AND, but it is important know the default for your chosen search engines as AND will narrow your search while OR will expand your search. Search engines will also drop small words from the search. All of these aspects of search engine functioning can affect the results provided. Sometimes, the search engine will treat the set of words as a phrase, which means that the words will be searched as a complete phrase and will only return results that show those words in the exact order they were put together. The outcome is determined by the relevance function of the search engine. If the group of words in the order you have arranged them shows up frequently as a phrase, the search engine is more likely to return those words as a group.

There is no need to give search engines that much power over your efforts to find information. There are steps that will enable you to take charge of your search queries!

Searching for phrases. Sometimes, you might want to find a specific phrase. When you put a phrase in quotes, only that exact phrase will be searched. Searching with quotations around "Ask not what your country can do for you" will return the quote, the source for the quote, as well as the historical implications of John F. Kennedy's inaugural address. Similarly, if you cannot remember the whole quote or phrase, you can use an asterisk in place of words that are unknown. For example, a search for "to * own self be true" reveals that the phrase is NOT "to thy own self " but rather "to thine own self be true." Moreover, we learn the source of the quote: Shakespeare's Hamlet Act 1, scene 3, lines 78–82. The asterisk can also be used to search for variations of a word. For example, a search for "educ*" will return results with the words *educational*, *education*, and *educate* included.

There are words that search engines typically do not search for. These words are simply ignored by the search engines to increase the speed it returns your results (like *a, about, and, are, as, be, from, I, in, is, on, or, that,* and *the*). Essentially, adverbs, conjunctions, or prepositions are automatically dropped from your search. There is no way to know the full list of words that are dropped from your search because the list varies from one search engine to another.

To ensure that every word you are looking for is included in your search, simply add a plus sign immediately before the word. For example, if we want to make sure that every term in the keyword search *gifted education graduate school* is included, we might arrange our search phrase as *+graduate +school +gifted +and +talented +education*. Notice that since the goal of our search was to find a graduate school to attend, we put the more relevant words at the beginning of the query. In the same way a plus sign ensures the word will be searched for, a hyphen removes words. If you want to remove a word from your search, simply use a hyphen immediately before the word you want to remove. For example, if you search for *electric vehicles*, hybrid vehicles show up within the first 10 results or so. A better search, since we are not interested in hybrid vehicles, would be *electric vehicles -hybrid*. This search removes the references to hybrid vehicles from the search results. Here are a few tips to help form your search phrase effectively:

› Be specific.
› Use nouns as keywords and use at least three keywords in your query.
› Put the most important word first in the search terms.
› Combine keywords into phrases using quotations whenever possible.

›   Avoid common words unless they are part of a phrase (remember to include quotations around the phrase).
›   Try to use the same phrases or words you would expect to appear on the webpage.
›   Use operators to specify your search (-, +, :, " ", *).
›   Combine phrases with keywords and operators (e.g., the hyphen or plus sign) to specify your search exactly.

These search techniques are important to understand when searching databases in libraries as well. The trend in searching the digital records in libraries is to have the search function more like searching on the Internet, so employing these techniques will help when students are ready to engage in advanced research.

What's in a name? There is a lot in a name, and this is never more so evident than in our web addresses on the Internet. Take for example the U.S. Census Bureau website: http://www.census.gov/geo/maps-data/maps/datamapper.html.

We'll break it down for you:
›   **http** is the "hypertext transfer protocol" and it is the format used for transferring the information from one location to another.
›   **www** is the "World Wide Web" and refers to the host server.
›   **census** is the second-level domain name and typically designates the server's location (in this case, the Census Bureau of the U.S. government).
›   **gov** is the top-level domain name. A list of top-level domains is provided below.
›   **geo** is the directory name.
›   **maps-data** is the sub-directory name.
›   **maps** is the folder name.
›   **datamapper** is the file name.
›   **html** is the file extension and in this case, stands for hypertext mark-up language. This is a standardized system or language that the computer can read.

Understanding the top-level domain name indicators is important particularly when we are assessing the quality of a website, specifically the biases a website author might hold and whether or not we can consider the information on a website to be reliable. A list of top-level domains follows.

Generally reliable information sources:
›   .edu—educational site (usually a university or college)
›   .gov—U.S. government site (nonmilitary)
›   .mil—U.S. military sites and agencies

Restricted use domains:
›   .aero—restricted use by air transportation industry
›   .coop—restricted use by cooperatives
›   .museum—restricted use by museums
›   .pro—restricted use by certified professionals and professional entities

Business and commercial use domains:
›   .org—nonprofit organizations and others
›   .com—commercial business site
›   .biz—general use by businesses
›   .net—networks, organizations, and Internet service providers
›   .info—general use by commercial and noncommercial sites
›   .name—general use by individuals

Ideally, when you are looking for factual information or information based in research, it is a good idea to go to an .edu or .gov site. Sometimes an .org site provides research-based information from nonprofit organizations, but the .org top-level domain is not regulated and almost anyone can get access to a .org domain. So, if you want to limit your search to an educational site, you can use an operator. An operator is a symbol or punctuation mark that tells the computer exactly your goal, thereby providing a more specific search result. In this case, you want to narrow your search to the top domain for an educational site so you would write, domain:edu. All of the results your search query returns will include websites that have .edu as their domain.

Assess the Quality of a Website

Website quality is important to be able to assess both from the perspective of consuming digital media and for the purposes of producing digital content. Therefore, understanding the criteria that defines quality will help students not only improve capacity for searching the Internet, but also improve the quality of their own personal website.

When students are searching for information on the Internet, they have to understand how to assess the quality of the content on the site. Other factors that might be important to students might be the design and attractiveness of the site, the organization of the site, and the usability of the site, but these criteria do not necessarily mean the site's content is accurate, unbiased, or up-to-date. Therefore, it is important that we help students distinguish between the quality of the content and other factors that may lead the student to trust the site despite a lack of meaningful content (see Table 9).

Other criteria for assessing the general quality of a website include:

Accessibility
› Does the site load quickly?
› Is the information viewable in different browsers and operating systems?
› Is access for people with disabilities and various backgrounds provided?

Design
› Is the website visually appealing, readable, and easy to navigate?
› Does the design reinforce the purpose of the site while providing a unified look and feel?

Take for example our search query *schoolwide enrichment pedagogy*. There were around 400,000 results, so how do we determine the most useful site for our needs? The Schoolwide Enrichment Model (SEM) dominated the results, and as we look closer at the SEM, we see that it was developed and researched at the University of Connecticut by Joseph S. Renzulli, Ed.D., Sally M. Reis, Ph.D., and their colleagues. The top result produced by the search appears to be high quality (developed by people with expertise) and from a reliable source (a well-known university with the domain .edu). Now there is a specific result that fits the original target and provides a whole host of valuable resources (http://gifted.uconn.edu/schoolwide-enrichment-model/sem3rd)!

Curating Content

Another important technology skill is curating. To curate is to select, organize, and present content using professional or expert knowledge. Teachers have been curating for generations as they select, organize, review, and take care of materials that support their work in classroom settings. Think about your "closet" (you know, that place where you try to store everything, but realize it is just not big enough!) or your bookshelves full of items that support instruction. You have been curating these materials over months and years and you can't get

TABLE 9
QUALITY CRITERIA FOR ASSESSING WEBSITE CONTENT

Timely information	<ul><li>Is the information up-to-date?</li><li>How often is the website updated?</li><li>When was the last time the website was updated?</li><li>Are links provided on the website? Are all of the links functioning?</li></ul>
Relevant information (the degree to which the information contained on the website addresses the visitor's interests and needs)	<ul><li>Is the information provided the information you were looking for?</li><li>Is the information useful?</li><li>What is the purpose of the website?</li><li>Is the information useful to the purpose of your search?</li><li>Does the information provide the level of specificity you were seeking?</li></ul>
Accurate information	<ul><li>Are the sources of the information identified?</li><li>Is the information reliable and free of errors?</li><li>Are there spelling, grammar, or punctuation mistakes?</li><li>Are the limitations of the information identified?</li><li>Can the facts be verified by at least two other sources?</li><li>Is the website author a trustworthy source (e.g., university, well-known service organization, research institution, U.S. government, etc.)?</li><li>Is the information reviewed, endorsed, or otherwise assessed by an outside source (i.e., not the website author)?</li></ul>
Objective information	<ul><li>What is the history of the website author?</li><li>What is the website author's purpose?</li><li>Is the website author trying to sell something?</li><li>What are the opinions expressed by the website author?</li><li>Does the website author have a bias?</li><li>Is the information presented objectively?</li><li>Are advertisements presented on the website? Who are the sponsors of the advertisements?</li><li>Who was the website created for?</li><li>Are there fees for obtaining the information?</li></ul>
Authority of website author	<ul><li>Who is the website author?</li><li>Is the author a qualified expert with credentials listed?</li><li>Does the author of the website provide a physical address?</li><li>Are the managers of the website specified?</li><li>Is contact information for the website author provided?</li><li>Is the website published at a .edu, .org, or .gov site?</li></ul>
Coverage of information	<ul><li>How comprehensive is the site?</li><li>How in-depth is the material?</li><li>What does the website offer that is not found elsewhere?</li><li>Is information cited correctly?</li></ul>

Note. See Hasan and Abuelrub (2011) and Moustakis, Litos, Dalivigas, and Tsironis (2004).

rid of anything because every item has a purpose. The concept of curating is not new to you, but you may not have considered your work as a process of curating and you may be just beginning to curate digital content.

The purpose for curating content varies from one teacher to the next—from providing exposure like that in Type I experiences, or technology tools and engaged learning opportunities like what might be used in Type II process, or for Type III productivity. Ultimately, you know that the content you curate will end up in the hands of your students.

DID YOU KNOW?

According to a 2012 Pew Research Internet survey of more than 2,000 middle school and high school teachers who participate in the National Writing Project or teach Advanced Placement courses, 83% of teachers responded that today's digital technologies discourage students from using a wide range of sources when conducting research (Purcell et al., 2012).

So you are ready to find open source content (i.e., free tools) on the Internet. With hundreds, maybe even thousands of free content sources available online, where do you begin? How do you find the right tool, for the right students, at the right time? Simple: Curate a collection of high-quality resources. That, however, is easier said than done. In an era where information is overabundant, we have to find ways to organize that information into meaningful categories. Curating content allows us to organize information by theme, topic, process, or relevance. Essentially any perspective we take, the goal is to define "like things" and group them together. It is a necessary skill for teachers and students alike. As teachers, curating allows us to work smarter, not harder, as we organize, manage, and collate resources. When students learn the techniques of curating, they develop digital literacy skills in addition to life skills like gathering, determining relevance, developing voice, categorizing, contextualizing, story telling, and so much more! Curating can simply be collecting with a purpose in mind or it can be a very intentional process of bringing a new perspective to a collection of carefully selected items.

In an ideal world, someone would do the curating for you. He or she would identify students' interests, abilities, challenges, and current needs, then curate content to reflect these criteria. Realistically, however, if someone curates the content for you, he or she is likely to first consider standards and then seek to identify tools that meet those standards for a particular grade level. This approach does not take into consideration the goal of your search for resources: To provide a student or small group of students with the right tool, for the right job, at just the right time. Letting someone else curate the resources does not necessarily work for *your* students. Your students may be passionately interested in a topic or may have already demonstrated a capacity to think and produce at levels well beyond that of their classmates. Curating content is an art, and curating content well requires one to consider the goal for collecting content, the audience of that content, and the unique perspective that organizes the collection into a meaningful whole.

Your audience is your student group and your purpose for curating. Whether you are thinking in terms of inspiring the entire school, engaging a class, helping a small group of students learn a skill, or supporting a single individual seeking to make progress on a passion project, curating content for education requires you to focus on their interests, needs, and capacity. In essence, it will be your students who help define the tools and resources you collect, and it will be your expertise, knowledge, and empathy for your students that create the perspective for the collection.

Collecting

Collecting content is a huge undertaking. The content available is endless. There are games, videos, simulations, interactive activities, virtual reality environments, real-time data, calculators, data analysis tools, and text of every kind. As you begin the search process, be specific about your needs: Are students requesting specific kinds of support? Have you identified trends in students' interests? Are there specific skills that students need? Letting all of your tool search decisions emanate from students' expressed interests and needs will help you narrow the focus of your search and make the time you spend searching more efficient. Certainly, you can spend time searching for tools and resources that reflect your interests, but you will get more from your efforts if you focus on your students' interests.

Anyone who has spent time collecting content can tell you it is easy to make a full-time job of the process. We're thinking you already have enough to do, so we recommend crowd sourcing as one option. Let everyone share in the work. When we say everyone, we mean everyone in your community who you trust to make good choices about content: teachers at every level, librarians, resource specialists, students, staff, principals, and anyone in the school community who would like to participate, particularly those who stand to benefit the most (teachers, specialists, and students). There are numerous online tools for collecting, social bookmarking, and sharing websites. Leverage these tools to create a community around the initial stage of curating, which is collecting a lot of high-quality tools and information.

Another option is to seek out those who have already curated lists of education resources. A simple Google search of *curated lists of education resources* provides more than a million results, but remember, those curated lists were not necessarily created with your students in mind.

A third option is to allow the collection to amass over time. This option is slower, and it may not be feasible given your situation, but just like becoming a master teacher, collecting high-quality resources takes years. There is no need to make the process overly cumbersome. Each time a student has a need, find a small number of tools that could meet that need and let the student make the determination about which tool will be easiest to use and enable him or her to reach his or her goal. This approach requires students to use skills like assessing quality, determining relevance, and prioritizing, but on a smaller scale than if they were provided a long list of resources and had no idea where to begin. Building the collection one item at a time is as valuable as having amassed the resources all at once, and it makes the job of curating that collection easier.

From Collecting to Curating

It is better to have 10 amazing tools that serve your students well and regularly than to have 1,000 and not be able to make determinations about which tool is the right one at any given time. So once you have amassed several tools based on students' expressed needs, how do you turn this collection into curated content? Curation denotes a carefully selected and organized group of resources. Typically there is a unique perspective or framework that connects the content. Think of it this way: If you have a collection of tools and you start to remove some because they are not the quality you seek or they don't quite fit your needs, you have begun the process of curating. So how do you make determinations about which tools stay and which ones should go?

We talked about allowing the collection to build over time. With a slow and intentional approach to collecting, the curated content may emerge with the care taken in the gathering process. Even if the collection builds over time, you may still want to review and evaluate tools. For example, did you find a tool that you thought would be so much fun with great potential for learning, but ultimately your students didn't use it because it was "too cutesy"? Or the reverse: You thought the challenging 15-minute video would stretch students' minds, only to find their attention span was stretched too far for any real growth in thought? Indeed, students' experience of using the resource is as important as quality. Consider whether the content is timely in both content and the user experience. For example, the 1990 version of *The Oregon Trail* computer software may be well loved, but its time has passed and would not only seem antiquated, but also laughable for students today.

A second option for curating the content is to gather a small group of individuals to provide a framework or set of criteria to focus and narrow the collection. You might consider creating a rubric that addresses your original intent for collecting these tools and then add in the criteria for assessing quality resources (see Table 9). Define your goals clearly. If you need tools that are free, make sure they are truly free and that students won't encounter in-app purchase requirements that would prevent them from moving forward and would potentially waste valuable learning time. Allow students to help you, too. Ask them to reflect on their experiences using the tool. Have them answer the following:

› How did the resource selected help you solve a problem or answer a question?
› Would you recommend this resource to someone else? Why or why not?
› What challenges did you experience when using the resource? What strategies did you use to persevere when faced with those challenges?

Include information about which tools students use most often, which ones they talk about the most, or which ones they share, and you will be well on your way to making determinations about which tools serve your students well and which ones may be great but not a match for your population.

TABLE 10
ONLINE TOOLS FOR CURATING CONTENT

Collecting	BagTheWeb (http://www.bagtheweb.com) EduClipper (https://educlipper.net/main.html)
Digital curating	LiveBinders (http://www.livebinders.com) Scoop.it (http://www.scoop.it) Storify (https://storify.com) Pinterest (https://www.pinterest.com) Themeefy (http://themeefy.com)
Social bookmarking and sharing	Diigo (https://www.diigo.com) Pocket (https://getpocket.com) TheHubEdu (https://secure.thehubedu.com) Padlet (https://padlet.com)
Content aggregators	paper.li (http://paper.li) Flipboard (https://flipboard.com)
Creating a "playlist" for students	LessonPaths (http://www.lessonpaths.com) Blendspace (http://www.tes.com/lessons) Learnist (http://learni.st)

Tips for Success

1. Curated content should reflect your student population—their interests, abilities, challenges, and current needs.
2. Remember, developing curated content takes time—months and years, not days.
3. Make sure the curated content enhances student learning through rigor *and* enjoyment.
4. Make sure the content is appropriate, relevant, and timely: Right tool, right job, right time.
5. Define the unique perspective you bring to the curated content. How did your perspective and expertise as an educator influence the tools you chose?
6. Review content occasionally for quality, relevance, and currency, continually adding to the compilation. (See Table 10 for suggestions on organizing your curated content.)
7. Share.

A technology tool may be new for your students, so it may take time for them to figure out how to use the tool effectively. Give them the time and if they get stuck, there are people who have blazed the trail. You would be hard-pressed not to find someone who has provided comments and information online—don't forget to go online to seek an answer to a problem, as you'll undoubtedly find a tutorial that can help.

CHAPTER 10

Type II— Processes and Skills in Action

Type II processes go beyond skill development. They are experiences designed to promote the development of thinking and feeling processes alongside the requisite skills of productivity and consumerism. It is important to remember that students are thinking and feeling beings, and while we develop the skills for success, we are also seeking to help students develop the dispositions for learning flexibly, joyously, and continuously throughout the course of their life. The objectives of a SEM:*Tech* Type II experience are to develop in students:

> general cognitive skills,
> effective communication skills,
> socioaffective skills,
> basic "how-to-learn" skills,
> innovation skills, and
> self-regulatory skills.

There are essentially three ways a Type II experience can develop:

1. Type II experiences can develop from students' interests. These interests might be generated during a Type I, determined through the use of interest inventories, or revealed on their personal introductory webpage.

2. Type II experiences can also result from the need for new information or skills as part of a Type III investigation. When a need for immediate skill development arises out of a Type III, we call this "just-in-time knowledge" because the student is primed to learn. he or she needs the information to progress forward, and if he or she cannot get the infor-

mation or skill, then the opportunity for deep, lasting, and transferrable learning may be lost.

3. Type II experiences can also be planned in advance, particularly when there are sets of skills that may be missing from your students' repertoire.

Here, we present several Type II experiences that embed the processes previously discussed. The focus of these experiences is on authentic outcomes rather than "accountability." As a result, the examples embed numerous skills and opportunities to be responsive to students' interests. The examples also enable you to bring your own talents and passions to bear on the curriculum. Use the information we provide and adapt it to your needs as you create your own version, include it within an interest development center, or use it as an anchor activity.

For each of the Type II experiences, we provide background information that supports the teaching processes, example student activities associated with the experience, and a list of resources that will support your extension of learning for students. Although we are providing you with illustrations of Type II processes, we are not suggesting that you must or should do these with your students. Even if you believe students would enjoy the processes, every student need not participate in these experiences. Before using these Type II examples, you should consider:

› Have students expressed an interest or need for the experience you have selected?

› Should the experience be adapted to better suit your students' readiness level, interests, or needs?

› Are there multiple students who would benefit from the experience? If so, how will these students work together while still maintaining a focus in their own interest area?

› Will the experience result in a product that is relevant to advancing a student's Type III work or extending a student's exploration of a Type I exposure experience?

Video Production: Lights, Camera, WAIT . . .

Smartphones, tablets, and digital cameras have the built-in capacity to capture video. This makes movie creation an affordable way to give students ownership of their learning. Movies, when done well, have an incredible capacity to communicate. They provide students with the opportunity to connect with an audience and elicit an emotional response. The challenge in having students make their own movie is supporting the creation of a quality product.

DID YOU KNOW?

More than a billion YouTube users generate billions of views and watch hundreds of millions of hours of video *daily* (YouTube, 2015), and Facebook hit 8 billion daily video views in 2015 (Facebook, 2015).

There are a variety of reasons students might want or need to make a video, but why should they make a video instead of giving a presentation? What is the difference between the two? For both moviemaking and presentation, you have to conduct research, write informative or explanatory text, create a story to anchor the concept, and create artwork or graphic representations to support the concept. The primary difference is the opportunity to practice the final product and make edits. Certainly, you can edit what you are going to say in a presentation, but once you are on stage, there is no going back. With moviemaking, you have the opportunity for multiple takes, and each time you film a section of your movie, you can reflect and review to make improvements for the next take.

Typically, the reasons for making a video fall into three main categories: entertain, educate, or inform. Regardless of the impetus for making a video, it is important that students understand the amount of work that goes into making a quality product. Students often have the misconception that moviemaking involves setting up a camera and filming. They may fail to see all of the planning, craft, editing, and time that goes into a good production. One way to help students understand how to create high-quality videos is to help them understand the work of professional moviemakers. When we think about the number of people and roles in professional moviemaking, it is overwhelming. The credits at the end of movies last so long that most people leave the theater before they are finished. Some of the basic roles students might consider taking on in a video production include:

> › writer,
> › producer,

> › director,
> › script supervisor,
> › director of photography,
> › camera operator,
> › chief lighting technician,
> › special effects supervisor,
> › production designer,
> › set designer,
> › props master and prop maker,
> › make up artist,
> › costume designer, and
> › video editor.

Many of these roles are self-explanatory, and the more students take on the role of acting like a professional, the more their movie will take on a real-world learning experience. Researching the roles will help students understand the responsibilities associated with each. When we consider the responsibilities of each role, it is useful to also consider the skills that will be brought to bear on the associated processes. Take, for example, the skills necessary for becoming a video editor:

> › active listening;
> › reading comprehension;
> › critical thinking;
> › communicating effectively (speaking, writing, and visual);
> › time management;
> › judgment and decision making;
> › complex problem solving;
> › monitoring progress;
> › systems analysis; and
> › managing personnel and resources.

These are just a few of the skills, and this is just one of the jobs needed for movie production. This is where the real value in allowing students to make movies comes in. When they are acting like professionals, they develop the skills for work and life success, but do so in a way that is meaningful to personal experience. Initially, allowing students to engage in this kind of learning and productivity can be scary and you may not have the expertise to guide them. Never fear: Google is here! A simple search of "how to make a movie" yields more than a million results. Examples of search results include a simple five-part solution with pictures from wikiHow, a YouTube video in 10 steps, and a 65-step film production checklist. Students can do the research on their own, or you can select some sources that provide them with the information they need to get started.

CHRISTY'S CORNER: SHOT REVERSE SHOT VIDEO

Christy's third graders created a video as part of an enrichment cluster. Chip Hackler, a parent from the community and a professor in the Department of Film Studies at a local university, led an enrichment cluster on filmmaking. The film was created with a focus on the theme of perspective. He used the Jack Johnson song "Shot Reverse Shot" and a filmmaking technique called *shot reverse shot*, to help students explore seeing things from a friend's perspective.

The project took on a life of its own. First, it grew beyond the enrichment cluster. Fortunately, the film professor was excited to share his knowledge and expertise after school and on weekends. It also grew beyond the gifted classroom as students who were not part of Christy's regular pull-out program were invited to participate. Of the experience, Christy said:

> It is not just for our gifted kids. I want to make these opportunities available for the whole school. We have so many kids at our school who are not identified as gifted, but could really grow and develop talents with these experiences.

The students learned a lot through the development of the film, and they participated in processes that were creative and required them to act like professionals in the film industry. Chip Hackler said of the experience:

> We engaged in a process that was *about* the creative process. You can break it down into five sections: development, preproduction, production, postproduction, and marketing and distribution. The basic process is similar whether it's a music video with kids or *Iron Man III*.

After a community screening of the film, it was entered into Wilmington's 2014 Cucalorus Film Festival. The film festival receives thousands of submissions each year, and *Shot Reverse Shot*, along with 144 other film shorts, was selected for screening. Before they knew it, *Shot Reverse Shot* was named one of the top 8 must-see short films in the festival (Ingram, 2014). Students received tickets to the event and were invited on stage after the screening for a Q&A about the film and their filmmaking experience. Most recently, the film was accepted into the NC Family Film Festival. It was one of only 20 films chosen out of almost 100 applicants (C. Hackler, personal communication, October 2015).

Embedded within the learning experience were transferrable skills like idea generation, visual storytelling, planning, monitoring progress, staying engaged in a project that lasted several weeks, editing, communicating effectively, and so much more! What more could you want from a learning experience for students? The learning experience combined an authentic audience, community expertise, enthusiastic learners, and a teacher willing to provide an enriched learning opportunity that extended beyond the walls of the school and resulted in a high-quality film recognized for excellence. See the results for yourself on YouTube (https://www.youtube.com/watch?v=x362ejRB4-Q).

High-quality outcomes are an important focus of the video-making experience. The budget of large production movies, the kind in theaters, may lead to significant revenue, but video produced by students should have the same five steps (development, preproduction, production, postproduction, and distribution) and result in a similar level of quality, but at a more junior level. Achieving a quality product requires two things: students' desire to make a video and time. Whether your students want to contribute an original story, make people laugh, share a newly learned skill, or even begin production on their own vlog (video blog), it is important that the impetus for engaging in the video production process comes from students' interest in doing that kind of work. The Internet provides an authentic audience that will support quality outcomes. When students know that the audience is someone other than the teacher or their classmates, the productivity takes on a different quality and the time and effort are a matter of course rather than optional.

Before the process ever begins, make sure it is the right product for students' work. Help students avoid making a movie merely because it is "fun" or as an exercise without authentic purpose. There are so many processes and skills that students utilize to produce a video that, when done correctly, is worthy of instructional time. The processes and skills students engage in are creative, making them transferrable to new settings, including college and career. To ensure students are making the right product choice, it is helpful for them to consider the process before selecting to make a video so that they understand that while the process may be fun, it is also rigorous. The questions below will help students understand that making a video is a lot of work and requires their best effort. Use these questions early in the development stages to help students determine if a video is the appropriate product:

› Why do you want to make a video? What is the purpose of your video?

› Who will watch the video? Who is the audience?

› Why will they be interested in your video? What makes your video idea unique or interesting?

› Have you chosen a topic for your video that you will be able to create content for and stay interested in for an extended period of time (weeks or even months)?

› What resources (e.g., video camera, tripod, costumes, etc.) will you need to make your video? Where will you get the resources you need?

› What steps are involved in making a video?

› What is the timeline for completing your video?

› Where will your video be filmed?

› Will you need help making your video? Who will you contact if you need help?

› What questions do you have about making a video? Where will you find that information?

Video Outlets

As your students complete their video projects, you should work with them to determine the appropriate audience and venue to share the project. Depending on the age of your students and the expectations of your school and parents, there may be some discouragement from publically sharing student products on the Internet. Additionally, many schools and districts still block access to video sharing sites like YouTube. Ideally, we would encourage you to share students' video projects with as wide an audience as possible, but we fully recognize that this may be against your school's policies.

To support your decision-making process, we have examined YouTube and three other popular video streaming services to provide a cross-platform comparison (see Table 11).

TABLE 11
VIDEO RESOURCE COMPARISON

	YouTube	Vimeo	TeacherTube	SchoolTube
Web Address	https://www.youtube.com	https://vimeo.com	http://www.teachertube.com	http://www.schooltube.com
Pros	◆ Widely known and recognized ◆ Offers massive real-world audience	◆ Completely ad free	◆ Education-focused ◆ Student accounts	◆ Ability to create school-wide accounts
Cons	◆ May be blocked by your school	◆ Limits on amount of uploading per week	◆ Some advertisements ◆ Primarily focused on instructional videos	◆ Less potential to reach an authentic audience outside of school
Videos can be downloaded	No	Yes	Yes	Yes
Upload limits	◆ 15 minutes for nonverified accounts	◆ Free basic account: 500 MB per week up to 25 GB per year	◆ Not mentioned	◆ Not mentioned
Max file size	No limit	No limit	300 MB	1.5 GB
Cost for premium version	◆ Free; account must be verified to upload videos larger than 15 minutes	◆ $59.95 per year ◆ Increase to 5 GB per week and 25 GB per year	◆ $4.99 per month or $39.99 per year ◆ Watch without ads ◆ Increase classroom storage to 30 GB	◆ No premium version
Bonus feature	◆ Cards ◆ Annotations	◆ Vimeo Video School offers tutorials on making videos in multiple platforms	◆ Includes ability to upload and store audio files, photos, and documents	◆ Videos can be shared publically or only with those in your school
Advertisements	Yes	No	Yes, but you can pay to remove them	No

For all of the services reviewed, the process of uploading the videos is remarkably similar. Users must first create an account and log in. By clicking the "upload" button, you are directed to a page that asks you to locate the file on your computer by selecting it from a list or by dragging and dropping the file into the appropriate box. Each of the services allows the user to select whether he or she would like for the video to be public, private, or unlisted. This provides the opportunity to maintain some control over the availability of potentially private information on the Internet. There may be times when you wish to post a video as private or unlisted. By posting a video as unlisted, others are able to view the video online only as long as you give them the link. A search of the web will *not* return results for the video, even if they know the title. In this case, you would have to share the link directly, post the link somewhere, or embed the video on your website. When a video is posted as private, only those users who you specifically invite will be able to view the video. Users would have to sign in to whichever service you might be using after they have been invited.

Again, we feel that students should try to reach the widest audience possible, but fully recognize that there are varying perspectives on just how much information should be shared and at what age. Having a real-world audience, however, can serve to make the experience a more authentic one for students. It is one thing to share a project with your class, but it is entirely another to have it presented on a worldwide stage. We have heard teachers routinely report that the quality of students' products increases as the audience size increases. What may be good enough when the audience is "the teacher" may *not* be good enough once students realize that the audience is everyone in the world because the video will be posted on YouTube.

When uploading videos to any service, you should be aware that the process can be time consuming depending on the upload speed of your Internet connection. Keep in mind that your upload speed is typically much slower than your download speed.

Going Beyond YouTube

Although YouTube is the most widely used video streaming site, we would like to provide some rationale for choosing options like Vimeo, TeacherTube, or SchoolTube, even if YouTube is not blocked at your school.

Vimeo. Vimeo is much more focused on high-quality and professional content than YouTube. As a result, there is much less fluff and potentially inappropriate content. The comments section on Vimeo tends to be more constructive in nature rather than the potentially vitriolic comments that can be left on

YouTube videos. That being said, YouTube does allow users to turn off the comments section on videos that they upload. The real advantage of Vimeo is that it is entirely free of advertisements. Even if you have not chosen to monetize your video uploads on YouTube, there remains the real chance that a 30-second advertisement will play before your video. Vimeo allows videos to be private and password protected as opposed to YouTube. When a video is private on YouTube, you must specifically invite users to be able to view, but Vimeo allows you to create a password that could be shared with those you wish to view the video.

Disadvantages of Vimeo are that the free basic service limits the number of videos that can be uploaded, which may inhibit students' productivity. Vimeo Plus significantly increases the amount of video that can be uploaded on a weekly basis from 500 MB per week to 5 GB per week, but this increase comes at a cost of $59.95 per year or $9.95 per month, which may be beneficial to you in order to be free of advertisements.

TeacherTube. More than just a video streaming service, TeacherTube describes itself as a "Content Management Community." Teachers have the ability to upload audio files, photos, and documents in addition to videos. Each user has a hub, which offers an organized view of all of his or her uploaded media as well as the ability to create classrooms and student accounts. There is also a strong emphasis on instructional videos. Consequently, many of the video projects that your students create may fall outside of the intended purpose for TeacherTube. When uploading videos, you are asked to categorize them according to academic subject. You also have the opportunity to identify which Common Core learning objective they address.

The biggest disadvantage of TeacherTube is the presence of advertisements throughout the site. These are in form of banners and sidebars on the webpages, as well as ads before and during the video in a way that is quite similar to what is seen on YouTube. We have noticed that the ads do tend to be far more educationally related than those that appear on YouTube. By upgrading to the TeacherTube Pro account for $4.99 per month or $39.99 per year, you are able to watch without advertisements. The Pro account also increases the amount of classroom storage space to 30 GB and allows teachers to create discussion groups for students.

SchoolTube. SchoolTube is dedicated to sharing videos created by both teachers and students and focused entirely on education. Videos are moderated by educators in an effort to ensure the content is safe and appropriate for school settings. SchoolTube is also exclusively endorsed by national education associations (http://www.schooltube.com/info/partners), including the American Association of School Librarians, the National Association of Elementary School Principals, and the National Honor Society. Schools, teachers, and students can create their own accounts and have them linked together. When posting a video, one can decide whether to make it public or to share it just with your school, which provides an alternative to only keeping videos private on a local level. Currently there is a 1.5 GB limit on the size of the file to be uploaded. However, this should still give you and your students enough flexibility. There seems to be no limit on the amount of content that can be uploaded, and there is not a premium version. SchoolTube is free from advertisements, which makes it an attractive alternative to YouTube. The only potential disadvantage is that there is no comment section for the videos.

Reasons to Choose YouTube

YouTube offers the most authentic and widely used platform for sharing videos and has the potential to reach an enormous worldwide audience. With any video that is uploaded to YouTube, the potential exists for the video to go viral. A viral video may be viewed thousands, if not millions, of times. If one contrasts a paper that might be read only by the teacher assigning it or an in-class presentation viewed by only one's classmates to having a video viewed by hundreds of people outside of the school walls, then you can see how this broader and more authentic audience might be a motivating factor for students.

By default, there is a 15-minute limit for video uploads; however, you may verify your account to remove this limit. For more information on this process, visit https://www.youtube.com/verify. The possibility of almost unlimited amounts of uploaded video content is a true advantage of YouTube over other platforms. Students will never feel restricted by the amount of content that can be created and shared via YouTube.

We would like to focus on a few options available on YouTube that are not part of any of the other services we have covered. Unlike videos posted to TeacherTube and SchoolTube, viewers can comment and rate YouTube videos. Although this does provide for open communication that may not be wanted, YouTube does allow you to moderate the comments by removing a comment, hiding a comment, or reporting a comment as spam or abuse. YouTube also allows you to set filters, blacklist certain words or phrases, and create a list of automatically approved users for your comments section. Additional information regarding filters and comments can be found at https://support.google.com/youtube/answer/6109622.

Although advertisements can be seen as a negative, YouTube does offer users the chance to monetize and profit from uploads. The amount of money that you might see from this may prove to be miniscule, but there exists the potential to be substantially and financially rewarded (although you should check school guidelines before signing up for this). For example, by the time vlogger Bethany Mota turned 18, she was not only a YouTube celebrity, but it was estimated that she was earning more than $40,000 per month in revenue from her videos being viewed on YouTube.

Two added features of YouTube are the ability to add cards and annotations to your uploaded videos. Cards (see https://support.google.com/youtube/answer/6140493) provide a small, interactive teaser icon that pops up in the corner of the video. When the viewer clicks on the icon, a card will open. It may include an image, title, and call to action task. This would be a great way for students to provide additional resources or information directly from the video. Up to five cards may be included in each video.

In addition to cards, YouTube also offers the ability to have users create annotations (see https://support.google.com/youtube/answer/92710) for their videos. Like cards, annotations will pop up as the video is being viewed, but these are not interactive like cards. Instead, they are intended to provide some just-in-time knowledge for the viewer. Speech bubbles may be added to your video and include text. The spotlight annotation tool is used for highlighting areas in a video. When the viewer moves the cursor or touches the area, then text will appear. Other annotations include notes, titles, and labels and can be used to emphasize specific parts of the video for the viewer.

Although at first it may seem like an overwhelming or difficult task to upload content to your YouTube Channel, there are an abundance of resources and tutorials to assist you and your students. Nearly any question imaginable is addressed in the YouTube Help Center at https://support.google.com/youtube. Beyond just uploading content, the folks at YouTube want to help you create quality content. After all, the more quality content that is uploaded, the more viewers they will have. This win-win approach supports YouTube and video artists alike with the Creator Academy (https://creatoracademy.withgoogle.com). Creator Academy is a series of free online courses and tutorials designed to teach you and your students how to create great content (https://creatoracademy.withgoogle.com/page/course/great-content), the importance of lighting and camera choices (https://creatoracademy.withgoogle.com/page/course/camera-lighting), and even the art of getting viewers (https://creatoracademy.withgoogle.com/page/course/viewership-bootcamp). We have provided a summarized list of steps in Table 12, but you will definitely want students to dig deeper to learn more about creating great videos!

TABLE 12
STEPS TO QUALITY VIDEO PRODUCTION

Step	Additional Information
Define the purpose of your video	Is your video designed to inform, entertain, or educate? **Informational:** • New content curation • Product reviews • Infomercial **Entertainment:** • Comedy • Drama • Horror **Educational:** • How-to guides • Interviews • Tutorials • Reviews • Demonstrations • Share research findings
Determine your audience	Who will be interested in this video? If you don't know, you might consider: • Searching trends online • Searching questions asked on social media related to your topic
Get your gear	You will need: • High-quality camera, but it need not be expensive; the camera on a smartphone typically has HD video • Tripod • Microphone (directional microphone preferred) • Selfie stick (optional)
Plan the content	Plan your compelling start to hook the viewer. You will need: • A script • A plan of the shots (storyboard) Define the content: • This will depend on the type of film you are making. For example you may have to do research about a topic to become an "expert" on the topic or you may have to have props, costumes, and actors. • Create a narrative (story) that makes the content cohesive. Remember to be original: • If your movie is to inform, synthesize. • If your movie is to entertain, be creative, do something different from others, or provide a new perspective. • Consider: What new perspective is my video providing?
Design the background	Plan your background: • What will be happening in the background of your video? • How does the background set the scene of your video? • How does the background enhance the narrative or story of your video?
Plan the lighting	How will lighting help set the scene? What elements of lighting do you need to consider? • Daylight versus artificial light • Direction
Practice, practice, practice	Practice before you start filming. Once you start filming, plan to do multiple "takes" for each scene. After each "take" review the video and see how you can improve the next time. Do this until you are happy with the outcome.

TABLE 12, *continued*

Step	Additional Information
Import video	Move the video from the camera to the computer.
	This will allow you to edit all of the video footage into a single, finished video.
Edit, edit, edit	It is estimated that for every hour of video recorded, there might only be 2 minutes of footage used in the final cut.
	Editing takes a long time, so be sure to start editing well before the deadline.
Upload	Choose the upload site and follow the instructions.

Your Students Want to Vlog?

A vlog, or video blog, is a regularly updated set of videos run by an individual or small group. Vlogs have a tremendous capacity to reach a large audience and young people have as much potential to build influence as any adult. Take, for example, the famous vloggers Bethany Mota and Marques Brownlee. Marques reviews technology gadgets of all kind and informs his viewers of the strengths and weaknesses of these gadgets. Bethany began her career sharing "haul" videos in which she focused on fashion purchases and style tips. Marques was 14 when he began vlogging. He has become very influential in the technology industry and attended college for business and technology marketing. Bethany was 13 when she started her vlog. Her original intent was to create so much content that the cyberbullies who had chosen her as a target would no longer have any influence. She certainly succeeded! She has nearly 10 million followers, a fashion line at a popular store, and in 2015, she had the opportunity to interview President Barack Obama. Marques and Bethany have a different purpose for their vlogs, but they both have one thing in common with all other popular vloggers: On a regular and recurring basis they produce and share high-quality videos, with a purpose, via the Internet.

When we talk about having students create a vlog, they could just as easily create a single video and develop many of the same skills. Both a single video and a vlog achieve the same primary goal: Create a high-quality product with a clear goal or purpose. The only distinction is that a vlog is multiple videos shared via a webpage or other Internet video outlet like YouTube, whereas a video alone does not need to be shared via the Internet and can be a single production.

Taking on a vlog is not easy and students need to know that in advance. A vlog is not just a series of videos, but rather an ongoing communication with an audience. A vlog must be maintained over time. Successful vloggers have done so over months and years and have maintained a commitment to consistency in quality over a long period of time. Matthias, a popular vlogger among tweens and teens, said of vlogging: "Make videos because of your undeniable need to be creative, because it's a lot of hard work, and if you don't have the passion, it makes it even more difficult to near impossible" (Vlog Nation, 2015, para. 11). Marques Brownlee said of vlogging, "The amount of time I put into it is equivalent to a full-time job" (Eisenhood, 2013, para. 12). He is always attending to detail to improve his videos and averages three videos a week (Eisenhood, 2013).

You may want to consider adapting this experience if a student has not developed sufficient discipline or commitment to an interest area. One alternative might be to have a group of students collaborate to create a vlog for the school community. The audience is real, but the stakes are not as high as putting the vlog online.

It is important to determine what a student or students want to achieve by making a vlog. Again, making a vlog takes a lot of time and a lot of commitment to the process, a level of commitment that far exceeds a singular video. We have provided a set of questions to help students think through the processes of vlogging. Without knowing the answers to these questions, students might not be able to maintain engagement and could lose their way in the video production process. These questions can be used as writing prompts, as part of a learning contract, as an online research activity, or simply as an "application" to be able to use the video production equipment.

Before starting:
› Why do you want to make a vlog? What is the purpose of your vlog?
› Who is the vlog for? Who is the audience?
› Why will they be interested in your vlog?
› Have you chosen a topic for your vlog that you will be able to create content for and stay interested in for an extended period of time (several months and potentially years)?

Plan your background:
› What will be happening in the background of your video?
› How does the background set the scene of your video?
› How does the background enhance the narrative or story of your video?
› How will your background be similar from one vlog to the next?

Plan your formula format:

› What are the parts or elements of your vlog that stay the same over time (e.g., a walking scene, inserted images, music, interviews)?

› How will you make the elements unique (e.g., abrupt ending, time lapse sequence, custom-designed graphics)?

› How will the elements be arranged into a pattern? How will this pattern get repeated in future vlogs?

Vlogging is not recommended for all students. Parents have to provide permission, students have to be committed to the process, and time needs to be carved out to make videos, whether outside the school day or during compacted learning. It is important to understand that the student's motivation for the vlog has to come from an authentic desire to entertain, educate, or inform others. Every vlogger will tell you that to be successful, you have to love what you are doing and want to share it with others.

Finding Quality Sources

Although the Internet holds the answer to many questions, the information found on the Internet is not always accurate. To assist students in learning to find quality sources, we have created the SEM:*Tech* Finding Quality Sources template (see http://bit.ly/sem-tech-quality-sources; see Figure 32). This template reorganizes the classic questioning strategy "who, what, when, where, why, and how" into order to better guide students in their search for a quality source.

1. How will I search?
2. What did I find?
3. Who said it?
4. When did they say it?
5. Why did they say it?
6. Where else did I find the same information?

You can either provide students with a printed copy of the guide or have them create their own digital copy by accessing the Google Document, going to the "File" menu, and selecting "Make a copy." This will then add an editable copy of the document to their Google Drive account that can then be shared with you.

Searches for information on the Internet all start with a question. Make sure students phrase this as an actual question. This may better frame what it is that

SEM:*Tech*

FINDING QUALITY SOURCES

WHAT IS MY QUESTION?

HOW WILL I SEARCH? (Key words and phrases)

WHAT DID I FIND? (Summarized notes)

WHO SAID IT? (Is this a person or an organization? Is the information from an expert? Is it a personal blog?)

WHEN DID THEY SAY IT? (Is the information current? Is there a date on the information?)

WHY DID THEY SAY IT? (What is the author's purpose? Is the information biased?)

WHERE ELSE DID I FIND THE SAME INFORMATION? (List two other sources.)

WHAT IS THE ANSWER TO MY QUESTION?

Figure 32. Finding quality sources.

they are looking for and help them to know when they have found the answer for which they are looking. See Chapter 9's section on "Searching the Internet" for a detailed description of Internet search strategies.

With the question in mind, the first step is for students to consider "how" they will go about searching for an answer. Keep in mind that this is different than the question that is being asked. Although search engines have become much more sophisticated, typing a question in the search box is not necessarily the best way to go about finding an answer. Instead, have students identify keywords and phrases. Be sure to list alternate search terms if the first attempt does not work out as planned. By spending some time considering what goes in the search box before heading straight to Google, students are more likely to find a better list of results.

Once the search engine returns the list of results, students should comb through the information and determine "what" they found. Note that this activity does not delve into how to read the search results. However, this is a skill that should be reviewed with your students to help ensure their success. Have students summarize what information they found that would answer their question. Be sure that they include the link to the website.

Depending on the question being asked, locating information online may not be enough. Instead, the real purpose of this activity is to get beyond simple answers to quick questions. When gathering information, students should question "who" said the information—identify the source. Have students determine whether this is a single person or an organization and whether or not it matters depending on the question. Decide if this source would be considered an expert and what qualifies him or her to be an expert. This information can usually be found on an "About" page. Students should also examine whether the site is a blog and contains mostly opinions or whether it is a site that contains mostly factual information. This discrepancy is something that many students have traditionally struggled with in print environments, and the Internet, where anyone has to power to publish anything, only further complicates matters.

Not only should students determine the source of the information, but it is also vital to determine "when" the information was posted. Is there a date on the website? Is the information current and still accurate, or has the information been disproven?

Next, it is critical for students to identify "why" the author said this. Students must consider if the source of the information is biased in any way or has a hidden agenda that would influence their perspective on the authenticity or factual nature of the information.

The next to last step in this process is perhaps one of the most important. Students should be highly encouraged to identify "where" else they could find the same information. It is important to verify any information with at least two other sources. By triangulating information in this manner, any potential for misinformation is greatly reduced.

The final step has the students going back to their initial question and identifying the answer. This helps to close the loop and ensure that students have accomplished their mission.

Creating a Quality Website

To help students in the process of designing a website, we have created the SEM:*Tech* Website Planner (http://bit.ly/sem-tech-website-planner; see Figure 33) as a Google Document template. You may choose to print this out for your students or have them create their own copy and add it to their Google Drive. To make a personal copy of the template, go to the "File" menu and select "Make a copy." This will add a new version of the document to your Google Drive that can be edited and shared. This guide can be used with any website building tool or blogging format. Although it is very tempting to simply jump in and start constructing a website from scratch, we have learned from personal experience that spending some time planning before you begin can save you hours in the long run in reorganizing content, deleting pages, and, in a worst-case scenario, starting over completely.

Whenever beginning a new website, one should consider what the purpose of the site is going to be. Is this a personal or professional website? Is this for a particular project or product? By keeping the purpose at the front of your mind, it will help to guide all of the other design choices. Closely related to the purpose should be the audience for the site. Web designers should aim to target who it is that they want to attract to their website. The overall design should relate directly to the purpose and audience. This includes things like color choices, types of images, fonts, and even layout.

A very important, but often overlooked, step in the planning process is to consider the number and types of pages that you will need in your design. Inexperienced web designers might be tempted to simply put everything on a single page. This can result in seemingly endless scrolling and can make it difficult for visitors to find content on the site. Instead, take some time in the planning stage to create a content outline of the types of information that each page

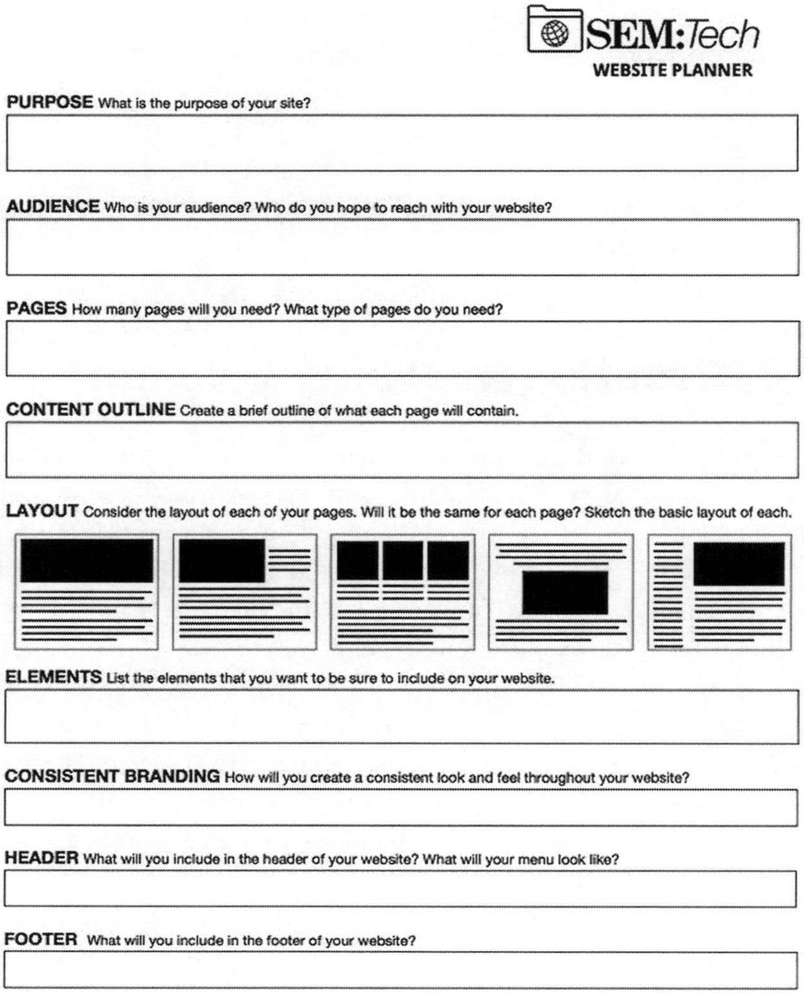

SEM:*Tech*

WEBSITE PLANNER

PURPOSE What is the purpose of your site?

AUDIENCE Who is your audience? Who do you hope to reach with your website?

PAGES How many pages will you need? What type of pages do you need?

CONTENT OUTLINE Create a brief outline of what each page will contain.

LAYOUT Consider the layout of each of your pages. Will it be the same for each page? Sketch the basic layout of each.

ELEMENTS List the elements that you want to be sure to include on your website.

CONSISTENT BRANDING How will you create a consistent look and feel throughout your website?

HEADER What will you include in the header of your website? What will your menu look like?

FOOTER What will you include in the footer of your website?

Figure 33. Website planner.

will contain. Consider the hierarchy or structure of the overall site. Although it is relatively easy to restructure or move content once it has been created, it is beneficial to give some thought before beginning. As a part of this step, consider how your page menus will be organized. Remember that you want to make your site as easy as possible to navigate.

Next, take some time to ponder the layout of each of your pages. We have provided some common options for websites. Think about how images might be employed. What type of column structure will be used? What about headlines or titles? Will the text be centered or right justified? We have found it quite useful to sketch out the basic layout for each of the pages before designing them. Again, this can give the designer an overall vision of what the end result will be. As part of creating the layout, consider what types of elements are going to be a part of the website. Elements might include items such as an embedded calendar, YouTube videos, SlideShare presentations, or images. How will these elements be organized? Will they be a part of every page or found in a single location?

One of the most important design considerations comes in determining how the designer will create consistent branding throughout the website. This branding should relate directly to the purpose and audience. Visitors to the website should recognize that they are on the same site regardless of what page it is that they are visiting. The use of themes helps make this much easier, but careful planning in the use of banners and images helps to create a cohesive structure to the website. Another part of this branding comes in the use of headers and footers that remain consistent across each page. As part of the planning process, have students indicate what types of information will be a part of the header and how they will structure the menu for the site. Finally, the footer section should provide some information about the designer and contact information.

Previously, we discussed how to assess the quality of a website. This is an important skill as students conduct research in online settings. It is also an opportunity for them to see examples of what constitutes quality products in digital environments. Now, we turn our attention from students as consumers to students as producers by allowing students to create their own website. As students begin producing a website, the quality criteria we covered in Chapter 9 are certainly applicable. Now, however, students must go beyond merely considering the quality of the content and information. They have to focus on design, accessibility, organization of the site, user-friendliness, and ways to include multimedia *in addition to* providing high-quality content. To help students in this process, Table 13 provides a series of questions to scaffold their thinking as they assess the quality of their own website throughout the design process. The Student Activity: Curating Content on a Website will also be helpful as students work on their sites.

TABLE 13
SCAFFOLDING FOR STUDENTS TO ASSESS THEIR OWN WEBSITE

Content quality	◆ Is the information provided accurate? ◆ Is the information reliable and free of errors? ◆ Are there spelling, grammar, or punctuation mistakes? ◆ Is the information provided supported by evidence? ◆ Is the information provided free of bias? ◆ Is the information provided current? ◆ Is the information provided comprehensive? ◆ Is the information cited correctly? ◆ Is the information provided useful for the intended audience? ◆ Have appropriate permissions or licensing been obtained for the use of copyrighted images and multimedia?
Accessibility	◆ Does the site load quickly? ◆ Is the site viewable from different browsers (e.g., DuckDuckGo, Google, Bing)? ◆ Is the site viewable from different operating systems (e.g., iOS 9 mobile operating system, Apple OS X, Windows 10)? ◆ Can the website be viewed by people with disabilities? ◆ Can the website be understood by people with various levels of education? ◆ Can the website be understood by people from different cultural backgrounds? ◆ Are clear instructions provided for using certain aspects of the website?
Organization	◆ Is the site easy to navigate? ◆ Is the page design overwhelming or confusing? ◆ Are links to various pages within the website available on every page? ◆ Are links to various pages within the website clear and easy to follow? ◆ Does the use of spacing, tables, borders, and dividers enhance the usability of the site? ◆ Is information presented in a clear and consistent manner across all pages within the website?
Graphic design	◆ Are the principles of good graphic design used (see p. 188)? ◆ Is the site visually appealing? ◆ Are color and shape used appropriately? ◆ Does the use of spacing, layers, tables, borders, dividers, and backgrounds enhance the look and feel of the site? ◆ Is the font readable?
Technology integration	◆ Does the way in which technologies are used fit with the purpose of the website? ◆ Does the use of technology detract from the purpose of the site? ◆ Are interactive technologies used (e.g., bulletin boards, surveys, search options)? ◆ Are multimedia technologies used (e.g., embedded videos, links to other websites, animations)?
Originality	◆ Is the website different from other similar sites? ◆ Is the website memorable? ◆ Does the website offer things not found elsewhere? ◆ Does the website offer original material?

Note. See Hasan and Abuelrub (2011) and Moustakis et al. (2004).

182

STUDENT ACTIVITY
Curating Content on a Website

You have developed your website as an important part of sharing your interests and passions with the world. Now, it is time to create a collection of resources, tools, or information about your interests that you can share with others to help them better appreciate or understand your passion area.

Start by doing some online research about curating content in your passion area. These questions will help you in your search:

› How is curating different than collecting?

› What are the steps in curating content?

› Where can I find content about my passion area? What content can I create related to my passion area? Why do I need both?

Nine tips for successful content curation:

1. Be specific about your topic choice. Your interest area might be "dinosaurs," but that is too broad. Make sure you have narrowed your topic to create a unique niche.

2. Choose content wisely. Does each piece of content reflect your goals and values? Is the content high quality?

3. Create your own content. Is there a good balance between your original work and that of others?

4. Organize your content in a way that is graphically appealing and easy to follow.

5. Rate each piece of content. Start with a scale like 1 to 5 or 1 to 10 and rank each piece of content on the same scale.

6. Be sure to add your own thoughts about the content. What are your unique insights?

7. Tell a story with your content. What is it about your collection of content that makes it better or more interesting than other similar collections of content?

8. Don't forget to cite your sources! Give credit where credit is due.

9. Share.

Mission Possible as a Type II

Maybe it was the notion of a one-way trip to Mars or the idea that as a species, we would colonize Mars in the same way that settlers colonized the Americas. Maybe it was the idea of traveling and living on the surface of Mars, or maybe it was simply the idea of exploring beyond the moon. Whatever the case, you have several students who are interested in learning more about surviving on Mars, but where to start?

Remember, Type II development activities cannot really be planned in advance. They will stem from a "need to know" because a student is actively engaged in Type III investigation and needs scaffolding to continue making progress. The need to develop a Type II process activity might also stem from student interest that was generated from having participated in a Type I experience. Here we suggest two activities that could have conceivably come out of interest generated as a result of participating in an engaging Type I experience. The activities presented teach critical thinking and require research. It is not expected that all of your students would want to participate in these activities. They are merely suggestions for if the need were to arise. Further, these activities are not new ideas, simply an effort to demonstrate how going beyond the Type I experience can lead to Type II processes.

Survival on Mars is a very real challenge scientists face as they plan and consider exploring the red planet, fourth from the sun in our solar system. The elementary edition of the unit "Survival on Mars" (http://www.angelahousand.com/elementary-mars-survival.html) is adapted from the NASA activity, "Survival! Exploration Then and Now." Here we ask students to rank 13 survival items from 1 (most important) to 13 (least important) based on whether or not they would help with survival on the surface of Mars. Collaborating in small groups, students have to justify their reasons for the rank order of the list. Providing this justification requires online research as students learn that items like a magnetic compass do not work on Mars because there is no magnetic field and matches won't light because there is no atmosphere. In the elementary edition, expert insights are provided afterward to help students compare their justification to that of scientists.

The secondary edition of "Survival on Mars" (http://www.angelahousand.com/secondary-mars-survival.html) takes 15 scientific innovations from the last 5 years and requires students to rank their importance for colonizing Mars. This version of "Survival on Mars" is far more open-ended. First, students simulate the role of an angel investor who funds projects for the advancement of society and the human race. They have to grapple with advancing the human race while taking into consideration the goal of colonizing Mars. When this activity has been done with students, several different kinds of conversations have emerged as part of debriefing the activity. For example, questions about whether or not an angel investor would put money into a project that might never turn a profit are often part of the content of the discussion. "Should we colonize Mars?" is a question that is often broached, followed by consideration of ownership of resources, setting up a government, and "Is money more important than human survival?" The secondary unit for "Survival on Mars" is rich with opportunity and introduces students to cutting-edge technologies, the field creating those technologies, and the universities or businesses that have the resources for research and development. Typically, students are not previously familiar with these cutting-edge technologies.

Selfies as a Type II

After the Type I Selfie experience, some students may be intrigued by the concept of self-expression and self-portraits using photographs. Although students will probably have some experience with taking selfies, this is a great opportunity to provide some how-to training on taking better photographs.

The Internet is full of many high-quality informational and how-to resources on almost any topic. Not surprisingly, selfies are no different. Consider starting with this article (http://www.wikihow.com/Take-Good-Selfies) from wikiHow, which is one of our favorite go-to resources on how to do almost anything. Students will quickly realize that taking a good selfie is much more than just pointing a camera at your face. One must also consider the pose, the scene, lighting, composition, and how the photo is edited. WikiHow provides a number tips and techniques for students to consider. Of course, YouTube is also a source for tutorial videos. In this 3-minute video (https://youtu.be/vbqIQcKNE7E) that has been viewed more than 4 million times, YouTube star Michelle Phan provides tips on how to take the perfect selfie. Topics include the importance of lighting, angles, and filters.

Although taking better selfies is one consideration, the real content to be learned here resides in training related to photography techniques. As students take more and more pictures, they may have a natural desire and interest in learning how to take better photographs. One simple strategy for improving the quality of your photos is using the rule of thirds. Ask students to explore this online tutorial (http://digital-photography-school.com/rule-of-thirds), and then try their hand at using the rule of thirds to take a series of photographs. The angle from which a photograph is taken can significantly change the perspective of photographs. After doing this online tutorial (http://digital-photography-school. com/photographing-people-from-different-angles), ask students to consider how taking a photo from a high angle can change the composition from taking the same subject from a low angle. Have them think about ways to take photos up close to fill the frame. In the third tutorial from the Digital Photography School (http://digital-photography-school.com/using-composition-create-powerful -portraits), tips from the first two lessons are utilized to discuss the importance of composition. When creating portraits, a photographer must also consider the story that is being told, how light is used, and the spacing within the frame. During the Type II, students should be encouraged to try to incorporate the photo techniques by taking a lot of pictures and examining how their photos improve over time.

Speaking the Language of the Future

"The principles of information design are universal . . . and are not tied to unique features of a particular language or culture."
—Edward Tufte

Technology pervades every dimension of human life and the advancement of technology is in many ways unfathomable. There are technologies being developed to alter the human genome, explore the outer reaches of space, create anthropomorphic robots, allow computers to learn and think for themselves, and even travel through time. No one can predict what life will be like even a decade from now, and although there will come a time when this advancement slows, where the wave of exponential growth will crest, that is not going to happen for a while. One thing we can be sure of is that the future our students will be participating in will be radically different than it is today. Naturally, this radical shift will change how we define our society, the ways we understand others, the ways we perceive similarity and differences, the ways we collaborate, and the ways we deal with conflict. Essential to a vibrant and peaceful society will be effective communication in a world that will be fundamentally different and therefore will communicate in fundamentally different ways.

Visual Communication

Visual communication is essentially the same as written communication, but instead of merely using words to communicate ideas, visual communication may use images, symbols, and words or some combination of these three. Have you ever heard the adage, "A picture is worth a thousand words"? This sentiment is aptly applied because the combination of images and symbols allows one to communicate complex ideas quickly and economically. For example, imagine learning human anatomy without any pictures! Visual communication simplifies information using patterns and connections to focus one's attention on the most important information. It allows one to convey information using a visual message, increasing its power to inform, educate, or persuade a person or audience. Given the increasingly short attention span and the vast information overloading our psyche, visual communication will only increase in popularity and use as technology evolves. Visual communication might take the form of signs, infographics, films, images, simple symbols, or graphic designs (just to name a few!).

A historical example that demonstrates the power of visual communication is Steve Jobs's introduction of the MacBook Air at MacWorld in 2008 (https://www.youtube.com/watch?v=OZ5fSDcAaCk). In Mr. Jobs's presentation, he begins with a picture of the competitor's tablet and talks about the competitor's tablet briefly. After providing general comparisons to other competitors in a table of information (a lot of information in a less than 20 words), he shares a graphic representation of the competitor's tablet profile. Then, he proceeds to overlay the MacBook Air's thin profile (in green) over the competitor's tablet profile (in white). It looked something like Figure 34.

That image is pretty powerful to demonstrate just how much thinner the MacBook Air was in comparison to the competition, but it still did not communicate powerfully enough. Steve Jobs then proceeded to take a common office manila envelope and pull the MacBook Air out of the manila envelope. That was the lasting image. After the presentation was over, remembering that the MacBook Air at its thickest point was less than the competitor's tablet at its thinnest point was not the memorable take away, albeit an important message. A tablet that would fit into a manila envelope is the image that elicited an emotional response. That was the information that remained vivid even after the presentation was over, and that is an effect that could not have been achieved with merely words—saying that it fits into a manila envelope is not the same as *seeing* that it fits into a manila envelope.

Steve Jobs was a master of visual communication, and the Apple logo, designed by Rob Janoff, is one of the most recognizable and iconic of all corporate

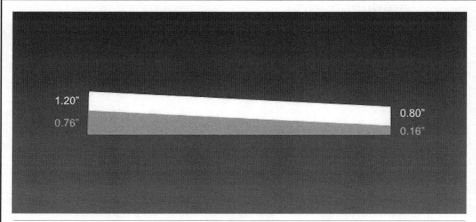

Figure 34. Approximation of graphic image from MacBook debut.

logos. Can you conjure an image of the Apple logo in your mind? It is a simple image of an apple with a bite out of it. That logo is part of Apple's brand or identity. You cannot imagine Apple products without also imagining their distinctive branding, part of the visual communication of the company. There are numerous examples. When you think of Coca Cola, what do you see in your mind? How about Nike or Disney? All of these have strong visual associations as part of their brand; whether it is the cursive words of Coca Cola, the distinctive swoosh of Nike, or the mouse ears of Disney, each of these companies has a clear visual component that communicates who it is simply and effectively—so effectively in fact that we challenge you to try and think about the companies without thinking about their logos.

Visual communication is not just about communicating identity. Visual communication allows us to find our way (e.g., road signs, restroom location signs), persuade people (e.g., advertising, product packaging), inform (e.g., infographics, graphs, charts), and entertain (e.g., graphic novels, games, décor). At the heart of all of this communication is design.

Graphic design. Chip Kidd, author of the 2013 children's book *Go: A Kidd's Guide to Graphic Design*, defined graphic design as the "purposeful planning that uses any combination of forms, pictures, words, and meanings to achieve one's goal" (p. 2). Graphic design is used in almost every form of media and in every aspect of life. In the same way that business, industry, and the arts use graphic design, students can use graphic design to enhance their communication, define their identity, and engage complex problems. For example, students can create a logo and business card to communicate who they are and what they value. They can use graphical representations to communicate their findings from research, or they can use mind maps to break large problems into smaller pieces. All of these require some graphic design and all of these allow students to communicate visually. These examples, however, can be produced with varying quality and varying levels of effective communication. For instance, a mind map can have clear and effective details, the organization of which is enhanced by the shapes and colors specifically chosen to enhance the connections and associations. In contrast, it also can be displayed as a simple branch system that suggests association without any clear connections. When information is intentionally planned using graphic design, it enhances the transfer of knowledge using visual cues.

Graphic design is both process and product. Graphic design can be considered the iterative process of developing representations that communicate using typography, space, images, and color. By the same token, the outcomes of the process, the graphic designs, are the websites, logos, signs, decoration, and visual representations of all kinds that communicate powerfully and quickly. There are a variety of methods graphic designers use to create these visual representations of ideas and messages, but it is important to understand the four main ingredients that provide the foundation for the design processes.

Typography. Comic Sans (yuck!), Helvetica (masterful), Arial (lovely), and Times New Roman (classic) are just a miniscule sampling of the available fonts used in typography. Typography is essentially the art of arranging type to make written words legible, easily readable, and appealing. The techniques that are used to make written language beautiful include selecting a font, changing the size of the font, moving the letters closer together or farther apart (a.k.a. tracking and kerning), and adjusting the space between lines (a.k.a. leading). In visual communication, there tends to be less text; therefore, it is even more important that the text that does appear is aesthetically appealing and easy to read!

Space. Space deals with how objects are placed within given parameters and how those objects relate to one another. Visual elements activate how we perceive space. Rubin's vase (see Figure 35) clearly illustrates how space can be defined and interpreted by the eye in visual design as your perception vacillates between two faces (the black space) and a vase (the white space).

Ironically, it is difficult to explain space in words, but visually it is an important element to understand. What "space" will remain empty? What part of the space will be filled? How does the relationship between these elements affect the overall composition? These are just some of the questions designers seek to answer when they address space.

Figure 35. Rubin's vase.

Images. An image is any likeness of a person, place, or thing. An image can be produced by an artist or a person using paint, sculpture, computer software, or a camera. Images can be two-dimensional or three-dimensional. Typically, though, images do not contain text; rather, they are the means to make objects visible and they communicate without words.

Color. The ingredient of color may at first glance seem very self-explanatory, but color at its essence is complex. Color is created by the reflection of light by an object and is determined visually by the measurement of hue, saturation, and brightness of the light reflected from the object. Colors convey meaning and affect our perception.

DID YOU KNOW?

In a study of perceptions of color, students associated colors like red with happy or fun, yellow with surprise, purple with curiosity, brown with "weird," black with fear and reluctance, and white with satisfaction or peacefulness (Jalil, Yunus, & Said, 2013).

Graphic designers compose these elements in a variety of ways. Whether they use existing ingredients (i.e., images created by artists, existing text, or photographs) or they create their own, there are numerous professional processes and skills that help support graphic designers to be successful. They have to be able to actively listen, write, speak, understand part-to-whole relationships, critically examine, problem solve, comprehend written text, manage time, make decisions, monitor progress, and most importantly, iterate. Technology once again provides students with the requisite tools to generate multiple ideas and substantive iterations in a short amount of time. Here are some tools to support that iterative process:

› *SVG-edit* (http://svg-edit.googlecode.com) is a web-based, open-source, free vector graphics editor. Vector graphics are simple shapes and simple color graphics that are not pixilated (i.e., they remain smooth at the edges). The SVG-editor allows students to create and edit Scalable Vector Graphics (SVG) images using a web browser of your choice.

› *Pixlr* (https://pixlr.com) is a cloud-accessible image editing application available for free. It uses effects, overlays, borders, cropping, resizing, and other enhancers to allow even novice image editing enthusiasts to make the most of their images. The apps provided by Pixlr range from simple to advanced, so even your most industrious student will find opportunities to continue challenging the image design capabilities. Although you have to download the applications to use them, they are available for both iOS and Android operating systems.

› *Sumopaint* (https://www.sumopaint.com/app) is a free web-based image editing application. It requires Adobe Flash Player to be downloaded to the computer, which means it cannot be used on the iPad. This image editor has many of the same features as Photoshop, such as brushes, pencils, shapes, text, cloning, gradients, layering, blending, shadows, filters, and more. To use the application without ads, simply download the affordable professional upgrade.

Using the computer for graphic design enables students to explore multiple ideas quickly and in more detail than they could achieve with hand drawings. Although it supports the process of iteration, it also makes critical assessment more challenging as students are faced with limitless choices. The vast number of options makes it more difficult for students to isolate the best design. Therefore, it is important with any design process that the audience is identified in advance and that a timeline is implemented to support students in managing their time well. The goal of graphic design is visual communication and problem solving through the correct use of typography, space, image, and color. It seeks to enhance the transfer of knowledge through visual messages and improve the readability and legibility of text through visual order and layout. You might be asking: Where do I start with the teaching of graphic design? Or, how will I get students interested in the skills of visual communication? Or, what steps should I take to engage students in meaningfully developing their graphic design skills? We recommend having students design a logo that represents their interests, values, and who they are as a person. This logo is a great addition to the website and because students are designing a logo for themselves, they quickly become vested in the quality and meaning of their design.

Student activity: Designing a logo. To help scaffold students in designing a logo, we have developed the SEM:*Tech* Logo Design Planner (http://bit. ly/sem-tech-logo) as a Google Document Template (see Figure 36). You may choose to print this out to guide your students or have them make a copy for themselves and add it to their Google Drive. To make a digital copy for yourself, go to the "File" menu and select "Make a copy." An editable copy will be added to your Google Drive folder. As students are planning the design of their logo, ask them to respond to each of the prompts in the textboxes that have been provided.

First, students should consider the product for which they are designing a logo. Is this a personal brand or is this for an existing product or service? What does the product do? Is there anything associated with that product that would serve as a visual reference point or a starting point for the design?

As students begin considering their logo, they should next identify inspiration for their design. Search for existing logos or images that have a style or a feel that the students might like to emulate. You should emphasize that an existing logo should not merely be copied, but instead, students should look for inspiration. Ask them to find at least five logos that might inspire their design. Once they are collected, have students examine what they have in common. Are there similarities in their design?

Next, students should consider what type of logo they want to design. There are three basic logo design types: font-based, literal image, and abstract image. For example, the Google logo is a colorful and playful example of a font-based logo that simply states the name of the product. The Apple logo, on the other hand, typically appears without any text. Instead, it is a stylized example of a literal icon. Over the years, it has transformed from a rainbow-striped image to one that typically appears as either a black or white image with a single bite taken out of the side of the apple. The abstract logo can be a bit more difficult

🌐 **SEM:***Tech*
LOGO DESIGN PLANNER

WHAT IS MY PRODUCT?

IDENTIFY INSPIRATION (Find five logos that might inspire your design. What do they have in common? Remember, inspiration does not mean copy!)

WHAT TYPE OF LOGO WILL YOU DESIGN? WHY?
(Font-Based / Abstract Image / Literal Image)

WHAT MESSAGE DO YOU WANT TO COMMUNICATE WITH YOUR LOGO?

WHAT COLOR PALETTE WILL YOU USE? (How does this relate to your message?)

WHAT FONT(S) WILL YOU USE? (How does this relate to your message?)

WHAT SHAPES AND FORMS WILL YOU USE? (How does this relate to your message?)

ITERATE THREE TO FIVE VERSIONS OF YOUR LOGO.

CONDUCT MARKET RESEARCH. (Which logo does your audience prefer?)
REFINE AND FINALIZE LOGO.

Figure 36. Logo design planner.

to identify. The Google Chrome logo is a good example of the third type. Here we see a circular icon with three different colored arms surrounding a blue center. Although it does not literally emulate a browser or operating system, it has become instantly recognizable to its users.

After deciding on a type of logo, students should consider what type of message they want to communicate with their logo. This should relate back to their product and audience, but it should also begin to indicate the feelings and emotions that they want the logo to convey. As they are narrowing this down, they should consider three different design factors: color, font, and shape or form. Each of these should specifically relate to the message that the logo is trying to convey.

At this point, students are ready to begin sketching their logo ideas. Although it is very tempting to start designing using a graphic design program, an important first step is to have them sketch out some ideas on paper. This allows for rapid prototyping of different ideas. Once some basic ideas begin to emerge, encourage students to iterate at least three to five versions of their logo. Professional graphic designers might produce hundreds of ideas before settling on the few that might work best. However, it is important to realize that you as the designer are not the only audience. Have the students conduct some market research with their three to five versions of their logo. Collect feedback from members of their intended audience as to which design they like best and why. After conducting market research, a logo may need to be refined or tweaked. This might include a change in color or even a complete redesign before it is finalized. Help students to realize that a good logo is not something that is completed on the first draft, but instead it is part of a long process with countless revisions.

There are a great number of graphic design skills that will be employed in the process of designing a logo. These skills, however, are not necessarily represented in this planner. Instead, this is meant to serve as a tool to help guide your students through the overall design process of a logo.

Information visualization. Going beyond graphic design is the visual display of vast quantities of information through data visualization. Data visualization, one form of information visualization, is a general term that describes efforts to help people understand data by placing it in a visual context. It is rapidly becoming a critical component in scientific research, particularly in the display of findings, and emerges from research on how we view and understand information. Research in computer science, visual design, psychology, business methods, and human-computer interaction have all informed the creation of approaches for conveying abstract information in intuitive ways, giving concrete visuals to abstract information.

One early author focusing on displaying quantitative information visually was Edward Tufte (1983). In his book, *The Visual Display of Quantitative Information*, he suggested that graphic displays of information should:

› show the data,
› induce the viewer to think about the substance rather than about the design or the technology used to create the graphic image,
› accurately represent the data,
› make large quantities of data coherent,
› allow for the comparison of different pieces of data,
› provide a broad overview of the data and also allow one to drill down into the information with careful inspection of the structure of the information, and
› serve a clear purpose.

Not unlike graphic design, a primary purpose of data visualization is to communicate information clearly and efficiently. The difference is that data visualization uses statistical graphs, plots, tables, maps, and charts that can be directly linked back to the data set from which they came. Effective data visualization aids the viewer in analyzing and understanding the data. It allows one to understand the associations between variables within data and focuses attention on specific aspects of the data, which creates ethical and analytical challenges for those responsible for creating these graphical representations. What data needs to be focused on? What questions are you asking of the large data sets? Are important variables being missed or disregarded in the visual display? Data visualization relies on the cognitive skills of humans to ask the right questions and seek meaningful insights. The process of creating graphical representations of data is both an art and a science, and the individuals responsible for displaying the data graphically bear a lot of responsibility for doing so fairly and wisely.

There are essentially five types of data visualization:

› *Time-series* designs document values over time (e.g., stock prices over several months).
› *Statistical distributions* reveal trends based on the probability density or how numbers are portioned along a single variable (e.g., a normal distribution).
› *Maps* represent geographical data (e.g., red and blue coloring on a map to demonstrate electoral results).

> *Networks* show relationships (e.g., social network analysis of Internet connections).
> *Hierarchies* communicate hierarchical data or data with parameters that vary at more than one level (e.g., students within classrooms within schools).

Data visualization is primarily focused on quantitative data, but qualitative data can also be presented visually in the form of information graphics, or infographics. Infographics are visual representations of information that can improve the viewer's understanding of complex descriptions by displaying the information concisely and incorporating graphics. The visual components enhance the display of patterns or trends within the information, making it easier to understand. Data visualization and infographics are more accessible to students than ever before as a variety of free online tools that are easy to use are available on the Internet:

> *Google Developers* (https://developers.google.com/chart) provides a chart tool that is powerful, easy to use, and free. The tool allows you to connect data, in real time, from a website to display information via pie charts, line charts, column charts, area charts, tree maps, geo charts, scatter charts, histograms, and more. This is a powerful tool that allows students to easily connect data with visual representations with just a few simple steps.
> *Infogr.am* (https://infogr.am/education) is another data visualization tool, not unlike Google Developers charts. This tool, a web-based and partially free tool, focuses on developing data literacy in students and supports the process of telling "data-driven stories." It also provides the option for classroom accounts and has numerous tutorials that support not only students' understanding of data visualization, but yours as well!
> *Easel.ly* (http://www.easel.ly) is a great tool to create eye-catching, informative, and fun graphics on the web. Easel.ly has made it possible for students to design their own custom infographic in minutes, and it's free. Within the web-based tool, there are thousands of existing templates that provide the jumping-off point for customizable designs. It relies on a drag and drop interface that is intuitive. The mission of Easel.ly is to allow users to create and share visual ideas online, easily.

Data visualization and infographics can be particularly useful to support students in having a deep understanding of complex information and is an excellent means for them to effectively communicate their findings from research. However, they may not have the time or the opportunity to collect large quantities of data for these types of interpretation. Never fear, the Stevens Institute of Technology and The Center for Innovation in Engineering and Science Education have partnered to bring you an inestimably valuable resource: http://www.k12science. org/materials/resources/realtimedata. More than 50 web links to real-time data across multiple domains and links to some of the most compelling data available for educational use are available at this site. You can use these data sources as you help students understand the data they are trying to visualize and what they want to communicate about the data, determine the most important information for their audience to understand, and convey the information in the best and simplest form possible.

Coding, Computer Science, and Software Development

For centuries, math has been a universal language, the only language shared by all human beings regardless of culture, religion, or gender—until now. Coding is emerging as the language that transcends cultures, religion, and gender. It is the language that allows individuals to express themselves and their ideas, feelings, thoughts, and vision using technology. It is a language that will be at the core of expression for most disciplines in the future. Just like learning a foreign language, the sooner students are exposed to code, the easier it will be for them to learn and effectively use. If we don't give students the language and tools to not only use computers, but to orchestrate their development and evolution, we run the risk of making students perpetual consumers rather than producers of technology.

Coding is also a bridge to learning other things. Coding requires an understanding of variables, the processes of design, breaking complex problems into smaller parts, how to find and fix existing problems, how to revise and fine-tune solutions, how to collaborate, and how to experiment with new problems and ideas. Coding places all of these skills into a context that provides meaning and relevance for the processes at hand while encouraging risk taking and perseverance through reciprocal processes of failure and solution.

Coding is obviously important for a job like computer programmer, but as coding becomes increasingly prevalent, job opportunities will decline. Instead, the future needs software developers and computer and information research scientists—the people who are the creative minds behind computer programs and technological advancement.

DID YOU KNOW?

According the Bureau of Labor Statistics (U.S. Department of Labor, 2015), jobs in the fields of computer and information research science and software development are growing fast, significantly faster than other industries. It is estimated that by 2020, there will be 1,000,000 more jobs in the field of computer science than there are students in computer science programs. Computer programming, on the other hand, is expected to decline.

We are not suggesting that every student will grow up to be a computer scientist or a software developer. Instead, we are saying that learning the language of code is no longer optional, but rather fundamental to an individual's success in the future. It is important to understand that numerous processes that are, and always have been, important for students to master are embedded within learning code. Whether it is thinking creatively, reasoning systematically, or working collaboratively, coding provides the playground for deep and complex learning. Research (Reynolds & Caperton, 2011) bears this out: When middle school students were asked to design web-based video games as part of their coursework, the skills they identified learning included teamwork, people skills, and social skills; proposing a project and following it through to completion; as well as perseverance and patience. Moreover, they perceived their experience in designing games made learning fun and not boring—it provided opportunities to engage in self-directed learning, teamwork, and cooperation; the learning environment was more relaxed and less pressured; they got to experience hands-on learning; they learned "new" things; and the work itself was hard and challenging, but also interesting. This example illustrated not only the importance of engaging students in authentic learning, but also the value of learning to communicate using computer code.

Learning code options for students. Although the ability to code is becoming a universal means of communication, there are several languages that make up the coding environment. Some of the most popular and easily recognized languages include C, C++, C#, Java, Objective C, PHP, JavaScript, Python, SQL, and Ruby. The names of these languages alone may sound foreign, but our students must become familiar with them. Fortunately, there are a plethora of sources with lessons and skill development opportunities already available and many provide free resources for teachers and students.

› *Code.org* (https://code.org), launched in 2013, seeks to expand interest and participation in the burgeoning field of computer science by making free introductory courses available to students and teachers. Code.org offers a wide range of tutorials and learning modules for students of all ages. The Hour of Code was designed as a tutorial for beginners to learn some of the basic concepts of computer science via a "drag and drop" programming tool. In the introductory course, students view video mini-lectures from Bill Gates, Mark Zuckerberg, and many other well-known computer scientists. Students then complete a series of game-based levels while learning about repeat loops, conditional statements, and other basic algorithms. Beyond the Hour of Code, Code.org offers tutorials to teach programming languages such as JavaScript and Python, resources for making your own apps, and tutorials on creating your own games. Additional learning modules and courses continue to be developed and added to the Code Studio (http://studio.code.org).

› *Codecademy* (http://www.codecademy.com) is different from Code. org, which tends to focus on introducing students to computer science. Codecademy offers a logical next step for students who are ready to learn core programming skills for popular and widely used languages. Set up as a simulation, users work their way through a set of increasingly difficult challenges to acquire the knowledge and skill set of each language. Codecademy also offers a collection of mini-projects for students to put their newly acquired skills to work in a real-world type setting.

› *Scratch* (https://scratch.mit.edu) is for your aspiring game developers. Scratch allows students to program their stories, games, and animations. Once they have a creation, they can share it with the ever-growing online community within the Scratch network. This resource is easy to use and has a friendly interface, which even the most novice computer programmer can use. Scratch was created by the Lifelong Kindergarten Group at the MIT Media Lab and it is available free of charge! It was actually designed with education in mind and there is an extensive online community for educators called ScratchEd (http://scratched.gse.harvard.edu). The ScratchEd community is vibrant and always being updated by educators.

› *Hopscotch* (https://www.gethopscotch.com) is unique in that its focus is less on education and more on play (and that is not a bad thing!). Students develop games, but in the process, they learn about variables, conditionals, and loops.

› *CS Unplugged* (http://csunplugged.org) is for teachers who are not ready to have students learn computer science on a computer. CS Unplugged provides a collection of activities that teach computer science concepts with simple materials like cards, string, crayons, and physical movement.

Don't be surprised if some of your students fall in love with coding. Coding allows you to solve complex puzzles, find solutions to problems, create something useful for others, and express yourself in a medium that is only limited by what the mind can conjure. Students may want to take their programming to levels beyond what is available with these Type II resources—they may want to embark on genuine Type III productivity. Once a student goes beyond your capacity to guide him or her, then it is time to find a mentor.

CHRISTY'S CORNER: "BEEN THERE, DONE THAT"

You may recall the Type I main event, an enrichment cluster experience on coding. For Christy, her students quickly surpassed her capacity to be able to guide them in the coding process, but as a group, they were able to continue learning collaboratively—pushing each other to higher levels of coding capabilities. There was one student, however, who stood out. Luis outpaced the other students in his learning. He did all of the Code.org learning modules. He had worked through Scratch animations and games development, but he wanted to go beyond Scratch and felt like he had "exhausted what MIT had to offer." He even began mastering core-programming skills using Codecademy, but he wanted to do real design—not just use other people's code.

Christy had already identified that Luis had a degree of interest that motivated him to work on his project outside of the regular school day. Christy said, "Luis would tell me what he was doing. I tried to ask questions to help, but I was slowing him down." She also realized that there was an opportunity to satisfy his curiosity and desire to create. At this point, to continue his learning he either needed to take a formal class in programming or he needed a mentor. Given that his goal was very focused (he wanted to create a web-based game), Christy chose to seek out a mentor.

She started the process of finding a mentor by asking her friends, "Do you know someone who is really good at coding, computer programming, or software development?" This led her to Cory, a professional software developer. When she first contacted Cory, he gave several suggestions for learning opportunities for Luis:

Cory: There is a program called Scratch out of MIT.
Christy: Yeah, we've been there and done that.
Cory: Well there is Code.org. They have a lot of learning . . .
Christy: Yes, he has completed all of those.

Christy said that it took Cory some time to understand that Luis was serious and that he had already, as a fifth grader, surpassed most adults in his learning. Once he understood that Luis had a real passion for programming design and going beyond merely using code that had already been developed, Cory was on board as Luis's mentor.

Cory and Luis's entire mentoring relationship was communicated via e-mail, and although Christy could have monitored the e-mails if she wished, she did not need to because, in his excitement to share his newly acquired knowledge, Luis read *every* e-mail to her. Christy said:

> Cory really loved nurturing Luis's passion, a passion Cory himself probably had as a kid, and Luis learned so much from him: things that I just wouldn't have had any idea about. Cory became the skill director and the skills that Luis developed are still skills I do not understand.

From programming to hardware. Although the vast majority of users are quite compelled to download the latest app or utilize the Internet to view YouTube videos, search for information of interest, or interact with others via social media, relatively few users will ever stop to wonder how all of this is possible. According to Arthur C. Clarke (1973) "Any sufficiently advanced technology is indistinguishable from magic" (p. 21). Indeed today's technologies might seem like just that. However, they are not magic, nor are they merely an expensive tool we use to tap, swipe, and key our way through the world. Instead, there is a whole world inside of the device, and we need to teach students that their devices are things that can be tinkered with.

DID YOU KNOW?

In one of the relatively few studies specifically related to gifted students and technology, O'Brien, Friedman-Nimz, Lacey, and Denson (2005) categorized technology-talented students as falling into two categories: interfacers and programmers. Interfacers are those students who are able to readily navigate a wide variety of applications and operating systems with relative ease. Programmers, on the other hand, are those students who are more interested in what is happening inside of the machine. O'Brien et al. primarily focused on students' interest in coding and programming computers, but they also categorized students who were drawn to the hardware rather than the software.

Since the dawn of the personal computer, there have been both a relationship and a divide between "interfacers" and "programmers"—those who use the computer and those who are concerned with the inner workings of the computer. Consider the creative dyad of Steve Jobs and Steve Wozniak, creators of the Apple Computer. Jobs was primarily interested in what the Apple computer was capable of doing and its applications, but he was dependent on Wozniak to figure out how to construct the hardware that would make it all possible. This yin and yang relationship is mirrored in many ways by the relationship between Bill Gates and Paul Allen, cofounders of Microsoft.

Learning to code a computer and create your own content and apps may be the first step toward creative productive giftedness in the technological domain; there exists something beyond the user interface that is also compellingly interesting to technologically talented students. For these students, like Steve Wozniak, the machine itself motivates them. Just as a growing number of coding resources for students have emerged, a number of hardware devices have been developed as well.

> › *Hello Ruby*—Hello Ruby (http://www.helloruby.com) is a resource that bridges software and programming with hardware design. The site is designed to be easily accessible for kids 5 years and older, but we admit enjoying it ourselves! The Hello Ruby website describes itself as, "the world's most whimsical way to learn about computers, technology, and programming." This is an ideal resource for developing technology know-how as early as kindergarten, and it provides lesson plans that engage young students in designing a computer, problem solving, and imagining the potential for designing the future. Using paper rather than

actual hardware, it is ideal for taking your first steps into understanding hardware and computer design.

› *Makey Makey*—Initiated by two graduate students at the MIT Media Lab, the Makey Makey Project (http://makeymakey.com) is described as "an invention kit for everyone." The kit costs $49.95 and includes a computer circuit board with a directional keypad and assorted buttons, as well as connector wires and alligator clips. The kit allows you to connect the circuit board to almost any physical object that is able to conduct electricity to control the associated keys on a connected computer. Up to 18 different objects can be attached to a single Makey Makey. Project ideas include creating an electric piano made from bananas and a video game controller made from Play-Doh. The Makey Makey website features a variety of lesson plans and project ideas as well as guides for teachers to get started with their students. The how-to page (http://www.makeymakey.com/howto/classic) presents a simple step-by-step setup guide, as well as a range of software created specifically for the Makey Makey to try out. This type of device can serve as an introduction to spark the creativity and imagination of talented students to further explore computer hardware devices.

› *littleBits*—Another option for introducing students to computer hardware is littleBits (http://littlebits.cc). More than 60 different interchangeable electronic modules are available for purchase in a variety of different kits and collections. The modules are designed to connect together to allow students to devise their own electronic circuits by clicking individual pieces together. Once assembled, the new device is capable of gathering input from a variety of environmental data, and provides a wide range of output options. littleBits also offers a wealth of educator resources and lesson ideas for teaching students how to imagine and create new computer devices (http://littlebits.cc/education).

› *Arduino*—Both Makey Makey and littleBits can serve as a gentle introduction into the world of computer hardware. A next logical step in this development is Arduino (http://www.arduino.cc). This is an open-source microcontroller motherboard that can be used to develop interactive objects that accept input from a variety of different sensors and switches, and is capable of producing a variety of outputs including control of lights, motors, and other devices. The Arduino is a simple computer that is capable of running one program at a time repeatedly. A variety of different Arduino kits are available for purchase depending on your desired project.

› *Raspberry Pi*—Finally, the Raspberry Pi (http://www.raspberrypi.org) is a general purpose computer that is typically used with a Linux or Windows XP operating system. Available for $35, the Raspberry Pi is a credit-card sized mini-computer that can plug into a HDMI TV or VGA monitor and USB keyboard. The device is capable of being programmed to do almost anything that a typical PC might be able to do. However, the relatively low cost and open architecture encourage students to create new types of devices and uses for this computer. As an added bonus, teaching resources and instructional units have already been developed for using the Raspberry Pi to teach students how to set up their own hardware. The Raspberry Pi help section (https://www.raspberrypi.org/help) provides all of the necessary information for getting started. Beyond the official site, a community of hardware hackers is growing online. For additional ideas, refer to the Instructables Raspberry Pi section (http://www.instructables.com/id/Raspberry-Pi-Projects). If $35 seems like too much, then you might be interested in the Raspberry Pi Zero that costs only $5. This tiny computer features a 1Ghz, single-core CPU with 512MB of RAM. Keep in mind that these costs are only for the computers themselves, and because they are fully customizable, all cords, connectors, and cases are sold separately. That being said, the Raspberry Pi is definitely a device that is only limited by your students' imagination.

If you or your students are wondering whether to use Raspberry Pi or Arduino, we suggest that you utilize *Make* magazine's (2015) simple rule of thumb for making your decision. Ask yourself what you want your hardware project to do. If you can describe the project with two or less "ands," then you should use an Arduino. For any project idea that has more than two "ands," you should get a Raspberry Pi.

As students learn the "how to" skills of computer programming and begin exploring the possibilities of using a number of introductory hardware devices like the ones listed above, natural curiosity leads them from this Type II skill development into the world of Renzulli's Type III.

Future Skills: More Than Technology

The skills of the future are so much more than merely being able to code or use technology effectively. There will continue to be the need for artists, craftsmen, mechanics, and every form of maker. The Maker Movement, for example, is an emerging and increasingly popular phenomenon that is finding its way from the world of hobbyists and amateur inventors into educational environments. In 2005, Dale Dougherty launched *Make* magazine (http://makezine.com) as a bimonthly publication focusing on do-it-yourself (DIY) projects involving technology, electronics, robotics, and various construction-related projects. As an increasing number of individuals and small groups developed new products and creations, they began seeking out opportunities to learn from and share with one another. In 2006, this need gave rise to Maker Faires, which have become regular events around the world. The 2014 flagship Maker Faire in San Mateo, CA, had a record-breaking 215,000 people in attendance, all there to learn more about robots, 3-D printing, and other do-it-yourself creations. Now, there are more than 120 independently produced Maker Faires around the world.

As the Maker Movement has gained popularity, community centers and many public libraries have begun establishing Makerspaces for inventors of all ages to come together to imagine, build, and create. According to the Makerspace (2016; http://spaces.makerspace.com), "Makerspaces represent the democratization of design, engineering, fabrication, and education" (para. 2). An increasing number of schools are exploring ways that they can incorporate Makerspaces into the learning environment.

New technologies that are going to change the way we work and interact with the world will also serve to support student creativity, design, and innovation. Additive manufacturing (AM), commonly known as 3-D printing, is a process whereby three-dimensional solids are made from a digital file. Objects are created as successive layers of material that are built up in a repeated fashion. AM technologies are notably suited for product development, data visualization, and rapid prototyping, and in recent decades, strides have been made to expand the use to mass production and distributed manufacturing. The use of 3-D printing continues to evolve. For example, exciting developments in the field include 3-D bioprinting, which uses cells and encapsulation material to print several kinds of tissue structures such as skin, bones, cartilage, tracheas, and hearts (Murphy & Atala, 2014). According to Wikipedia, the uses of 3-D printing are numerous: bioprinting, nanoscale printing, apparel production, automobile prototyping, construction, motors and generators, firearms, as well as art and communication. 3-D printing itself is an area for Type I and II exploration, but the use of a 3-D printer in classroom settings holds significant promise for encouraging innovation, supporting design processes, developing and producing finished products, and even testing products to determine its success or failure. In other words, 3-D printing is a meaningful tool to enable students to engage in the basic elements of technology and engineering.

Although current 3-D printers are cost prohibitive, like any rapidly advancing technology, the price is already dropping to within reasonable ranges. A simple Google search leads to examples of personal 3-D printers for a mere $349 and certain educationally focused printers for around $1,400. So, as the price drops, the future of classroom printers will evolve.

Another technology that can support innovation and creativity across all domains is augmented reality (AR). In the not-so-distant future, technology will put an overlay of digital information on the world around us. We will move away from stagnant computer screens and use an interface that is an extension of our body, wherever we are in space. Neuroscientists will be able to look at the inside of a brain and use proprioception to maneuver and manipulate a three-dimensional model of the brain. Investigators will be able to run scenarios in real time at a crime scene. Architects will be able to design buildings in the same ways we build—connecting the designer and builder like never before. It will infiltrate our day-to-day lives as we receive calls and a holographic image of the caller is projected in front of us. It will change the way we share information, collaborate, and interact. Sure, it may be another 10–20 years before the technology is affordable and readily available, but for our students, 10–20 years from now means they will be in their late teens, twenties, and maybe early thirties. In the meantime, you might want to give students the opportunity to learn how to create in three-dimensional virtual environments with some of these free 3-D creator tools:

> *Blender* (https://www.blender.org) is an open-source 3-D content creation suite. It supports every aspect of the 3-D creation process: modeling, rigging, animation, simulation, rendering, compositing and motion tracking, and video editing and game creation. The mission of the Blender Foundation's project is to build and continually develop a free and open-source complete 3-D creation pipeline for artists and teams. Your students are free to use Blender for any purpose including commercial or education.

> *Sculptris* (http://pixologic.com/sculptris) also focuses on creating in a three-dimensional space. Pixologic created this digital sculpting software that is perfect for multiple skill levels, particularly for students who

have some knowledge of design software. There is no limit to what your students can create and the level of challenge is limited only by your students' imagination.

› *Houdini Apprentice* (http://www.sidefx.com/apprentice) is a 3-D animation and visual effects tool. This type of tool is used broadly in film, broadcast, entertainment, and visualization. This free version is designed for noncommercial use only, but your students can learn the software and create real 3-D products. It is a junior version of the professional software and has many of the same features as the professional version.

It is hard to imagine the many ways students will use and create with technology. We are in a time of unprecedented evolution in the way that we work, create, collaborate, and communicate. We have to make sure that the products we ask students to create are not just about today, but also about tomorrow, because we are preparing students to develop as-yet-unimagined future products.

CHAPTER 11

Type III— Investigations of Real Problems

"From the standpoint of the child . . . he is unable to apply in daily life what he is learning at school. That is the isolation of the school—its isolation from life."—John Dewey (1907)

The third service delivery component of the SEM, Type III investigations, combines inquiry and the examination of real problems with the development of creative products. In these investigations, students assume roles such as analyst, programmer, engineer, designer, entrepreneur, or other types of practicing professionals. Although students pursue these kinds of involvement at a more junior level than adult professionals, the overriding purpose of Type III Enrichment is to create situations in which young people are thinking, feeling, and doing what practicing professionals do, even if at a less sophisticated level than their adult counterparts.

When students act as practicing professionals, it creates authenticity, which breeds acceptance and trust in the learning process. For many learners, this is the first time they have the opportunity to produce something in an educational setting that has the capacity to make a difference in the world, either within the school community or beyond the school walls. This authenticity serves to validate the learning and productivity in which students engage, and supports the creation of lifelong learners as it connects the learning to students' lives in meaningful ways.

Authentic Learning

How do we help students experience authenticity in their learning? Authentic learning means different things to different people. For us, this type of learning includes an authentic problem, an authentic audience, and authentic outcomes. In short, the components that make learning opportunities relevant. The need for clarity about authenticity is paramount, as the phrase *authentic learning* is used over and over in educational settings, but rarely is the definition of "authentic" articulated in a way that can be understood by everyone, both those in education and the constituencies beyond. Moreover, the importance of authentic learning to support students' engagement in learning cannot be overstated in the Type III experiences because authenticity helps students to find personal meaning in the processes, establish the immediate usefulness of the learning process, and understand the relevance of the learning to their own lives and future aspirations.

Authentic Problems

What characteristics of a problem allow students to explore and solve problems that are real? In his 1982 landmark article, *What Makes a Problem Real: Stalking the Illusive Meaning of Qualitative Differences in Gifted Education*, Renzulli suggested that four characteristics of a problem make it authentic:

1. The problem is based on personal interest.
2. Authentic methodology (i.e., conventions of the field) are used to solve the problem.
3. The problem has no existing solution or "right" answer.
4. The solution to the problem is designed to have an impact on an audience other than or in addition to the teacher.

Interest. When we think about these four characteristics, it is clear that Type III experiences address real problems. First and foremost, students self-select to participate in Type III experiences. It deserves repeating that we should not expect that every student can or would want to complete a Type III. Type III investigations are reserved for those students who have an intense interest in a particular topic or a high level of commitment to solving a problem that affects their family, community, or the world. Students must choose to pursue Type III investigations because the rigor, commitment, focus, and hard work required for successfully engaging a Type III cannot be achieved by a student who is slightly interested. Success can only be attained by students who have an intense interest, a willingness to work hard, the motivation and grit to persevere in the face of obstacles, the desire to learn, and the understanding that mistakes and missteps will be made along the way. This level of commitment on the students' part cannot be achieved if the project is prescribed by the teacher, is presented as a requirement, has predetermined processes for achieving the goal, or has an expectation for a product—an expectation that would suggest the product was determined in advance.

Authentic methodology. Each domain of problem solving exists within a content field and each content field is defined, in part, by the methods and techniques used to solve problems or create new knowledge within that field. For students to achieve high levels of competence within a domain, there are certain methodologies and conventions within any field that must be adhered to. For example, there is an identifiable heuristic (process or method) software programmers use when they are designing their software. Essentially, there are questions that fall into four broad categories that enable programmers to successfully create new code. Category 1, finding initial focal points, focuses on finding initial points in existing code that are relevant to the task. These are the questions that are asked at the beginning of a coding session or when coders explore a new part of the system. Category 2, building on those points, focuses on questions that help programmers build from an existing entity. These questions allow them to explore relationships. Category 3, understanding a subgraph, focuses on questions that help programmers understand the multiple relationships and entities within the code. Here programmers are really looking at the part-to-whole relationships. Finally, Category 4, questions over groups of subgraphs, includes questions that help the programmers refine their understanding of the relationships between subgraphs, as well as the interaction between those subgraphs (Sillito, Murphy, & DeVolder, 2006). The point here is not to dissect programming conventions as much as it is to demonstrate that no matter the field, there are professional conventions and methodologies that define how one attacks a problem to be solved within that domain. It is important that as students engage in Type III investigation and problem solving, that they learn and adhere to the conventions of the field in which they are working, keeping in mind that their involvement in these processes will be at a more junior level than their adult counterparts. The goal is that students will be thinking, feeling, and doing what practicing professionals do, even if at a less sophisticated level than adult professionals.

No right answer. We have said it before and we will say it again: If you can Google the answer, then you are asking the wrong question. Real questions and subsequently real problems have not already been solved. Even if students are working at a more junior level, their problem may already have a solution, but not one that is found on the Internet or addresses their *specific* problem or audience. It may be that the product idea or problem solution is new or creative for the individual student, but it may not be new in the sense that it never existed before. However, when a student comes up with a truly unique and practical solution and develops the personal commitment to follow the process to its logical conclusion, then we have accomplished the true goal of a real problem: adding new knowledge to an existing domain. Even as adults, we do not generate perfect solutions in our fields, and there is no one right answer for the problems we endeavor to solve; we seek to provide the best solution to a problem that can be achieved given the limitations of existing technologies, materials, and resources. We are asking students to do the same, as we allow them to solve the kinds of problems that will prepare them to engage society's most pressing need for solutions.

Authentic Audience

Authentic audience is a component of an authentic problem, but in education it serves an even greater role than being one aspect of a real problem: It helps define the parameters of the process, identify appropriate methodologies, and provide criteria for the assessment of quality. An authentic audience is technically defined as any audience for a student outcome other than the teacher. In the case of Type III authentic audience, we like to take this a step further and say that an authentic audience is any person or group of people who will be positively and directly affected by the product of a Type III exploration. For example, when fourth-grade students use GoAnimate to create a set of Greek mythology stories for K–2 students, the younger students receive the direct and positive benefit of having age-appropriate access to timeless stories of gods and goddesses.

The importance of an authentic audience is the positive effect that it has on the quality of the work students produce, the engagement that students have in the learning process, and the ownership and responsibility that students take for the outcomes. You have likely experienced this phenomenon before, when the audience of a learning outcome is someone other than the teacher. How would you describe the quality of students' outcomes when the audience was someone other than the teacher? During the process of creating the outcome or product, how would you describe students' engagement? Was their commitment to success and engagement in learning beyond what you would normally expect when the product would merely be "graded" by the teacher? Did students seem to take pride in the work that they had accomplished?

We live in a day and age when the Internet provides access to a global audience. For students in classrooms today, social media platforms have advanced sharing to the echelon of cultural norm, and the sharing of authentic outcomes is for many, a daily behavior. Beyond social media, we live in a world where access to authentic audiences for Type III investigations is merely access to the Internet and a process of just a few keystrokes. Moreover, these authentic audiences can be connected to right from the classroom, as access to the Internet creates a bridge to the much larger world beyond the school walls.

Type III outlets for authentic audiences. The search for an authentic audience for student projects has historically been a challenging one for teachers. Traditionally, student work is seldom presented beyond the classroom setting. Occasionally, students might have been able to share their work with another class or at the school level. However, thanks to the Internet, our students have unprecedented access to worldwide audiences, and regardless of their interest area, students are able to find and connect with others who share similar interests. The Internet has become an ever-growing enclave of creators and makers. To help you find appropriate outlets for your students' Type III products and ideas, we recommend that you explore the following resources related to creative virtual spaces and competitions.

Creative virtual spaces.

Websites/Blogs. We are living in a time where everyone has the ability to "dot com" themselves. We believe that we should encourage our students from an early age to begin to build a digital presence and a portfolio of their best work. Regardless of the type of creative product, a personal website or blog is the best place to showcase one's work. We have discussed the creation of websites and blogs and a variety of potential tools and services to utilize elsewhere in this book. Additional websites may be created if a project is completed by a group of students or has a more specific purpose than a personal website. However, a personal website or blog should also provide a link and information about the project. Additionally, a project website can be promoted through other social media outlets such as Twitter or Facebook to target specific audiences.

DIY. Students might choose to build their skills in an area of interest by completing projects in an online community like DIY (https://diy.org). DIY has more than 120 different skill areas for students to explore. Each skill contains a collection of challenges for students to complete. As students complete these challenges, they are invited to post proof that they have successfully completed the task. In this online community, students can view and comment on the projects of others.

YouTube. As previously discussed, YouTube has become a global phenomenon and part of our daily lives. YouTube also represents a worldwide audience for students' projects. Whether it is an original short film, a public service announcement, a vlog, or a stop-motion animated movie, YouTube provides a platform where any video posted has the potential of going viral. Video projects can easily be viewed or even embedded into a personal website or blog.

SlideShare. If your students are creating some type of presentation using PowerPoint or Keynote, then they might share their slides using SlideShare (http://www.slideshare.net). You might think of this as the YouTube of PowerPoint, as there are millions of presentations that have been uploaded to the site. Presentations are categorized into different collections by theme. Those interested in either slide design or in a particular topic are able to search for and view presentations online. SlideShare also permits users to embed their presentations onto websites.

Book publishing. Writing and publishing a book was once a goal that an author would work toward over the course of a career or even a lifetime and was dependent on obtaining a contract from a willing publishing company. For students, the idea of publishing their own book was something that was far out of their reach. However, there are a multitude of services that allow anyone to publish their own book in a variety of formats. With services like Blurb (http://www.blurb.com) and Lulu (https://www.lulu.com), would-be authors can create their own photo book, magazine, or novel in hardcover, paperback, or even eBook format. Similarly, Amazon Kindle Direct Publishing (https://kdp.amazon.com) offers a variety of services to interested authors, including the ability to sell their work directly on Amazon.

Apple also offers creators interested in publishing their own interactive books for the iPad or Mac a free tool called iBooks Author (http://www.apple.com/ibooks-author). This free app, available for the Mac, allows anyone to create and edit a book that can include photos, videos, web elements, and other interactive components to support the text. Creators can then upload and share for free or even sell their books through iTunes. This or any of the publishing options can serve as an authentic audience for student projects. For example, Katie Morrow and Jennifer Troester's eighth-grade students from O'Neill, NE, conducted a community-learning project in which they expressed their ideas on what patriotism means to them. The students and teachers used iBooks Author to create and sell their book on iTunes and donated 100% of the proceeds from the sale of the book to Nebraska Troop Support. You can purchase their book for only 99 cents at https://itunes.apple.com/us/book/48-ways-to-show-patriotism/id764177284.

iTunes app store/Google Play. If students are interested in computer programming and creating their own apps, then why not encourage them to develop and sell their apps on the app store? You and your students can hear about this process from two 12-year-olds who have found success with this. Thomas Suarez delivered a TED Talk (https://www.ted.com/talks/thomas_suarez_a_12_year_old_app_developer) discussing his journey in creating and publishing a whack-a-mole game involving Justin Bieber called *Bustin Jieber.* On the NPR show Here and Now (http://hereandnow.wbur.org/2014/08/13/avery-miller-bill-murray), 12-year-old Avery Miller discusses his app development experience and selling his Android apps on Google Play. In both of these instances, the app developers describe the relative ease in publishing an app and sharing it with the world.

Competitions. In educational settings where group achievements are given credence over individual accomplishments, students' need for recognition may go unsatisfied. Competitions provide substantial challenge and the opportunity for students to find worthy opponents—the kind of opponents that will push them to higher levels of achievement. Competitions also provide authentic audiences for products that are useful in "real world" settings, as many of the competitions in virtual environments are designed to solve a problem and require students to create products that reflect professional practices. We are not suggesting that competitions are for all students, but it is important that students have the opportunity to work with and compete with students who have similar interests, similar capacities, and a willingness to go beyond regular curricular expectations. For these students, competitions can serve as catalyzing experiences that lead students to deeper learning and potentially help students set a course for their future aspirations. Here, we provide some examples of the kinds of competitions that are readily available online.

Discovery Education and 3M have teamed up to present the *Young Scientist Challenge* (http://www.youngscientistchallenge.com). Claiming to be the nation's premier science competition for students in grades 5–8, this competition asks students to create a 1–2 minute video describing a new, innovative solution that could solve an everyday problem. This annual competition has been running since 1999 and has had hundreds of thousands of students compete over the years. Winners of the competition are given the opportunity to work directly with 3M scientists to develop their concept from idea to reality.

eCybermission (https://www.ecybermission.com) from the Army Educational Outreach Program is an annual web-based competition open to sixth–ninth grade students focused on STEM. Teams of students identify real problems in their community and propose solutions in a range of areas, including alternative sources of energy, national security and safety, robotics, and technology.

FIRST (For Inspiration and Recognition of Science and Technology) hosts a number of programs and competitions for students of all age levels. Perhaps best known for the LEGO League and robotics competitions, FIRST (http://www.firstinspires.org) has many similarities to Renzulli's original conception of the Enrichment Triad Model (1977) and to the SEM:*Tech*. Each competition involves students in engaging in a solution to a real problem using a variety of technology resources.

NASA sponsors a number of student competitions throughout the year (https://www.nasa.gov/audience/forstudents/stu-competitions-current-opps.html). These include one-time competitions, as well as those that occur on an annual basis. If your students are intrigued by any of the multitude of fields related to space science, then this may be a outstanding set of competitions for them to explore.

The Tech Museum of Innovation in Silicon Valley hosts an annual team design challenge for students called *The Tech Challenge* (http://www.thetech.org/tech-challenge-presented-emc). Teams of students in grades 4–12 compete to solve a real-world problem involving the engineering design process. A companion video contest invites teams to submit short videos detailing their creative process. Check with local museums and science centers in your state or community to see if they have similar programs. If none are available, you and your students might consider organizing a local event.

The *Future City Competition* (http://futurecity.org) starts with a simple question, "How can we make the world a better place?" Students in grades 6–8 imagine, research, and design their vision of a city of the future. Each year, students are presented with a different citywide issue that must be addressed. Students construct a virtual city design using SimCity in addition to a scale model, and a project plan. Students compete at a regional level and present their solution to a panel of judges.

The *National STEM Video Game Challenge* (http://stemchallenge.org) presented by the Joan Ganz Cooney Center and E-Line Media, invites students in grades 5–8 to design or program a video game that teaches or employs STEM concepts. A project may be a written video game design document that clearly describes the overall vision of a game to be designed; a playable game created using a free platform such as GameMaker, Scratch, or Gamestar Mechanic; or a playable game using an open platform. A range of categories and awards are granted, and an outstanding collection of free tools and resources are presented for teachers and coaches to help support young game designers.

Microsoft's *Imagine Cup* (https://www.imaginecup.com/category/index) is a global technology program and competition that encourages students to team up and use their creativity, passions, and interest in technology to create applications, games, and solutions to a range of problems and challenges in an effort to make the world a better place. A range of online contests are held on a rotating basis in addition to global competitions. The contests and competitions offered include those for the beginner with little or no coding experience, those with some familiarity with coding, and advanced teams of developers.

Finally, for your students who are more advanced in their coding skills, they might be interested in competing in the annual Google Code Jam (https://code.google.com/codejam). Each year, a new set of challenging problems are posed, and contestants are given a limited amount of time to devise and submit a solution to the problem. Students can begin by reviewing the past challenges and putting their advanced programming skills to the test. Since the competition began in 2008, there have been seven problems in the Code Jam rounds that were not solved in the given time. Indeed, this represents a worldwide stage for your most advanced coders.

Authentic Outcomes

In a sense, the very crux of technological advancement is creativity and innovation, but these have little benefit if they are not combined with a productivity component. Type III investigations require students to create products. These products are the result of students encountering real problem situations (e.g., student sees a market for a new video game or a student identifies a need for her peers to learn a second language). These problem situations, by virtue of the problem itself, should and do serve as vehicles whereby the processes can be applied in an authentic way. For example, a student identifies a market for a new type of video game, which requires her to learn how to design code to create the game. Designing new code requires the student to function using the conventions and processes of a software or app designer. Another example is the student who conducts research on the best way to teach a language and creates an interactive blog to teach her classmates Spanish. As a digital instructor, she uses the processes of best practices for online learning as part of her development phase. As you can see, both of these examples require students to create a tangible outcome that reflects the conventions of the domain in which they have produced the work. Authentic outcomes can essentially be defined as products that fulfill a need.

When it comes to authentic learning, the onus is on educators to provide the opportunity, resources, and encouragement that will allow students to engage in advanced problem solving and bring their talents to bear on the creation of products that fulfill the needs of an authentic audience. Type III investigations provide the opportunity for individuals or small groups of students to intensely engage their interests by addressing problems in their local community or beginning the process of solving society's immediate and future challenges.

CHRISTY'S CORNER: ACTING LIKE PROFESSIONALS IN THE FIELD

Christy works with K–2 students to nurture their talents and looks for students who might not normally be identified for gifted services through traditional means. She really works to seek out students who would thrive in the Academically and Intellectually Gifted program at her school. A lot of Christy's work with K–2 students includes practices to develop creativity, critical thinking, and problem solving. Two girls in Christy's fifth-grade classroom felt that everyone in the school should have opportunities to be creative and develop their ability to generate ideas. Specifically, the two girls wanted to develop the imaginations of their peers.

The girls came up with the idea for an afterschool club, The Imagination Station. At first glance, it didn't seem like there was an authentic audience for this Type III project, but when the girls really got started there was a lot of work and multiple audiences. They first made a plan for The Imagination Station, including a budget for materials, a schedule for club meeting dates, plans for recruiting participants, and a detailed description of the club's purpose. They then took their proposed plan to the principal to get approval. Essentially they were doing the job of a teacher sponsor, and although Christy was the "official" sponsor, the girls did all of the work.

Once their plan was approved, the girls set their sights on recruitment. This was a matter to which they gave a lot of consideration. The girls decided that as part of their efforts to recruit participants, they should translate the informational announcements, invitations, and reminders into Spanish. There were so many students interested that they had to create a lottery system to determine who would be chosen to participate. All the names of interested students were placed into a hat and drawn to fill the available slots. As it turned out, more than half the students selected were English language learners. For the remaining students, the girls sent home personal letters thanking people for their interest. Christy noted, "The girls learned a lot about being inclusive. If they had not translated communications into Spanish, there would have been a lot less interest, and a lot of students left out."

Once the logistics of setting up the Imagination Stations were settled, the girls had to actually create the activities that club participants would engage in. They conducted research on the Internet to find activities that they could use or adapt. They created original activities as well, and they planned "anchor activities" for when participants might finish the main activities early. Most of their anchor activities were available as iPad tools or games that club participants could start and end at any time. The club began to take the form of an enrichment cluster as the two girls planned 6 weeks of activities. Christy highlighted that they learned a lot about writing proposals, making a budget, and planning activities, but they really learned a lot about people. The participants became the biggest variable as the girls dealt with their peers not really liking the activities, finishing early, talking at unexpected times, or not paying attention. This is when Christy stepped in to scaffold their learning:

> I didn't want to leave them hanging, I wanted to give them the
> support that they needed, but at the same time, I wanted them
> to have the independence they deserved after doing all of that
> work and taking the initiative.

The girls took on the roles of teacher and guide, acting as the professionals. They really engaged in processes similar to the processes a teacher would work through in developing an extracurricular program for learning. Even though their Type III product did not extend beyond the school walls, the audience was still authentic, as it was an audience other than the teacher.

Technology really made the learning more authentic as well. Access to the Internet allowed the girls to connect to a larger reservoir of information and potential activities than they would have otherwise. Christy noted:

> Using the Internet provided students the independence, respon-
> sibility, and initiative to really be in charge of their own learning.

> That responsibility piece is so important, not just for the work
> we do in school, but for everything they do in life.

Motivation

Have you ever thought that you loved something, and as soon as it became part of your job, you realized that you weren't as passionate as you thought, or worse, the fact that it became an activity being done for money or payment took all of the joy out of the process? This happens all the time with our students. They believe they are truly interested in a topic, only to get deeper into the content and processes to realize that they are interested, but not necessarily passionate. Take for example, a student who believes she is passionate about basketball. She watches every basketball game, both historic and current, that she can find on the Internet. She plays on multiple basketball teams, and even practices daily, but realizes that her 1–2 hours a day of practice needs to be more like 5–6 hours of practice a day if she is going to achieve her goal of becoming a NCAA athlete. She doesn't want to spend that many hours a day practicing because she has other interests, like maintaining an active social life and doing well in her classes. Her "passion" for basketball begins to wane as she realizes that her previous goal of becoming an NCAA athlete no longer aligns with her current values. Another example might be the student who wants to write a novel; he has written several short stories, some of which resulted in acclaim and awards, but sitting down to write a novel proved to require too much effort and time and detracted from the time he could spend reading and critiquing fiction in his online book community, Goodreads (https://www.goodreads.com), and on his blog. Writing the novel, while interesting, no longer aligned with how he enjoyed engaging with the literary community.

There is a similar inherent problem with prescribed outcomes like those in projects that are assigned and subsequently assessed in educational settings. They have the potential to take fledgling interests and mire them in contrived constraints (as opposed to the constraints encountered in solving real problems) that do not align with personal values, thereby undermining commitment to the process and preventing the opportunity to shift gears when priorities and goals shift. Moreover, when projects add an assessment component, the judgment and pressure of being assessed on outcomes that no longer align with true passions or no longer hold inherent value may squelch the future potential of pursuing that interest or similar passion. Once the motivation is gone, the grade being assigned is not enough to motivate continued and future exploration of the topic.

Motivation is essentially being moved to do something. We aspire to generate intrinsic motivation in our students, the kind of motivation that drives students to do something just for the fun of engaging in that process or activity. Researchers Ryan and Deci (2000) have a model of intrinsic motivation that identifies how individuals move from amotivation, a state of unwillingness or lacking the intention to act, to intrinsically motivated action (see Figure 37). When we think of motivation and learning, you can think of extrinsic motivation as the lowest form of motivation, where the regulation of students' behavior is driven by rewards (e.g., grades, candy, stickers, stars on a chart) and compliance with requirements (e.g., completing assignments, fulfilling the requirements prescribed by a rubric). As students progress toward being intrinsically motivated, they may act to gain approval or please the teacher, but they do not fully understand, nor are they directing their own engagement in particular learning activities. This phase is called *introjection*. As students continue to move toward intrinsic motivation, the learning behaviors become personally meaningful. They start to understand why they are participating in certain learning. They may be able to identify the learning objectives and can identify the value of learning about a topic or engaging in the processes. This phase is called *identification*. The next step toward truly intrinsically motivated learning is *integration*. This is when engaging in the learning process becomes central to a student's identity. The process of learning is personally interesting, viewed as useful for his or her future, or it fulfills an internally motivated desire to learn (Figure 38).

When we compare Type III's to interest-driven projects, there are some inherent differences. Type III's are intrinsically motivated because they are initiated by a student's desire to pursue a topic, create a product, investigate a problem, or answer a question. The behaviors that students engage in to participate in Type III investigations are integrated with their identity. The impetus for action comes from the student and is supported by the teacher. Projects differ significantly. Projects can be regulated externally as teachers require every student to identify their interests and pursue a problem or answer a question in their interest area. A project can fall on any of the lower levels of motivation from externally regulated to identification. Ideally, in project learning, students are pursuing problems that have some personal meaning, thereby making for an engaging endeavor. A project at its highest level of motivation allows students to identify with the problem, proving some personal importance. A Type III at

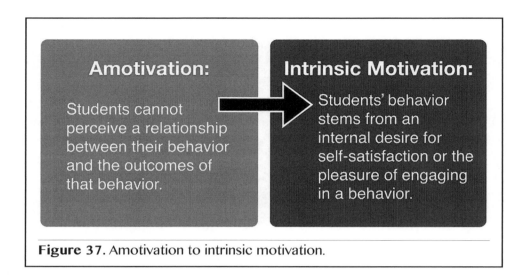

Figure 37. Amotivation to intrinsic motivation.

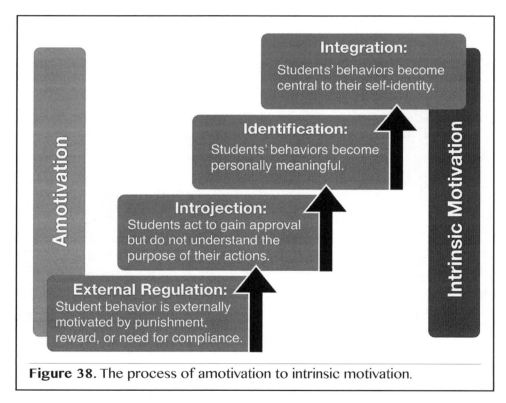

Figure 38. The process of amotivation to intrinsic motivation.

the lowest level allows students to engage in work that is personally meaningful, but instead of being contrived by requiring students to identify their interests, Type III's emerge naturally as a student seeks to learn more, do more, and engage more. A Type III at the lowest level is in the identification stage of motivation, but typically is a true integration of students' learning with their sense of self. The learning is an expression of who they are, what they value, and what they want to achieve in life.

Type III Investigation Versus Projects

Type III productivity is unlike projects that might be assigned to all students. As a matter of fact, Type III investigations should *not* be completed by every student, because not every student is truly passionate about a topic, motivated to engage in advanced learning, and committed to doing the hard work. That said, every student who exhibits these dispositions should have the opportunity to engage in a Type III investigation. The primary difference between a Type III and typical prescribed projects, those assigned by the teacher, is that individuals or small groups of students initiate their own Type III because they want to, not because they are required. Type III's are conducted purely for the joy of learning and ideally, no formal "grades" are assigned at the completion of such an undertaking because the authentic product is judged by an authentic audience—an assessment that is far more important, far more memorable, and far more critical than any grade could ever hope to be. If a student were going to put a Type III on their resume or college application, it would *not* be the kind of thing that is rolled into a grade; it would be an outcome that was worthy of being highlighted as a *real* accomplishment in a real-world setting. This is not to say that the academic exercises of education are not important or that students should not engage in activities that are long term, but that a Type III may go well beyond the school walls and have an effect on a larger audience (e.g., the local community, a group of individuals, one person).

Another important aspect that differentiates Type III investigations from projects is that Type III investigations are not contrived because students are forced to develop a topic for exploration. Projects are often interest-based, which serves to heighten students' level of engagement, but there is a difference between mild interest and intense interest—true passions. Projects ask students to identify their interests for the purposes of completing an academic task whereas Type III's tend to evolve from Type I and Type II experiences—experiences designed to introduce and immerse students in topics and processes that help lead them to their own self-discovery. Only through the process of self-discovery and self-awareness can Type III's emerge. Certainly, it is important to help students identify their interests, but not every student must pursue his or her "passion" now. Projects are a great way to learn and some Type II processes may resemble projects, but a Type III is truly unique in a world where learning is often prescribed with predetermined pathways and products. The differences between Type III and projects are clearly illustrated through comparison (Table 14).

Project-based learning is important, particularly when it is based on students' interests; however, by imposing requirements, the joy in the process of learning is diminished because there is a fundamental shift from achieving a self-initiated goal to fulfilling a set of requirements for a grade. One of the key elements of Type III's is that the assessment and judgment of the project is left to the authentic audience and the intrinsic reward is doing hard work and generating quality outcomes that have the potential to make a difference in the world.

Initiating a Type III

We commonly assume that when a student excels in a given area that he or she has a special interest in that topic. This is just not always the case, particularly with gifted students. For example, you might have a student who excels in math, but his passion lies in music or a student who writes exceptionally well, but she is driven by scientific discovery. Examples of students' Type III independent or small-group projects vary, but all require extensive student effort. Also, all Type III investigations should be initiated by the students and started because they are personally interested in learning and producing in a particular domain.

Another thing to consider in this initiating of a Type III are the structures that need to be in place to support students in communicating their desire to pursue a Type III investigation. For example, students might approach their regular classroom teacher with an idea, but are systems in place that allow the teacher to easily and seamlessly move the student's request to the enrichment specialist? Does the student have access to the enrichment specialist to communicate his or her request or idea directly? A simple way for students and teachers to advance a Type III investigation request is to provide a link to a survey on the school webpage. The survey might include the following information:

› Today's date
› Name of student or students interested in pursuing a Type III investigation

TABLE 14
COMPARISON OF TYPE III VERSUS PROJECTS

Type III	Project
Student initiated	Teacher initiated
Based on students' passions	Based on students' interests
Teacher's role: • Open doors • Facilitate progress • Find mentors • Support students in setting realistic goals • Support real-world processes • Provide direction in navigating real-world encounters	Teacher's role: • Set guidelines • Require goal setting • Prescribe format • Manage process • Observe navigation of real-world encounters or obstacles • Assess outcomes
Students' role: • Self-motivated • Engage in passionate learning • Think, feel, and do like practicing professionals	Students' role: • Fulfill requirements of the project • Be assessed (usually via a rubric)
Completed by: • Students who self-select • Individuals or small groups	Completed by: • Every student • Individuals
Duration is open-ended; Type III may not be complete at end of academic term	Duration is prescribed via a deadline
Students review what is already known about a topic and creatively contribute a product that goes beyond existing information	Students create an outcome that synthesizes existing knowledge
All that is known is identified at the beginning of the process	Students plan project and may run into barriers that prevent them from completing their goal
Solves an authentic problem or requires inquiry and investigation	May require inquiry
Requires developmentally appropriate self-regulation with scaffolding from teacher	Requires self-regulation
Authentic audience	Teacher is the audience

> › Name of teacher primarily responsible for student during school day
> › General domain of inquiry
> › Topic for investigation
> › Problem to be solved or question to be answered
> › Potential product
> › Evidence of high levels of interest and commitment to learning
> › Justification for expenditure of resources (e.g., teacher time, potential materials support, time out of class)

This survey is essentially the initial proposal. It brings the student to the attention of a teacher, specialist, or mentor who can support this potential independent investigation process. This, however, is only a first step. Just as individuals in professional settings have to propose their ideas to pursue tasks or present themselves well to get a job, so too must students. Therefore, we suggest students participate in an interview or submit a proposal as a request to follow a certain line of inquiry independently from the regular curriculum, or have students apply for the job of lead investigator. The two different approaches to doing this, the interview and the pitch, respond to different styles of expression.

The Interview

The interview is an approach that works well for students who may work better in small groups or prefer more one-to-one communication. When the enrichment specialist, classroom teacher, or assigned mentor receives a Type III investigation request, more information needs to be gathered. First and foremost, the person who will be responsible for supervising students' work needs to learn as much as he or she can about the students. The Type III supervisor will need to ascertain the level of students' interest, the ability to engage in advanced learning over an extended period of time, and their areas of strengths and weaknesses. Time has to be found in the regular school day for students to pursue their proposed problem or line of inquiry, because if they are not given time, all of the planning in the world will not lead to advanced-level learning and Type III productivity. The goal of the interview is to determine the capacity for the student or students to successfully engage in the process, understand the scope of the proposed project, and determine what kinds of supports might need to be in place to ensure that students grow from the experience.

The first phase of the interview is designed to understand the true level of interest and commitment to the topic in mind. Ask questions like these:

> Have you conducted any research about the topic online?
> What do you already know and understand about the topic?
> How long have you been interested in this topic?
> How did you become interested in this topic?

Note the last question. It is particularly important, as it helps you determine if the students' interest is intrinsically motivated or if there is a level of motivation at the introjection stage—the stage of trying to please others.

The second phase of the interview helps you to further analyze the student or students' desire to complete the task, and includes questions about procedures. Questions might include:

› What do you think your first steps might be?
› Who will benefit from your efforts?
› How many hours do you think it will take to successfully pursue your idea to its conclusion?
› Are there other students who might want to get involved?
› How many other students do you think might want to participate? Who do you think these students might be?
› Do you have any ideas about how your solution or line of inquiry might result in something different from what already exists?

It is important to note here that these questions help you determine if the student has really considered the amount of work, effort, and time that will likely be involved in pursing a topic of interest independently. The interview process is not designed to frighten students away from engaging in independent study, but it will help teachers, mentors, and specialists use their time efficiently to support only those students who possess the motivation, task commitment, ability, and interest to see the process through to a natural end.

The Pitch

In professional settings, when someone wants to present his or her idea for consideration or funding, it is known as a pitch. The pitch approach to presenting an idea for a Type III investigation might be best suited to students who enjoy being the center of attention and feel comfortable speaking in front of a group. In this approach, students "pitch" their idea to a panel, a group of peers, their class, or even the whole school. The process requires students to plan a presentation in advance and convince others that their idea is a good one. There are nine distinctive steps in developing an effective pitch:

1. *Define the idea.* Here the student needs to clearly articulate the idea in a way that others will understand its intent or goal. The idea should solve a problem or provide evidence of a need it will fulfill.
2. *Define the scope of the idea.* This might include the amount of time it will take, the extent of the potential impact, or the size of the product outcome. The students should explain how the idea will work.

3. *Identify the person with the power to say "yes"(the key master).* It is important that the student clearly knows who has the final word because perspective taking will be key.

4. *Think from the key master's point of view.* Students have to answer the questions:
    a. What might make the key master say "no"?
    b. What might make the key master say "yes"?

5. *Show the team's expertise.* The student has to demonstrate that he or she is capable of being successful.

6. *Prepare materials to support the presentation of the proposition.* This might include slides, a model, a sample, or a first step toward achieving the final goal. Creativity here is a plus!

7. *Practice, practice, practice!* It is a presentation and the more prepared a student is, the more confident he or she will be, which increases the likelihood of success.

8. *Be prepared to answer questions.*

9. *Be ready to ask questions, particularly if it does not go in your favor.* The pitch model allows students to ask questions to better understand how they might be successful in future attempts to pitch their idea.

Student initiative in the process of proposing a Type III cannot be overstated. Even going through the proposal processes will help make determinations about a student's readiness to pursue independent investigations. If significant scaffolding is required for a student to pitch his or her idea, for example, that might be an indicator that the student does not have sufficient self-regulatory skills or motivation to be successful. The alternative—if little to no scaffolding was required in the development of the pitch—might suggest that the student is ready, willing, and able to take on the challenge of independent study. Here are some tips for students to consider as they develop their pitch or prepare for an interview:

›   Inspire confidence by being able to provide facts and evidence to support your idea.

›   Get your friends and teachers excited about the idea—share your passion about the topic.

›   Show that you understand the logistics—whether managing your time or managing your resources, you have to prove you can do all aspects of the work.

> › You don't have to be the smartest person in the room—through your pitch, you might find a classmate who is equally interested or who can provide useful knowledge and skills to the project.
> › If the key master says "no," you can always try to propose the idea after some more research and planning or you can try to do it on your own time.

The process of presenting ideas for a Type III investigation will look very different depending on the grade level of the students. It is important to remember what is developmentally appropriate and that while the idea may not be entirely new, if it is new to the student, it does in fact pose a novel investigation opportunity.

Type III investigations are an opportunity for students to examine a self-selected topic of interest in a way that requires the commitment of time, deep review and understanding of advanced content, the development of authentic products, the use of advanced skills like those used by professionals in students' domain of interest, as well as the skills of innovation, self-regulation, resource management, decision making, and reflection and evaluation. Type III investigations are long-term assignments that may take weeks, months, or even years to complete. For example, a student may start a project in third grade that is not complete at the end of the academic year. Moreover, the project may not be brought to fruition until fifth grade. The commitment to these investigations may well be extensive; however, that should not stop a student from having the opportunity to begin the process of engaging in authentic learning, of pursuing a Type III. That said, what might technology based on Type III's look like in classroom settings? The next chapter answers this question.

CHAPTER 12

Type III— Student Initiative and Productivity

"For the gifted person, the person who really wants to learn something, too much instruction is insulting."—Mortimer Adler (in Renzulli, 1982, p. 151)

Type III investigations are the means through which everything from basic skills to advanced content and process skills blends together into student-developed products and services. This kind of learning represents a synthesis and an application of content, process, and personal involvement. The student's role is transformed from one of lesson-learner to firsthand inquirer, and the role of the teacher changes from an instructor and disseminator of knowledge to a combination of coach, resource procurer, mentor, and "guide-on-the-side."

Students accomplish this by pursuing self-selected topics of interest and developing authentic products that require task commitment, application of content knowledge, an understanding of methodology, and creativity. In earlier chapters, we discussed instructional processes and planning that are often didactic in nature. In the Type I exposure experiences, students are presented with new information or a learning opportunity that is based on a topic, person, place, or thing. Type I experiences are content-knowledge driven. In Type II processes, the goal of instruction is to engage students in activities to develop transferrable skills and understandings that are necessary for successful learning, achievement, and creative productivity.

CHRISTY'S CORNER: HELPING STUDENTS IDENTIFY THEIR PASSION

As you may recall, Christy does a lot of work to help her students communicate their interests. She uses strategies like large paper with circle maps and has the entire class review the ideas of others with a "museum walk." Christy uses these approaches to get a rich resource of interests, but she also found that her gifted students have a *lot* of interests and on any given day their interests can change quickly. Rather than focusing on what they are interested in this week or might be interested in next week, Christy helped students define the difference between interests and passions for the purposes of pursuing individual and small-group productivity like that of a Type III product. So, she took a couple of steps to scaffold students as they moved in the direction of projects. Her reason for scaffolding the process is clear:

> I was constantly surprised how much scaffolding was needed. I really thought that this group of kids, because they were identified as gifted, would take an idea and run. They really needed help. I don't know if it was help to think differently, because a typical school setting can be more traditional, or if it was just a natural thing that they needed all of this scaffolding.

Either way, Christy set out to find ways to support the transition from identifying interests to defining passions. The first time Christy attempted to support students in the process of narrowing their interests down to real passion areas, it was in the middle of March Madness (that time of year when NCAA college basketball teams compete for the National Championship, the structure of which is a bracket system). Using the same bracket system as basketball's March Madness, Christy had students list their interests on the outside brackets (see Figure 39). Then, for each bracket pair, students had to choose only one interest to move onto the next round. By the time they got to the center, they were left having to decide between their two favorite interest areas rather than a long list of potential interests. Christy said of the process, "It worked so well, we have been doing it ever since!"

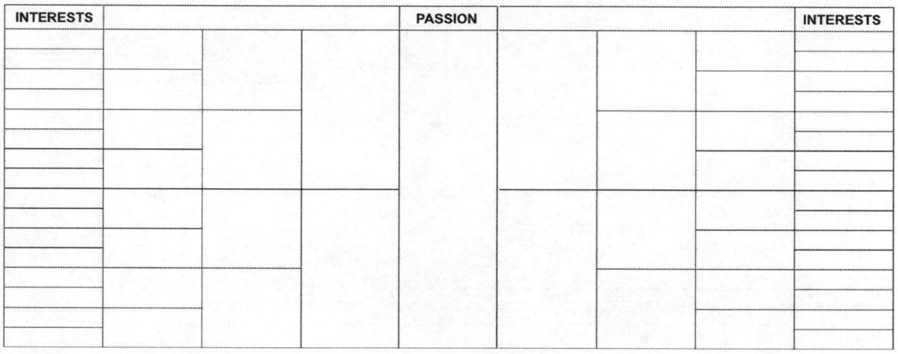

Figure 39. Interest bracket.

Once students have identified their true passion and successfully pitched an idea, planning must necessarily take place. For most students, this independence is best supported through a learning contract. Learning contracts are pretty straightforward. This is an agreement between teacher and student that outlines and supports students' responsibilities. Students' independence and autonomy are supported with the inclusion of a timeline and the opportunity for students to be integral in the planning and support process. A key feature of effective learning contracts is that all stakeholders have a place to sign. For a Type III, stakeholders might include the teacher, the resource specialist, the principal, or mentors. Regardless, the key stakeholder is the student and the power of the signature cannot be overstated. Learning contracts provide clear communication between the student and those responsible to ensure his or her continued growth. The contract itself communicates and clearly defines the resources, expectations, timeline with benchmarks, and responsibilities for the student. The SEM:*Tech* Management Planner (Figure 40), a learning contract designed to support Type III Investigations specifically, is available online for your use (http://bit.ly/sem-tech-planner).

Mission Possible as a Type III

The resources listed in this Type III section are provided for inspiration *only*. They are not meant to be copied, nor are they intended to be assigned as a project for your students. Instead, our aim is to provide examples of the kinds of directions students might pursue when they are inspired. Moreover, our goal

233

SEM:*Tech*

MANAGEMENT PLANNER

NAME(S)	
GRADE	
TEACHER	
SCHOOL	

START DATE	COMPLETION DATE

DATES FOR PROGRESS CONFERENCES

PURPOSE
Write a brief description of the problem you want to solve, the question you want to answer, or the product you want to produce. What do you hope to discover?

GETTING STARTED
What are the first steps that you should take to begin your investigation? What information do you need to get started?

EXPERTS AND MORE KNOWLEDGEABLE OTHERS
Lists the names and contact information of persons who might be able to provide assistance to you in your investigation.

Figure 40. The SEM:*Tech* Type III management planner.

is to show you that students can reach much farther and climb much higher when they are passionate about their investigation, so they need not be limited to "kid-friendly" inquiry, when they are often capable of exceeding our expectations. For instance, the Mission Possible Type III examples should be viewed as potential starting points or ideas for directions that students might pursue when considering going deeper into the exploration of sending humans to Mars.

Although space is cold, vast, and deadly, humans persist in exploring it anyway. One jumping-off point for students to consider when they are thinking about sending humans to Mars is the 12 greatest challenges for space exploration presented in *Wired* magazine (http://www.wired.com/2016/02/space-is-cold-vast-and-deadly-humans-will-explore-it-anyway). Here are the 12 problems that have to be solved so that humans can colonize Mars:

1. The cost of breaking free from Earth's gravity
2. Propulsion systems that work in a vacuum
3. Navigating through and protecting against space debris
4. Navigating in deep space
5. Radiation
6. Providing sufficient food and water for astronauts
7. Bone and muscle wasting in zero gravity
8. Maintaining mental health on long space voyages
9. Touching down on another planet without injury to the passengers
10. Transporting resources of all kinds (e.g., seeds, machines, building materials, etc.)
11. Robot technologies to support colonization
12. Attaining warp speed

Of course, another option would be to save Earth so that we are not forced to colonize other planets, so there is a lot for our students to consider. There are a variety of online opportunities for students to engage in Type III investigations that support the goal of colonizing Mars. Past examples include NASA's Centennial Challenges: 3-D Printed Habitat Challenge, the Engineering for YOU Video Contest, and Future Engineers *Star Trek* Replicator Challenge. Simply visiting NASA's current competition website might inspire a student (http://www.nasa.gov/audience/forstudents/stu-competitions-current-opps.html). Even if the challenges they suggest are for university students, there is no reason why a gifted elementary student could not start working the problem and following the research as it emerges.

SpaceX is another source of competitions. These competitions are incentive prize competitions. The 2015–2016 competition was the Hyperloop, which asked students to build a subscale prototype transport vehicle to demonstrate the technical feasibility of Elon Musk's Hyperloop concept (i.e., a high-speed transportation system incorporating reduced-pressure tubes with pressurized capsules that travel at speeds up to 760 mph). The Hyperloop technology is open-source, meaning that any student who wants to explore the feasibility of the concept can do so, free of charge.

Once you name the student's interest in Mars, you can likely find some direction and support for his or her Type III investigation. This Type III investigation might even be as simple as researching and filling out a scholarship application for Space Camp (http://www.spacecamp.com/scholarships). These applications, for 4th through 12th graders, open in the fall each year. On another note: They have educators and adult Space Camp opportunities too!

Selfies as a Type III

Now that students have begun to explore the art of photography and selfies, some students may wish to conduct their own Type III project related to selfies and self-portraits. Encourage students to consider what impact their project could have. We have collected some ideas that might inspire a student project, but keep in mind that these are here merely to serve as possible inspiration and not meant to be projects to be assigned. Students should feel free to explore well beyond what is suggested here depending on their own interests.

In *Me* (https://youtu.be/vGdc_qcmFF0), we see a collection of selfies taken every day for 3 years assembled in a time-lapse film. A shorter one-minute version has been viewed more than 9 million times. There are numerous other versions of this type of project constructed by different people. However, *Me* was the first one to be posted on YouTube. Students might wish to start their own selfie-a-day project.

In partnership with the Sundance Institute, *Dove Selfie* (https://vimeo.com/84649988 or https://www.youtube.com/watch?v=BFkm1Hg4dTI) is directed by Academy Award-winning documentary filmmaker Cynthia Wade and produced by Sharon Liese. More than just an advertising campaign, this short film is the journey of a group of high school girls and their mothers who create a new type of selfie that celebrates their unique beauty. This film reveals how we have the power to redefine what is beautiful in all of us. Ask interested students to consider how this type of campaign could be expanded to include their school or community.

If you have students who are interested in how selfies could highlight the good deeds and actions that people are completing, then look no further than the #soulselfies project (http://www.soulselfies.com/sys). Who says selfies have to just be photographs? This project asks that individuals record short videos on a set of given prompts. For example, "If you really knew me, you'd know that . . . ," "I am grateful for . . . ," and "My purpose in life is . . . ." Although students may wish to contribute to the project, a better Type III project would be for them to start their own campaign and share it with the school, the community, and the world.

Again, the resources listed in the Type III section are meant to be only inspiration and not intended to be copied as is or assigned to your students as a project. Instead, our hope is that students might view these as beginning points. As students are contemplating a Type III investigation related to selfies or self-portraits, we suggest that you use the SEM:*Tech* Management Planner (http://bit.ly/sem-tech-planner) to help students launch their projects. With careful initial planning, you can ensure the success of your students and outline ways for you to provide guidance and support in their endeavors.

CHRISTY'S CORNER: THE LEGWORK

Christy often finds herself in the position where students ask her questions to which she does not know the answer. Certainly she wants to help her students, but she always makes sure that they have gone online to seek the answer for themselves prior to helping them. This helps to ensure that students are developing self-regulation skills to be able to find answers even when she is not there to help them. Sometimes, however, their questions are so advanced and the search is more in-depth, so rather than having students spend time doing the legwork and potentially stalling progress on their project, she does try to find resources to enable them to keep moving forward instead of getting bogged down by the details. For Christy, it really depends on the situation—if she feels the student has clearly made the effort to find the answer on his or her own, then it is better to help than leave the student stuck.

The legwork is ongoing. At the beginning of each class, students outline their goals and at the end, they reflect on their accomplishments and determine whether or not they met their goals.

> The first year I did this, I remember [that in] one of the first few classes I realized that we could spend the whole class just goal setting. One of the things I tried to do this year was model the goal setting in our first few classes. I also asked them to have their goals set before arriving to class. This made the process go a lot faster, and students were thinking about their projects on an ongoing basis.

To reflect on whether students had met their goals, Christy provided students with exit tickets, which at times take the form of a Google survey. To ensure that the process was meaningful but quick, she provided self-evaluation checklists with a single open-ended question. For example, it might be a prompt like, "This is where I need Mrs. Howe to help me" or "These are the next questions I need to explore." Christy intentionally used the questions to get students to think about their next steps. The prompts also provided her with information about the help they might need or a direction for doing the legwork to be ready for them when they arrived to class the next time. Christy worked to prevent the goal setting and exit survey from becoming cumbersome or something the students dreaded. Instead, she helped them to become mindful of how they were using their time and thinking ahead to really consider what they would need to continue forward.

Christy does take work home. Using the information from their reflection on the exit ticket, she can identify the questions students have or how they need help:

> Oftentimes, based on what students need help with, I just have to search online. If I can find it online, that's great and I can help them that way, but if I can't, I search for a person I can connect the student with—either from the school family database or the broader community like our local university professors.

Students tend to do a lot of work outside of class, and Christy found that a lot of back and forth happens. For example, a student might give her project goals on a Tuesday, and Christy will do the legwork that night and have information to give her the next day or when she returns to her class. She has found that the students who do some of the work at home seek her out during the week to get help, so the process is really ongoing, keeping the students moving forward.

PART III
Putting the Pieces Together

CHAPTER 13

From the Enrichment Triad Model to the Classroom

For a century, many in the United States took for granted that most great inventions would be homegrown—such as electric power, the telephone, the automobile, and the airplane—and would be commercialized here as well. But we are less certain today who will create the next generation of innovations, or even what they will be. We know that we need a more secure Internet, more-efficient transportation, new cures for disease, and clean, affordable, and reliable sources of energy. But who will dream them up, who will get the jobs they create, and who will profit from them? (National Research Council, 2007, p. 40)

Integration

An integrative curriculum focusing on connections between disciplines allows students to find different points of entry, connect their interests to the academic content, and combine information from a variety of fields to develop novel and insightful solutions to problems they encounter within sufficiently advanced learning opportunities. We know that this makes learning more engaging and relevant for students. It allows them to make cross-curricular connections, place their learning and knowledge within the context of their own lives, and solve real problems that are worthy of their time and effort. The curriculum must then be useful in contexts beyond the classroom, allow for meaningful collaboration, use the conventions of the appropriate discipline, and clearly and unequivocally be relevant to students' life experiences.

Take for example, something as simple as a STEM extracurricular program. In one such program, 146 students participated in fully integrated learning activities like robotics and applied science learning. The experience led to increased interest in STEM topics, which was the goal. More importantly, however, students considered the activities appealing because they were comprehensive (e.g., science, math, and engineering were required to design the robotics technology) and students reported feeling more productive, successful, and happy because they were fully engaged in the activities (Sahin, Ayar, & Adiguzel, 2014).

We do face challenges in our efforts to implement curriculum that is integrative, meaningful and relevant for students, develops technology talent, and increases technology literacy. One challenge we face is that historically core curriculum areas have been mathematics, English language arts, science, and social studies, yet the spectrum of domains has been eroded in recent years with math and reading replacing time spent on science, social studies, and the arts (McMurrer, 2008). This leaves little room or opportunity in the instructional day for time to be spent focused on multidomain or cross-curricular pursuits— the kind that lead to advancing a society into the future

Another challenge is the current focus in classrooms on test performance over innovation. We cannot deny the reality that we are living in an educational climate that is governed by accountability and is guided by standards. Although these are in service to improving education, we cannot forgo innovation and enjoyment in learning for the sole purpose of improving test scores. Otherwise, outside of classrooms, technology will continue to advance at an unprecedented rate and the United States will lose its entrepreneurial edge.

The Enrichment Triad can be a linear process:

› Step 1: Students are introduced to a new experience with a Type I that gets them curious and excited about a specific topic.
› Step 2: The Type I leads to the need for more information and the development of skills, thus becoming a Type II.
› Step 3: Skills are developed in the Type II that will allow students to independently go deeper into the specific topic, resulting in a Type III investigation and ultimately a product that solves a real-world problem.

The reality, however, is that the Enrichment Triad is not a linear process. Let us demonstrate what we mean with an idealized example.

A Type I is presented in the form of a short video of the first Orion launch (see Figure 41). The short video highlights the seconds leading up to the launch and ends with the commentator saying, "the dawn of Orion and a new era of space exploration." A debriefing occurs and students are asked about the implications of the launch of Orion and what is meant by the commentator's statement about the dawn of Orion. The video, alone, might be enough to get students to want to learn more about Mars, space travel, and future plans for space exploration.

In an effort to connect to students whose interests lie in reading and language arts, a book hook is read as if it were a "movie trailer" for the book. The goal of this book hook is to build suspense and increase students' interest in learning more about how to survive on Mars. By simply ending the reading of a brief excerpt from *Mission: Mars* by Pascal Lee before the resolution to an impending problem, students are left wondering: What next?

Either of these very simple exposure experiences (Figures 41 and 42) has the potential to engage students' curiosity. This curiosity leads very simply and naturally into the Type II experience or the "how-to" processes for skill development. Instead of answering students' questions, we simply teach them how to find the answers for themselves. At first, this may be frustrating for students, but once they learn that the teacher will not offer the answers, they begin to engage in a variety of skills that are transferable. Figure 43 lists some of the skills students might use to learn more about surviving on Mars.

After doing some research and learning more about what is required for surviving on Mars, a few of the students become completely engrossed in the idea of developing spacesuits that are more fashionable and provide greater mobility compared to the giant space suits current astronauts wear. Another student, an aspiring architect, has set out to design space habitats that would enable people to colonize Mars. These two sets of students are primed for small-group and independent productivity. This is how the Type III is initiated (See Figure 44 for Type III examples): through student interest and a desire to go beyond the regular curriculum.

Although it seems that the two sets of students have completely different interests for going deeper, the skills they will need are very similar. We have successfully set the stage for greater depth of learning and more complexity as they work through the problem-solving processes of designing spacesuits and habitats. As the spacesuit designers are working and doing research, they find out about the "Biosuit," a new kind of spacesuit being designed at Massachusetts Institute of Technology by Dava Newman and her team.

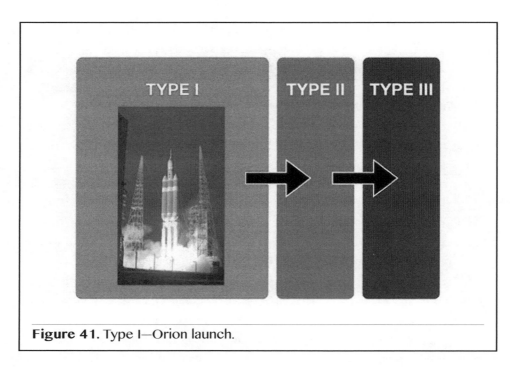

Figure 41. Type I—Orion launch.

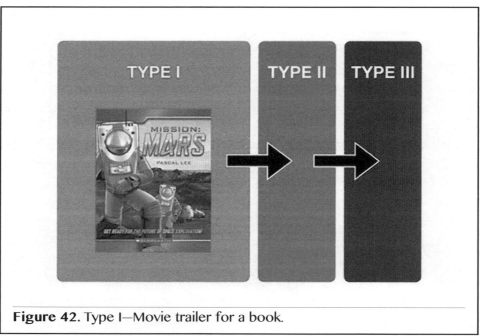

Figure 42. Type I—Movie trailer for a book.

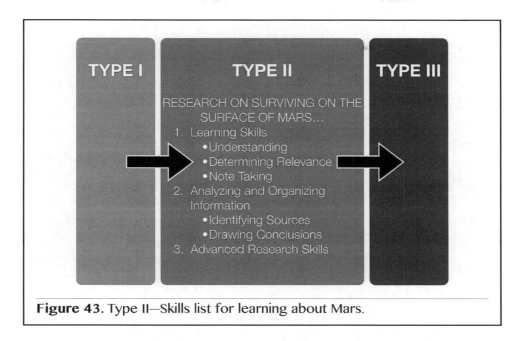

Figure 43. Type II—Skills list for learning about Mars.

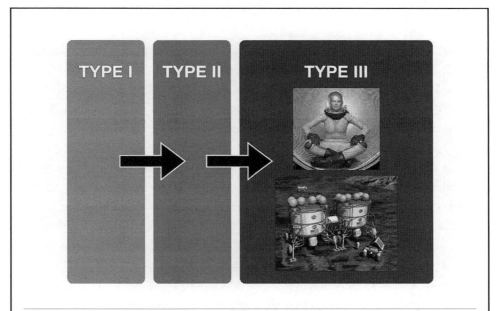

Figure 44. Type III examples. *Note.* Photo credit: Professor Dava Newman, MIT: Inventor, Science and Engineering; Guillermo Trotti, A.I.A., Trotti and Associates, Inc. (Cambridge, MA): Design; Dainese (Vicenza, Italy): Fabrication; Dougas Sonders: Photography.

So, the teacher decides to contact Dava Newman to ask her if she might be available to talk with her students via the latest video conferencing technology. What was previously merely something a small group of students were learning about—technological advances in spacesuit design—has now become an opportunity for a Type I (see Figure 45).

The Type I experiences mentioned, the Orion launch video and the book hook, got another student excited about the idea of getting to Mars. Sure, the Orion spacecraft is the latest technology, but there is still a lot of work to do in developing electrostatic ion thrusters if we are really going to Mars, because the ion thruster is more energy efficient (i.e., requiring less fuel) than the chemical thrusters used to accelerate out of Earth's gravity field, or so we've been told. Off the student goes to do his or her own research to find out what work has already been done by experts, and what still needs to be done to advance the technology. As part of this research, the student also learns which universities and private industries are doing work in this field—a real boon for setting an educational trajectory beyond the K–12 setting (see Figure 46).

After showing the Type I video of the Orion launch, a student approached the teacher with this tidbit of information: She has been working on a design for the SpaceX Hyperloop Pod competition. Unbeknownst to the teacher, this student had been engaging in very advanced research and design work outside the class. Essentially, the student was engaging in a Type III—an individual investigation of a real problem (see Figure 47). The connection here, and the reason the student thinks the teacher might be interested, is that the SpaceX corporation is also working on the Mars Colonial Transporter, and the CEO of SpaceX, Elon Musk, has a personal goal of enabling human exploration of Mars.

The teacher was so impressed with the girl's work on the project that she asked the student to share her design with the class. You might consider the student's presentation a Type I, but remember, the Type I includes a process of debriefing that this presentation may or may not have had. It did, however, get one student interested who up until now was not impressed. This particular student was interested in going fast: fast cars, fast bikes, fast planes, etc. The mere mention of the name Elon Musk engaged this student. You see, this student wanted a fast car and believes that petroleum-based fuels will be obsolete when he is an adult. Therefore, he has been enamored with the Tesla, an electric car that can go 125 miles per hour and reach 60 miles per hour in 3.7 seconds. The idea of the Hyperloop was also mind-boggling for this student, as he did not know that there were plans to create a ground transportation system that could go more than 750 miles per hour! Now, this student is *hooked*. He wants to learn

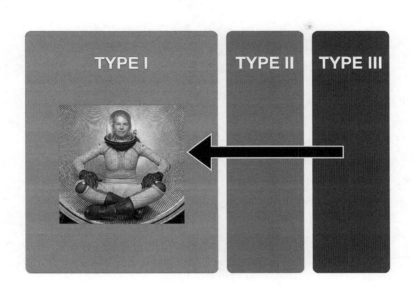

Figure 45. Type III becomes a Type I. *Note.* Photo credit: Professor Dava Newman, MIT: Inventor, Science and Engineering; Guillermo Trotti, A.I.A., Trotti and Associates, Inc. (Cambridge, MA): Design; Dainese (Vicenza, Italy): Fabrication; Dougas Sonders: Photography.

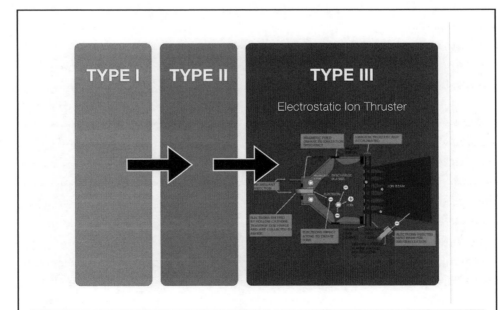

Figure 46. Type I leading to Type II processes and Type III investigation.

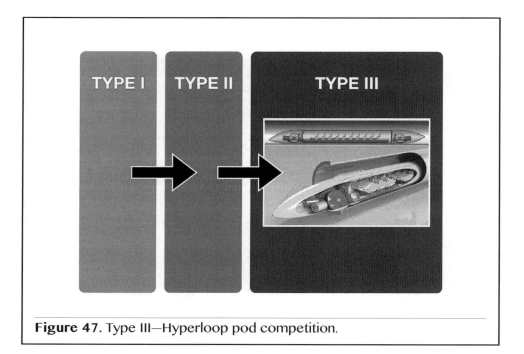

Figure 47. Type III—Hyperloop pod competition.

more about the Hyperloop technology and the work that Elon Musk is doing, beyond the Tesla. Although the Hyperloop Pod design presentation was not planned as a Type I, it has had the effect, for at least one student, of being a Type I—a general exploratory activity that provides exposure to a new experience or new information (see Figure 48).

This fortuitous series of learning events enables the teacher to connect her students in myriad ways. You have the speed connection, the Mars connection, the designs connection, and all of them are working on real problems. For example, the student working on the ion thruster works with the Hyperloop Pod student so that they can determine how their ideas are similar and different and see if there is any crossover in their work or if there could be. The student who is interested in going fast starts to work with the Hyperloop Pod student on speed designs. The collaborations naturally evolve as students work together when doing so allows them to individually advance their work in their interest area.

From a teaching perspective, supporting these students may seem overwhelming, but the skills they will need to develop prototypes of their designs are essentially the same (see Figure 49). Some students are in the early stages, where the research skills will be important and they will begin to prepare for independent work, while other students will develop skills "just in time" to advance their work.

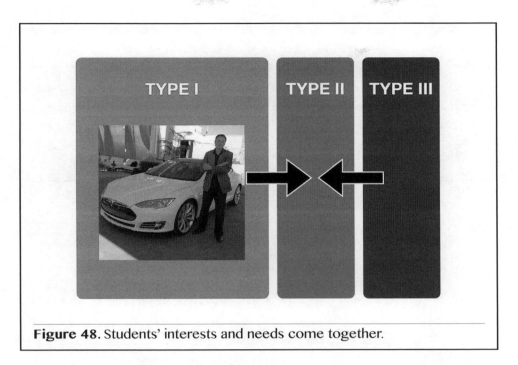

Figure 48. Students' interests and needs come together.

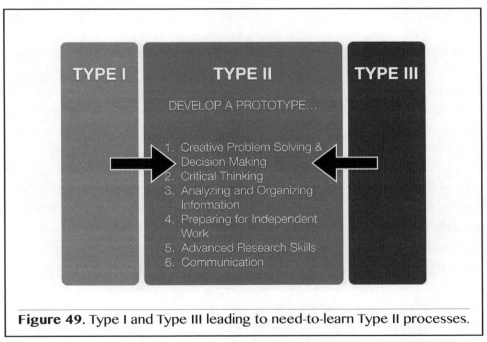

Figure 49. Type I and Type III leading to need-to-learn Type II processes.

Although this example is fictional, it illustrates the ideal—the thing we hold out as something to work toward. This idealized example, although something we strive for, does in fact represent the way the professional world of design and innovation really works. Information is transferred, ideas are shared, research is conducted, inspiration comes from a variety of sources, and connections are made. Sometimes there is competition and sometimes collaboration, but as a society, we keep moving forward.

CHRISTY'S CORNER: MANAGING THE PIECES AND PROVIDING "JUST-IN-TIME" INSTRUCTION

Oftentimes, there are patterns or trends that Christy can identify in the work she has students do. For example, when students are conducting research, they may have similar questions or problems at the same time. This is when the Type II learning can take place in a small-group or whole-group discussion. There are times when she does bring all of her students together to say, "We are beginning our research. Let's talk about a good question. How do we use the Internet? Or, how do we make our searches better so that we can find the information we need?"

Typically, the skill instruction is embedded in the larger framework of a Type III project, for example. As students get to points in their work where they need more scaffolding to move forward, Christy steps in to provide the instruction they need when they need it.

As time goes on and students get deeper into a Type III development process, students' needs, and thus the conferences, become increasingly individualized or turn into smaller groupings. Christy sometimes notices that although students may all have different topics or projects they are working on, they may all be stuck in a similar place. This provides Christy with the opportunity to work with multiple students at the same time. For instance, multiple students may be stuck on developing an essential question to guide their research. As a result, Christy might focus on specific instruction about question development or she might provide modeling.

If they are stuck in more varied places, she focuses her instruction on the behavioral strategies they might use to get unstuck (e.g., learn from other people, seek additional information, take a break and come back to it later, visualize where you want to be, etc.). More often, though, the skills are specific to the student's project, so she teaches in a one-on-one fashion. This happens either in the pull-out program time or she pulls individuals out separately at another time. One thing Christy really understands is that if she does not possess the requisite skills or knowledge to help the student, and she cannot find that information online, it is time to find an expert for that student.

Christy does a lot of individual conferencing because, as she puts it, "The needs are typically unique and specific to each student's project." This allows her to take on the role of "consultant." Students set up a time to meet with her and she provides feedback to their questions or gives direction for their next steps.

Organizing the Pieces

When it comes to creating experiences for your students, we feel that it is important to get organized and to present the information in a way that is logical and well-designed. Joe Renzulli has long advised his students to "Get yourself a folder!" Although Renzulli originally meant this to be an actual file folder where one might put articles, newspaper and magazine clippings, handouts, quotations, and other random notes, technology has significantly advanced to a point where the vast majority of the information that we come in contact with is digital. As a result, we must find a digital folder system to work for us across multiple devices.

Blendspace

If you are looking for a tool that allows you to efficiently organize and present information and resources to your students in a format that allows for student engagement and assessment, then Blendspace (https://www.blendspace.com) may be the tool for you. With the promise of creating digital lessons in 5 minutes, Blendspace features a dynamic interface that allows you to create interactive lessons by dragging and dropping resources into a grid template. Within a Blendspace, you are able to add links to any Internet-based resource by copying and pasting the link or by using Blendspace's built-in search tool. Blendspace provides easy access to videos from YouTube, images from Flickr, and websites from Google. You can link directly to your Dropbox accounts or even upload files from your computer to your Blendspace. When inserting a Google Drive document, Blendspace allows you and your students to interact with the document just as you would normally without leaving the lesson.

When organizing your resources, you are able to label each resource and provide a description or instruction for your students to help them understand what to do or look for. As a part of each resource that you add, a separate discussion board is provided. Users must log in with a free account to leave a comment. This allows you to track the activity of your students and how they are interacting with the Blendspace. For example, you might ask them to view a YouTube video clip and then post their reaction to it on the Blendspace. Using this feature, you can capture students' thoughts whether you are using this synchronously or asynchronously with your class.

Blendspace also provides the ability to insert quizzes within your lessons. This can provide formative assessment checkpoints for you and your students to quickly check for understanding before proceeding. To access this feature, you must create a class account and provide your students with the class code. More information regarding this process can be found at https://www.tes.com/lessons/register. Blendspace allows you to create free lessons using its online toolbox; you are able to create either public or private lessons. You are also able to search its library of public lessons for inspiration or for lessons to remix as your own. The hosting company for Blendspace, TES, has also created a storefront for teachers to sell the Blendspaces that they have created. This could serve as an authentic audience for your students if they choose to design and create their own Blendspaces as part of a Type III.

To get a better idea of how Blendspace can be used to facilitate a SEM:*Tech* experience, we have created two examples for you: Selfies (http://bit.ly/sem-tech-selfie-blendspace) and Mission to Mars (http://bit.ly/sem-tech-mars-blendspace). The advantage of using Blendspace to organize and present your SEM:*Tech* experiences lies in the ease of use and flexibility of the tool. It can use a wide range of media types and online resources. The discussion feature is a nice addition, but it does not allow for threaded discussions. Another disadvantage is that the quiz feature currently only permits multiple-choice responses. That being said, Blendspace is a worthwhile tool that can definitely enhance and better organize your lessons for your students.

TED-Ed

Created by TED as an educational initiative to target a youth audience, TED-Ed's (n.d.) goal is to "spark and celebrate the ideas of teachers and students around the world" (para. 2). What began as an open call to teachers to submit their best lesson ideas has evolved into an ever-growing collection of video lessons designed to capture the imagination of students and to help provide them with some answers and intriguing content related to a wide range of topics. Each of the TED-Ed lessons follows a four-step lesson format that can be seen in Figure 50.

After students "Watch" the video, they are asked to "Think" about what they have just seen. This takes the form of a combination of multiple choice and open-answer questions. The purpose here is to check for students' comprehension and understanding of the information. If students answer one of the multiple-choice questions incorrectly, TED-Ed invites them to go back and review the section of the lesson that covers that content. Next, the "Dig Deeper" section contains additional resources and lessons for students to explore if they enjoyed the lesson and want to learn more about the topic. This serves as a nice extension activity for students who want to delve deeper into the subject. Finally, there is a "Discuss" section that poses an interesting question for students to consider as part of a guided discussion. Students and teachers also have the ability to start an open discussion for others to participate.

Every TED-Ed lesson follows this same format, but lessons can be customized for your students. By clicking on the "Customize This Lesson" button, you are able to alter the title, provide an opening statement, add up to 15 multiple-choice or open-answer questions in the "Think" section, insert additional resources in the "Dig Deeper" section, customize the discussion board section, and add a "And Finally" section to leave your students with some closing thoughts or something to ponder. This customization puts your name on the lesson and can easily be shared with your students by providing them with the unique URL generated for each lesson. To access your lesson, students would need to use the link that you provide to them and log in with a free student account. You will then be able to see each of your students' responses to the questions and their discussion posts.

Not only does TED-Ed allow you to customize any of its original lessons, but you can also utilize this same platform to create a lesson using any YouTube video (http://ed.ted.com/videos). This would be of particular use for designing Type I experiences for individual or small groups of students who might not be completing the activity at the same time. TED-Ed is not necessarily the best tool to use for whole-class lessons that are face to face, but instead is a wonderful technology platform if you are interested in flipping your classroom instruction.

Figure 50. TED four-step process.

Weebly

Although there are certainly a growing number of website building tools to choose from, including Wix (http://www.wix.com), Squarespace (http://www.squarespace.com), and WordPress (http://wordpress.com), when it comes to building a site for education, we feel that there is one tool that stands above the rest. Weebly for Education (http://education.weebly.com) allows you to create free classroom websites, and it integrates student accounts to allow students to contribute to your site and build their own sites as well. With Weebly, you can easily create a classroom website and blog, manage your students' activity on your site, and even accept student assignments online. You are able to create accounts in bulk for your students, and student accounts do not require an e-mail address. You have the option to make your website publically viewable or password protected.

Unlike TED-Ed and Blendspace, Weebly is a very open-ended platform for organizing your lessons and SEM:*Tech* experiences. We would recommend trying the blog feature to facilitate student discussion and comments. The blog allows you to post content and then have your students post responses. You can also create an unlimited number of pages and posts within your Weebly website. On any of these pages, you are able to insert images, text, audio, video, and other elements. You can easily create hyperlinks to other online resources. For example, you could create a TED-Ed lesson and link to it from your Weebly site. No knowledge of coding is required to create a professional-looking website. Instead, Weebly uses a drag and drop menu to allow you to easily organize the elements on your pages. You can insert files, documents, YouTube clips, or even embed assorted web-based resources, including Blendspaces you have created. Weebly offers a wide range of design templates to choose from and helps you look like you know far more than you actually do about web design.

The advantage of using Weebly is that you have a greater degree of flexibility in what you are creating than with TED-Ed or Blendspace. Also, Weebly is able to serve a variety of different purposes and can provide you and your students with a homebase from which to operate. Weebly provides an excellent level of support and tutorials on how to make the most of your website. An Education Pro account is available for $39.95 a year. This raises the storage limit of your site from 500 MB to an unlimited amount. With the free version, Weebly is part of your domain name, but the Pro account allows you to remove all of the Weebly branding from your site. The Pro version also provides an enhanced level of technical support and the ability to password-protect pages within your site.

CHAPTER 14

Casting a Future Plan

The demands of preparing students for an unknown future can seem daunting and require an approach to instruction that meaningfully prepares students for college, career, and citizenship. All too often, education emphasizes math, science, language arts, and history as the core of learning necessary for college and career readiness. The problem is that this narrow focus eliminates opportunities for students to explore music, the arts, foreign language, design, speech, technology, and myriad other topics that reflect not only the richness of potential learning, but also the richness of life.

There is so much diversity in life that we would be doing our students a disservice by not exposing them to as many and as varied topics as we can. The bigger disservice, however, would be to not even ask students about their values, interests, or aspirations and assume that our instruction connects to their lives. The ways schools are arranged (advancement by age rather than readiness) and the way curriculum is designed (start with the standards and pick topics/ skills to meet the standards) prevents us from ever really knowing our students beyond the classroom environment. Sure, we give them interest inventories like the ones we showed you in Chapter 3 to determine the ways in which we might connect our content and instructional goals to their interests, but we still worry that standards will not be achieved and students will not be prepared for the test that comes at the end of the year. Admittedly, these are valid concerns, but what if we asked students on the first day of class to *really* introduce themselves? Not just their name, but their interests, how they like to spend their time outside of school, their friends and families, and so on. Could we stop working *from* the standards, which obligate students to learn, and instead invite students to engage in rigorous learning experiences designed around their passions that allow them to naturally meet the standards? What might that look like?

You Get Me!

In 2013, we had the opportunity to work with students at the Renzulli Academy's Summer Institute. We only had one short week with them, but we managed to really get to know them in a short amount of time, not to mention we had a *lot* of fun working with these gifted, energetic, and strong-willed individuals. Teaching these students meant a lot to us because these students, many of whom came from high-poverty backgrounds, helped remind us how much we both loved teaching and both loved to learn from students. They showed us so much and were so willing to engage (at least most of the time).

There was one student—we'll call him Dion—who came up to Brian and I at lunch, a nonstructured time to eat, play games, run around, etc. (it used to be called recess). You have to imagine Dion in your mind: He was at least 6 feet tall and had broad shoulders and seemed to tower over both of us. He was gregarious, liked to talk, and was the kind of student that you instantly felt a rapport with because he was so open to experience and so willing to learn everything he could about people. He seemed to always have a smile on his face and was more than willing to share his thoughts. On this day, he walked up with a mischievous smile on his face, and pointing his finger at me said, "You, you, you . . ." Then he chuckled, stepped closer (right into my personal space!), and said, "You." I won't lie, I immediately wondered, "What did I do? Did I do something to mislead this student?" Thankfully Brian was standing right there, so some of my concerns were alleviated, but I was at a loss for how to respond. Then Dion said, "You get me! You are the first teacher to ever understand what I care about, and that's me. You are the only teacher to ever let me work on what I want to work on. Can I shake your hand?" Keep in mind that for Dion, this was the summer between eighth and ninth grade, so his comment about caring only about himself was honest and developmentally understandable. Regardless, the comment was moving. Even now, hearing that we have done something that made a student enjoy learning brings a rush of personal and professional joy. I shook his hand (he was really strong, but certainly had the soft skill of the handshake mastered), and mutual smiles were had by all.

You might wonder what we were doing with these students that made Dion so excited about the work and made him feel the need to tell us that we were doing something right. We were using the FutureCasting® (Housand, 2014, 2015) process. This process helps students communicate their interests and passions, connect their passions to learning goals, and ultimately define *who* they want to be in the future. At this point in the process, students had created a webpage and begun the process of conducting online research to find out more about their interest area. The instructions for developing the webpage were simple:

Create a website page that tells us WHO you are as a person. Identify yourself with:

1. Text
2. Images
3. Graphic organization and design that reflect who you are

For this activity, we had students use Weebly, but you can use any website creation tool out there (e.g., WordPress, Wix, Squarespace, Google sites). We chose Weebly for several reasons:

› It is a free tool available on the Internet.
› It is easy to use.
› Teachers can manage students' accounts.
› Students do not need an e-mail address to have a website.
› Students can create professional-looking website pages in a short amount of time.

Dion, in particular, focused his webpage on Dubstep, an electronic dance music that has syncopated rhythms and a bass that "wobbles." Although it might seem like there is no educational content, knowing how important Dubstep is to Dion and how much his current interests align with the music form gives us several entry points for teaching skills that Dion needs. For example, he can:

› Compare and contrast Dubstep with other music genres.
› Research the origins of Dubstep and do a historical retrospective embedded in the larger historical milieu—demonstrating the societal factors that gave rise to Dubstep as a unique music form.
› Analyze the oscillation of the bass "wobble" to identify patterns unique to Dubstep.
› Evaluate the oscillation patterns to determine the mathematical function that best illustrates the pattern.

› Create variations on Dubstep patterns to evolve the music into a new genre.

The beauty is that now we are engaging Dion in higher order thinking and problem solving by leveraging his interests. The website he created gets a new page each time he creates another product related to Dubstep. Over time, a *cohesive* portfolio demonstrating Dion's best work (i.e., work that is academically rigorous and personally interesting to Dion) is created.

Essentially, we have created the opportunity for personalized learning. When we refer to personalized learning, we are talking about providing students with learning opportunities that reflect their interests, aspirations, and learning needs. Personal learning opportunities enable us to provide sufficiently challenging work for gifted students and allow us to customize the learning in a way that honors the cultural backgrounds of individual students. In the case of Dion, we assessed his basic technology skills, identified his interests, and determined instructional objectives that challenged him through increasing levels of Bloom's taxonomy. Most importantly however, we valued the things he values, enabling us to leverage his love of music—a very specific type of music—to teach transferrable skills that lead to short-term achievement and support future success. Once we have identified the students' readiness level, interests, and aspirations, we can provide learning experiences that are customized, to varying degrees, for each student. This allows us to facilitate their long-term success while imbuing the learning process with joy.

You might recall in Chapter 3 that we discussed two students who love music. Do these images jog your memory (Figure 51; See also Figures 6 and 7 in Chapter 3)?

Once again, you probably noticed differences and, as you may recall, the first student was quiet, reserved, and very thoughtful about what she says as well as the way she treats others. She was so quiet that it took 4 days before we heard her say anything to us directly. She loves playing the piano and she prefers classical music, but will listen to other genres of music. She practices several hours a day and aspires to play classical piano professionally.

The second student, also female, loves music with solid rhythms and rhyming lyrics like rap and hip-hop. This student was personable, very outgoing (not a day went by that she did not contribute), affably ambitious, and enjoyed engaging with others. If you were to scroll down her first page, you would find the following text:

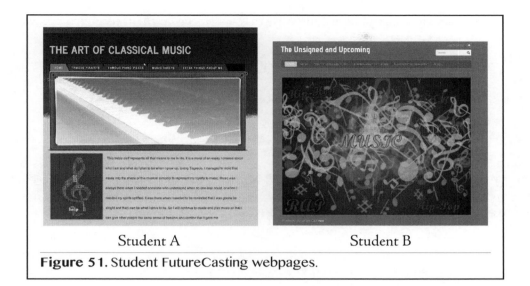

Student A   Student B

Figure 51. Student FutureCasting webpages.

Me, I want to become a performer.
I want to travel the world.
I want to be an inspiration to others; grown and young.
I want to work with the stars.
I want to be a star.
I want to help.
I want to create something beautiful.
I want to be famous.
I want the muny [sic].
I want to help.
I want to be free.
I WANT TO BE ME!!!!!

After reading this, do you think she will be a musician or a singer? Did you notice that she used the phrase "I want to help" more than once? Did you also notice that it was the only phrase used more than one time? As you work through Jayla's site, she has embedded instructional videos and provided information about recording, getting your song on the radio, and working a soundboard. She has even created a community where up-and-coming songwriters can share their lyrics and get feedback on their work. Needless to say, although she wants to be a star and a performer, it is more likely that she will be a music producer working behind the scenes. Once again, you might be thinking: What does this have to do with the curriculum? Here are just *some* of the skills Jayla will need to develop in order to be a music producer:

> effective communication for appropriate audiences, including speaking and writing;
> collaboration;
> critical thinking;
> monitoring and assessing the performance of others;
> reading comprehension;
> active listening;
> time management;
> complex problem solving;
> decision making and being able to conduct cost and benefit analyses;
> systems analysis and evaluation; and
> managing time, material resources, and people.

By asking individuals who they want to be, FutureCasting® focuses the exploration of future options on core competencies and personal satisfaction. The process really helps students focus on attaining a fulfilling life rather than acquiring money or social stature. Focusing on *who* one wants to be allows for a concentration of efforts, time, and energy that minimizes distractions and increases engagement in learning—learning that is happening for meaningful reasons.

You might also notice that the technology has taken a backseat. Sure, Jayla knows how to embed videos, create text boxes, form interactive communities, and create a visually appealing website using the software, but the goal was not to create a website for the sake of using technology; it maintained a pedagogical purpose, one we could have achieved without the use of technology. The technology is merely a tool that has helped us understand Jayla's interests, aspirations, and values. Once we have identified Jayla's motivations, we can then support her as she develops the skills of a practicing professional—in this case, a music producer. The goal is to shift the focus of learning and instruction from academic achievement (important, but not the end game) to promoting the long-term development and success of our students. Ultimately, we want to help students take meaningful steps to prepare for college, career, and civic engagement while enjoying learning. You will know you have accomplished these goals when students are:

> engaged in learning that results in products that address the needs of an audience beyond the school walls;

> experiencing some level of personalization in their learning by creating products that reflect their interests, values, aspirations, and cultural background; and

> challenged at a level that forces them to grow beyond where they are now or where they have been before, both personally and academically.

Technology and access to the Internet provide unique curricular opportunities to connect youth to communities where they can find individuals who share their interests and advanced knowledge, provide opportunities to share their insights, and find mentors who can serve to advance gifted students' knowledge to expert levels while encouraging continual advancement in fields of interest.

Those who promote talent development must seek to go beyond textbook-style instruction, consider the many and varied ways that talent manifests, and be willing to take risks in their instructional settings to set a new course for students' futures and for the futures of every individual who might benefit from technological innovation, which, when you think about it, is everyone.

We are preparing students for jobs that do not yet exist using technologies that have yet to be imagined. We have to move beyond a 21st-century skills mindset and seek a "change and innovation" mindset. We have to embrace the notion that technology is evolving at an alarmingly fast pace and the projection of that pace will inevitably continue to increase. To be competitive now and in the future, individuals will have to take more initiative, be more responsible, and produce more than ever before. They will have to be flexible, comfortable with ambiguity, and continually create and recreate to stay viable in a world that will, evermore, be in a state of flux. They will have to go where no one has gone before.

APPENDIX A

Taxonomy of Type II Enrichment Process Skills

Taxonomy of Type II Enrichment Process Skills

I. Cognitive Training
  A. Creativity. Developing and Practicing the Use of:

Fluency	Attribute Listing
Flexibility	Fantasy
Originality	Imagery
Elaboration	Association
Brainstorming	Comparison
Forced Relationships	Risk Taking

   Modification Techniques:

- Adaptation	- Multiple Uses
- Magnification	- Rearrangement
- Minification	- Combination
- Substitution	- Reversal

  B. Creative Problem Solving and Decision Making. Developing and Practicing the Use of:

   Creative Problem Solving:

- Mess Finding	- Idea Finding
- Fact Finding	- Solution Finding
- Problem Finding	- Acceptance Finding

Decision Making:
    Stating Desired Goals and Conditions Related to a Decision
        That Needs to Be Made
    Stating the Obstacles to Realizing the Goals and Conditions
    Identifying the Alternatives Available for Overcoming Each
        Obstacle
    Examining Alternatives in Terms of Resources, Costs,
        Constraints, and Time
    Ranking Alternatives in Terms of Probable Consequences
    Choosing the Best Alternative
    Evaluating the Actions Resulting From the Decision

C. Critical and Logical Thinking. Developing and Practicing the Use
   of:

Conditional Reasoning	Analogies
Ambiguity	Inferences
Fallacies	Inductive Reasoning
Emotive Words	Deductive Reasoning
Definition of Terms	Syllogisms
Categorical Propositions	Probability
Classification	Dilemmas
Validity Testing	Paradoxes
Reliability Testing	Analysis of:
Translation	- Content
Interpretation	- Elements
Extrapolation	- Trends and Patterns
Patterning	- Relationships
Sequencing	- Organizing Principles
Flow Charting	- Propaganda and Bias
Computer Programming	

II. Affective Training

Understanding Yourself	
Understanding Others	Moral Reasoning
Working With Groups	Sex Role Stereotypes
Peer Relationships	Assertiveness Training
Parent Relationships	Self-Reliance
Values Clarification	Dealing With Conflict
	Coping Behaviors

266

Analyzing Your Strengths
Planning Your Future
Interpersonal
Communication
Developing Self-Confidence
Developing a Sense of
Humor

Showing an Understanding
of Others
Dealing With Fear, Anxiety
and Guilt
Dealing With the Unknown

III. Learning How-to-Learn Skills
A. Listening, Observing, and Perceiving. Developing and Practicing
the Use of:
Following Directions
Noting Specific Details
Understanding Main
Points, Themes, and
Sequences
Separating Relevant
From Irrelevant
Information
Paying Attention
to Whole-Part
Relationships

Scanning for the "Big
Picture"
Focusing in on Particulars
Asking for Clarification
Asking Appropriate
Questions
Making Inferences
Noting Subtleties
Predicting Outcomes
Evaluating a Speaker's
Point of View

B. Notetaking and Outlining. Developing and Practicing the Use of:
Notetaking:
Selecting Key Terms, Concepts, and Ideas
Disregarding Unimportant Information
Noting What Needs to Be Remembered
Recording Words, Dates, and Figures That Help You Recall
Related Information
Reviewing Notes and Underlining or Highlighting the Most
Important Items
Categorizing Notes in a Logical Order
Organizing Notes So That Information From Various Sources
Can Be Added at a Later Time

Outlining:
Using Outlining Skills to Write Material That Has Unity and Coherence
Selecting and Using a System of Notation Such as Roman Numerals
Deciding Whether to Write Topic Outlines or Sentence Outlines
Stating Each Topic or Point Clearly
Using Parallel Structure
Remembering That Each Section Must Have at Least Two Parts

C. Interviewing and Surveying. Developing and Practicing the Use of:
Identifying the Information Being Sought
Deciding on Appropriate Instrument(s)
Identifying Sources of Existing Instruments
Designing Instruments (e.g., Checklists, Rating Scales, Interview Schedules)
Developing Question Wording Skills (e.g., Factual, Attitudinal, Probing, Follow-up)
Sequencing Questions
Identifying Representative Samples
Field Testing and Revising Instruments
Developing Rapport With Subjects
Preparing a Data-Gathering Matrix and Schedule
Using Follow-up Techniques

Note. The Taxonomies displayed in Appendix A are not intended to be a complete listing of every thinking and feeling process, nor are the processes listed here mutually exclusive. Rather, there are many instances in which the processes interact with one another and even duplicate items from various categories. Because of this interaction and the need to use several processes simultaneously in their application to real problems, it is important to teach them in various combinations rather than in an item-by-item fashion. Whenever possible, we have attempted to list the process skills in a logical hierarchy, but it is important to point out that the appropriate use of thinking skills often proceeds in a cyclical rather than linear fashion. For this reason, it is not necessary to teach each set of skills in a rigidly sequential fashion; however, there may be instances when a sequence will facilitate comprehension and application.From *The Schoolwide Enrichment Model* (3rd ed., p. 128) by J. S. Renzulli and S. M. Reis, 2014, Waco, TX: Prufrock Press. Copyright 2014 Prufrock Press. Reprinted with permission.

APPENDIX B

SEM: *Tech* Templates

To support teachers and students throughout all stages of the SEM:*Tech*, a collection of templates has been created using Google Drive. Although these templates may be printed, the real power comes in the interactive nature of the documents. To help you access the templates, the full collection is listed below. Directions for how these templates are used are included within the various chapters of this book.

To view any of the templates, use the bit.ly link that is provided. This will allow you to see the information to determine whether or not it matches the needs of you and your students. If you wish to make a personal copy that can be edited and modified, a bit.ly link has been provided. This will prompt you to add a copy of the template to your Google Drive account.

Once a copy has been added to your Google Drive account, you may choose to make edits or additional copies. To make a copy of any Google Drive document, simply go to the menu bar in Google Drive and select "File." A menu of options will appear. Select "Make a copy . . .". You will be prompted to rename the document and asked where you would like to save it within Google Drive.

Interest Surveys

Interest Bracket
To view, go to http://bit.ly/sem-tech-interest-bracket
To make a copy, go to http://bit.ly/sem-tech-interest-bracket-copy

Interest-A-Lyzer
To view, go to http://bit.ly/sem-tech-interest-a-lyzer
To make a copy, go to http://bit.ly/sem-tech-interest-a-lyzer-copy

Remember Your Future
To view, go to http://bit.ly/sem-tech-future
To make a copy, go to http://bit.ly/sem-tech-future-copy

Type I Templates

Type I Planner
To view, go to http://bit.ly/sem-tech-type-i-planner
To make a copy, go to http://bit.ly/sem-tech-type-i-planner-copy

3-2-1
To view, go to http://bit.ly/sem-tech-321
To make a copy, go to http://bit.ly/sem-tech-321-copy

AEIOU
To view, go to http://bit.ly/sem-tech-aeiou
To make a copy, go to http://bit.ly/sem-tech-aeiou-copy

Color Symbol Image
To view, go to http://bit.ly/sem-tech-csi
To make a copy, go to http://bit.ly/sem-tech-csi-copy

Compass Points
To view, go to http://bit.ly/sem-tech-compasspoints
To make a copy, go to http://bit.ly/sem-tech-compasspoints-copy

Connect Extend Wonder
To view, go to http://bit.ly/sem-tech-cec
To make a copy, go to http://bit.ly/sem-tech-cec-copy

Frayer Model
To view, go to http://bit.ly/sem-tech-frayer
To make a copy, go to http://bit.ly/sem-tech-frayer-copy

Hexagonal Thinking
To view, go to http://bit.ly/sem-tech-hexagon
To make a copy, go to http://bit.ly/sem-tech-hexagon-copy

I Used To Think, But Now I Think
To view, go to http://bit.ly/sem-tech-used-to-think
To make a copy, go to http://bit.ly/sem-tech-used-to-think-copy

KWL
To view, go to http://bit.ly/sem-tech-kwl
To make a copy, go to http://bit.ly/sem-tech-kwl-copy

One of These Things Is Not Like The Other
To view, go to http://bit.ly/sem-tech-other
To make a copy, go to http://bit.ly/sem-tech-other-copy

Question Starts
To view, go to http://bit.ly/sem-tech-question-starts
To make a copy, go to http://bit.ly/sem-tech-question-starts-copy

SWOT Analysis
To view, go to http://bit.ly/sem-tech-swot
To make a copy, go to http://bit.ly/sem-tech-swot-copy

The Bull's Eye
To view, go to http://bit.ly/sem-tech-bullseye
To make a copy, go to http://bit.ly/sem-tech-bullseye-copy

Why? x Five
To view, go to http://bit.ly/sem-tech-why
To make a copy, go to http://bit.ly/sem-tech-why-copy

Type II Templates

Finding Quality Sources
To view, go to http://bit.ly/sem-tech-quality-sources
To make a copy, go to http://bit.ly/sem-tech-quality-sources-copy

Logo Design
To view, go to http://bit.ly/sem-tech-logo
To make a copy, go to http://bit.ly/sem-tech-logo-copy

Website Planner
To view, go to http://bit.ly/sem-tech-website-planner
To make a copy, go to http://bit.ly/sem-tech-website-planner-copy

TYPE III Template

Management Planner
To view, go to http://bit.ly/sem-tech-planner
To make a copy, go to http://bit.ly/sem-tech-planner-copy

A full list of the SEM:*Tech* Templates is also available at http://sem-tech.org/templates

References

Arnone, M. P., Small, R. V., Chauncey, S. A., & McKenna, H. P. (2011). Curiosity, interest, and engagement in technology-pervasive learning environments: A new research agenda. *Educational Technology Research and Development, 59,* 181–198.

Bloom, B. S. (Ed.). (1985). *Developing talent in young people.* New York, NY: Ballantine.

Brigandi, C. B. (2015). *Gifted secondary school students: The perceived relationship between enrichment and achievement orientation* (Unpublished doctoral dissertation). University of Connecticut, Storrs. Retrieved from http://digital commons.uconn.edu/cgi/viewcontent.cgi?article=6972&context=dissertations

Bruner, J. S. (1960). *The process of education.* Cambridge, MA: Harvard University Press.

Bruner, J. S. (1966). *Toward a theory of instruction.* Cambridge, MA: Harvard University Press.

Bruner, J. S. (1973). *Beyond the information given: Studies in the psychology of knowing.* New York, NY: Norton.

Clark, B. (2002). *Growing up gifted* (6th ed.). Upper Saddle River, NJ: Merrill/Prentice-Hall.

Clarke, A. C. (1973). Hazards of prophecy: The failure of imagination. In A. C. Clarke, *Profiles of the future: An inquiry into the limits of the possible* (Rev. ed., pp. 12–21). New York, NY: Harper & Row, Publishers.

Common Sense Media. (2015). *Digital citizenship in a connected culture.* Retrieved from https://www.commonsensemedia.org/educators/scope-and-sequence

Common Sense Media. (2016). *The Common Sense census: Media use by tweens and teens.* Retrieved from https://www.commonsensemedia.org/research/the-common-sense-census-media-use-by-tweens-and-teens

Cooper, C. R., Baum, S. M., & Neu, T. W. (2004). Developing scientific talent in students with special needs: An alternative model for identification, curriculum, and assessment. *The Journal of Secondary Gifted Education, 15,* 162–169.

Delcourt, M. A. B. (1988). *Characteristics related to high levels of creative/productive behavior in secondary school students: A multi-case study* (Unpublished doctoral dissertation). University of Connecticut, Storrs.

Delcourt, M. A. B. (1994). Creative/productive behavior among secondary school students: A longitudinal study of students identified by the Renzulli three-ring conception of giftedness. In R. Subotnik & K. Arnold (Eds.), *Beyond Terman: Longitudinal studies in contemporary gifted education* (pp. 401–436). Norwood, NJ: Ablex.

Delcourt, M. A. B. (2008). *Project POTENTIAL.* Washington, DC: Jacob K. Javits Gifted and Talented Education Act.

Dewey, J. (1907). *The school and society.* Chicago, IL: University of Chicago Press.

Dewey, J. (1910). *How we think.* Amherst, NY: Prometheus Books.

Dewey, J. (1913). *Interest and effort in education.* New York, NY: Houghton Mifflin.

Dewey, J. (1916). *Democracy and education: An introduction to the philosophy of education.* New York, NY: The Free Press.

Dweck, C. S. (2006). *Mindset: The new psychology of success.* New York, NY: Random House.

Eccles, J., & Wigfield, A. (1995). In the mind of the actor: The structure of adolescents' achievement task values and expectancy-related beliefs. *Personality and Social Psychology Bulletin, 21,* 215–225.

Eisenhood, C. (2013). *Ultimate's most famous YouTuber is not who you think.* Retrieved from http://ultiworld.com/2013/08/22/ultimates-most-famous-youtuber-is-not-who-you-think

Facebook. (2015). *Facebook Q3 2015 results.* Retrieved from http://investor.fb.com/releasedetail.cfm?ReleaseID=940609

Frasier, M. M., & Passow, A. H. (1994). *Toward a new paradigm for identifying talent potential.* Storrs: University of Connecticut, The National Research Center on the Gifted and Talented.

Guo, P. (2013). Optimal video length for student engagement. *EdX MOOC Research.* Retrieved from http://blog.edx.org/optimal-video-length-student-engagement

Hasan, L., & Abuelrub, E. (2011). Assessing the quality of web sites. *Applied Computing and Informatics, 9,* 11–29.

Hébert, T. P. (1993). *An ethnographic description of the high school experiences of high ability males in an urban environment* (Unpublished doctoral dissertation). University of Connecticut, Storrs.

Henson, K. T. (2004). *Constructivist teaching strategies for diverse middle-level classrooms.* Boston, MA: Allyn & Bacon.

Hockett, J. A. (2009). Curriculum for highly able learners that conforms to general education and gifted education quality indicators. *Journal for the Education of the Gifted, 32,* 394–440.

Hollingworth, L. S. (1926). *Gifted children: Their nature and nurture.* New York, NY: Macmillan.

Housand, A. M. (2014, November). *FutureCasting: Making inroads to a successful future.* Presented at the National Association of Gifted Children 61st Annual Convention, Baltimore, MD.

Housand, A. M. (2015, Fall). Deceptively simple and exceedingly rich: Using gifted pedagogy for technology integration. *Gifted Education Communicator.* Retrieved from http://giftededucationcommunicator.com/gec-fall-2015

Housand, B. C., & Housand, A. M. (2012). The role of technology in gifted students' motivation. *Psychology in the Schools, 49,* 706–715.

Hunter, M. (1982). *Mastery teaching.* El Segundo, CA: TIP Publications

Ingram, H. (2014). 8 short films to see at Cucalorus 20. *Star News Online.* Retrieved from http://www.starnewsonline.com/article/20141113/ARTICLES/141119889?tc=ar

International Society for Technology in Education. (2016). *ISTE standards for students.* Washington, DC: Author. Retrieved from http://www.iste.org/standards

International Technology Educator's Association. (2000). *Standards for technological literacy: Content for the study of technology.* Reston, VA: ITEA.

International Technology Educator's Association. (2007). *Standards for technological literacy: Content for the study of technology* (3rd ed.). Reston, VA: ITEA.

Jacobson, M., & Ruddy, M. (2004). *Open to outcome: A practical guide for facilitating & teaching experiential reflection.* Oklahoma City, OK: Wood 'N' Barnes Publishing & Distribution.

Jalil, N. A., Yunus, R. M., & Said, N. S. (2013). Students' color perception and preference: An empirical analysis of its relationship. *Procedia-Social and Behavioral Sciences, 90,* 575–582.

Jonassen, D. H., Peck, K. L., & Wilson, B. G. (1999). *Learning with technology: A constructivist perspective.* Upper Saddle River, NJ: Prentice Hall.

Kaplan, S. N. (1986). The grid: A model to construct differentiated curriculum for the gifted. In J. S. Renzulli (Ed.), *Systems and models for developing programs for the gifted and talented* (pp. 180–193). Mansfield Center, CT: Creative Learning Press.

Kashdan, T., & Steger, M. (2007). Curiosity and pathways to well-being and meaning in life: Traits, states, and everyday behaviors. *Motivation and Emotion, 31,* 159–173.

Keengwe, J., Onchwari, G., & Wachira, P. (2008). Computer technology integration and student learning: Barriers and promise. *Journal of Science Education and Technology, 17,* 560–565.

Kidd, C. (2013). *Go: A Kidd's guide to graphic design.* New York, NY: Workman Publishing.

Kolb, D. A. (1984). *Experiential learning: Experience as the source of learning and development.* Upper Saddle River, NJ: Prentice Hall.

Lenhart, A., Duggan, M., Perrin, A., Stepler, R., Rainie, L., & Parker, K. (2015). *Teens, social media & technology overview 2015.* Retrieved from http://www.pewinternet.org/files/2015/04/PI_TeensandTech_Update2015_04091 51.pdf

Macaca nigra self-portrait large.jpg [Digital image]. (2010). Retrieved from https://upload.wikimedia.org/wikipedia/commons/4/4e/Macaca_nigra_self-portrait_large.jpg

MacDonald, M. (2016). How asking 'Why' 5 times can change your life. *Entrepreneur Media.* Retrieved from http://www.entrepreneur.com/article/253820.

Make. (2015). *Raspberry Pi or Arduino? One simple rule to choose the right board.* Retrieved from http://makezine.com/2015/12/04/admittedly-simplistic-guide-raspberry-pi-vs-arduino

Makerspace. (2016). *What's a Makerspace?* Retrieved from http://spaces.makerspace.com

McMurrer, J. (2008). *Instructional time in elementary schools: A closer look at changes for specific subjects.* Washington, DC: Center for Education Policy.

Murphy, S., & Atala, A. (2014). 3D bioprinting of tissues and organs. *Nature Biotechnology, 32,* 773–785.

Mönks, F. J., & Katzko, M. W. (2005). Giftedness and gifted education. In R. J. Sternberg & J. E. Davidson (Eds.), *Conceptions of giftedness* (2nd ed., pp. 187–200). New York, NY: Cambridge University Press.

Moustakis, V. S., Litos, C., Dalivigas, A., & Tsironis, L. (2004). Website quality assessment criteria. *Proceedings of the Ninth International Conference on Information Quality* (ICIQ-04). Cambridge, MA: MIT.

National Aeronautics and Space Administration. (2008). *NASA technologies benefit our lives.* Retrieved from https://spinoff.nasa.gov/Spinoff2008/tech_benefits.html

National Consumers League. (2012). *Parents, tweeners and cell phones: Attitudes and experiences.* Retrieved from http://www.natlconsumersleague.org/images/PDF/tween_cell_survey.pdf

National Research Council. (2007). *Rising above the gathering storm: Energizing and employing America for a brighter economic future.* Washington, DC: The National Academies Press. Retrieved from http://www.nap.edu/catalog.php?record_id=11463

Net Market Share. (October, 2015). *Realtime web analytics with no sampling: Desktop search engine market share.* Retrieved from http://www.netmarket share.com/search-engine-market-share.aspx?qprid=4&qpcustomd=0

O'Brien, B., Friedman-Nimz, R., Lacey, J., & Denson, D. (2005). From bits and bytes to C++ and websites: What is computer talent made of? *Gifted Child Today, 23*(3), 56–64.

O'Dwyer, L. M., Russell, M., & Bebell, D. (2004). Identifying teacher, school and district characteristics associated with elementary teachers' use of technology: A multilevel perspective. *Education Policy Analysis Archives, 12*(48). Retrieved from http://epaa.asu.edu/ojs/article/viewFile/203/329

Ofcom. (2015). *Children and parents: Media use and attitudes report 2015. Independent regulator and competition authority for the UK communications industries.* Retrieved from http://stakeholders.ofcom.org.uk/market-data-research/other/research-publications/childrens/children-parents-nov-15

Organisation for Economic Co-operation and Development. (2015). *Students, computers and learning: Making the connection.* Paris, France: PISA, OECD Publishing. doi:10.1787/9789264239555-en

Partnership for 21st Century Learning. (2009). *Framework for 21st century learning*. Washington, DC: Author. Retrieved from http://www.p21.org/storage/documents/P21_framework_0515.pdf

Pea, R., Nass, C., Meheula, L., Rance, M., Kumar, A., Bamford, H., . . . Zhou, M. (2012). Media use, face-to-face communciation, media multitasking, and social well-being among 8–12 year old girls. *Developmental Psychology, 48,* 327–336.

Pearson. (2014). *Pearson student mobile device survey 2014: National report students in grades 4–12.* Retrieved from http://www.pearsoned.com/wp-content/uploads/Pearson-K12-Student-Mobile-Device-Survey-050914-PUBLIC-Report.pdf

Pfeiffer, J. W., & Jones, J. E. (Eds.). (1985). *Reference guide to handbooks and annuals* (Rev. ed.). San Diego, CA: University Associates Publishers.

PIA20316: Curiosity self-portrait at Martian sand dune [Digital image]. (2016, January 19). Retrieved from http://www.jpl.nasa.gov/spaceimages/images/wallpaper/PIA20316-800x600.jpg

Piaget, J. (1976). *To understand is to invent: The future of education* (G. Roberts, Trans.). New York, NY: Penguin.

Purcell, K., Rainie, L., Heaps, A., Buchanan, J., Friedrich, L., Jacklin, A., . . . Zickuhr, K. (2012). *How teens do research in the digital world.* Retrieved from http://www.pewinternet.org/2012/11/01/how-teens-do-research-in-the-digital-world

Reis, S. M. (2005). Feminist perspective on talent development: A research-based conception of giftedness in women. In R. J. Sternberg & J. E. Davidson (Eds.), *Conceptions of giftedness* (2nd ed., pp. 217–245). New York, NY: Cambridge University Press.

Reis, S. M., Burns, D. E., & Renzulli, J. S. (1992). *Curriculum compacting: The complete guide to modifying the regular curriculum for high ability students.* Waco, TX: Prufrock Press.

Reis, S. M., Renzulli, J. S., & Burns, D. E. (2016). *Curriculum compacting: A guide to differentiating curriculum and instruction through enrichment and acceleration* (2nd ed.). Waco, TX: Prufrock Press.

Reis, S. M., Westberg, K. L., Kulikowich, J., Caillard, F., Hébert, T. P., Plucker, J. A., . . . Smidst, J. (1993). *Why not let high ability students start school in January? The curriculum compacting study* (RM93106). Storrs: University of Connecticut, The National Research Center on the Gifted and Talented.

Renzulli, J. S. (1976). The enrichment triad model: A guide for developing defensible programs for the gifted and talented. *Gifted Child Quarterly, 20,* 303–326.

References

Renzulli, J. S. (1977). *The Enrichment Triad Model: A guide for developing defensible programs for the gifted.* Mansfield Center, CT: Creative Learning Press.

Renzulli, J. S. (1978). What makes giftedness? Reexamining a definition. *Phi Delta Kappan, 60,* 180–184, 261.

Renzulli, J. S. (1982). What makes a problem real: Stalking the illusive meaning of qualitative differences in gifted education. *Gifted Child Quarterly, 26,* 147–156.

Renzulli, J. S. (1986). The three-ring conception of giftedness: A developmental model for creative productivity. In R. J. Sternberg & J. E. Davidson (Eds.), *Conceptions of giftedness* (pp. 53–92). New York, NY: Cambridge University Press.

Renzulli, J. S. (1994). *Schools for talent development: A practical plan for total school improvement.* Waco, TX: Prufrock Press.

Renzulli, J. S. (1996). Schools for talent development: A practical plan for total school improvement. *School Administrator, 53*(1), 20–22.

Renzulli, J. S. (2001). Gifted education in the new century: Identification and programming issues. *Australasian Journal of Gifted Education, 10*(1), 23–32.

Renzulli, J. S. (2002). Expanding the conception of giftedness to include co-cognitive traits and to promote social capital. *Phi Delta Kappan, 84*(1), 33–40, 57–58.

Renzulli, J. S. (2005). The three-ring conception of giftedness: A developmental model for promoting creative productivity. In R. J. Sternberg & J. E. Davidson (Eds.), *Conceptions of giftedness* (2nd ed., pp. 246–279). New York, NY: Cambridge University Press.

Renzulli, J. S. (2010). *The Interest-A-Lyzer: Adult version.* Waco, TX: Prufrock Press.

Renzulli, J. S., Leppien, J. H., & Hays, T. S. (2000). *The multiple menu model: A practical guide for developing differentiated curriculum.* Waco, TX: Prufrock Press.

Renzulli, J. S., & Reis, S. M. (1985). *The Schoolwide Enrichment Model: A how-to guide for educational excellence.* Mansfield Center, CT: Creative Learning Press.

Renzulli, J. S., & Reis, S. M. (1994). Research related to the Schoolwide Enrichment Model. *Gifted Child Quarterly, 38,* 2–14.

Renzulli, J. S., & Reis, S. M. (1997). *The Schoolwide Enrichment Model: A how-to guide for educational excellence* (2nd ed.). Waco, TX: Prufrock Press.

Renzulli, J. S., & Reis, S. M. (2014). *The Schoolwide Enrichment Model: A how-to guide for talent development* (3rd ed.). Waco, TX: Prufrock Press.

Renzulli, J. S., Smith, L. H., & Reis, S. M. (1981, March). Identifying and programming for the gifted student. *The Education Digest*, 45–47.

Resnick, M. (2006). Computer as paintbrush: Technology, play and the creative society. In D. Singer, R. Golikoff, & K. Hirsh-Pasek (Eds.), *Play = Learning: How play motivates and enhances children's cognitive and social-emotional growth* (pp. 192–208). Oxford, England: Oxford University Press.

Reynolds, R., & Caperton, I. H. (2011). Contrasts in student engagement, meaning-making, dislikes, and challenges in a discovery-based program of game design learning. *Educational Technology Research and Development, 59,* 267–289.

Riddle, M. (2015). *Digital citizenship in schools: Nine elements all students should know* (3rd ed.). Arlington, VA: ISTE.

Robert Cornelius, head-and-shoulders [self-]portrait, facing front, with arms crossed [Digital image]. (1839). Retrieved from https://en.wikipedia.org/wiki/Self-portrait#/media/File:RobertCornelius.jpg

Ryan, R. M., & Deci, E. L. (2000). Self-determination theory and the facilitation of intrinsic motivation, social development, and well-being. *American Psychologist, 55,* 68–78.

Sahin, A, Ayar, M. C., & Adiguzel, T. (2014). STEM related after-school program activities and associated outcomes on student learning. *Educational Sciences: Theory & Practice, 14,* 309–322.

Schack, G. D. (1986). *Creative productivity and self-efficacy in children* (Unpublished doctoral dissertation). University of Connecticut, Storrs.

Schack, G. D., Starko, A. J., & Burns, D. E. (1991). Self-efficacy and creative productivity: Three studies of above average children. *Journal of Research in Education, 1*(1), 44–52.

Self-portrait with straw hat by Vincent Van Gogh [Digital Image]. (1887). Retrieved from https://upload.wikimedia.org/wikipedia/commons/thumb/9/95/Van_Gogh_Self-Portrait_with_Straw_Hat_1887-Detroit.jpg/800px-Van_Gogh_Self-Portrait_with_Straw_Hat_1887-Detroit.jpg

Sharp, V. (2006). *Computer education for teachers: Integrating technology into classroom teaching* (5th ed.). New York, NY: McGraw-Hill.

Sillito, J., Murphy, G. C., & DeVolder, K. (2006). Questions programmers ask during software evolution tasks. *SIGSOFT' 06/FSE-14.* Portland, OR. Retrieved from http://people.ucalgary.ca/~sillito/work/fse2006.pdf

Sparrow, B., Liu, J., & Wegner, D. M. (2011). Google effects on memory: Cognitive consequences of having information at your fingertips. *Science, 333,* 776–778.

Starko, A. J. (1988). Effects of the Revolving Door Identification Model on creative productivity and self-efficacy. *Gifted Child Quarterly, 32,* 291–297.

Sternberg, R. J. (1997). A triarchic view of giftedness: Theory and practice. In N. Colangelo & G. A. Davis (Eds.), *The handbook of gifted education* (pp. 43–53). Boston, MA: Allyn & Bacon.

Swan, G. E., & Carmelli, D. (1996). Curiosity and mortality in aging adults: A 5-year follow-up of the Western Collaborative Group Study. *Psychology and Aging, 11,* 449–453.

TED-Ed. (n.d.). *About TED-Ed.* http://ed.ted.com/about

Tomlinson, C. A., Kaplan, S. N., Renzulli, J. S., Purcell, J. H., Leppien, J. H., Burns, D. E., Strickland, C. A., & Imbeau, M. B. (2009). *The parallel curriculum: A design to develop learner potential and challenge advanced learners* (2nd ed.). Thousand Oaks, CA: Corwin Press.

Torrance, E. P., & Safter, H. T. (1990). *The incubation model of teaching: Getting beyond the aha!* Buffalo, NY: Bearly, Ltd.

Treffinger, D. J., Young, G. C., Selby, E. C., & Shepardson, C. (2002). *Assessing creativity: A guide for educators* (RM02170). Storrs: University of Connecticut, The National Research Center on the Gifted and Talented.

Tufte, E. R. (1983). *The visual display of quantitative information.* Cheshire, CT: Graphics Press.

U.S. Department of Labor, Bureau of Labor Statistics (2015). *Occupational outlook handbook, 2016–17 edition.* Retrieved from: http://www.bls.gov

VanTassel-Baska, J. (2011). An introduction to the Integrated Curriculum Model. In J. VanTassel-Baska & C. A. Little (Eds.), *Content based curriculum for high-ability learners* (2nd ed., pp. 9–32). Waco, TX: Prufrock Press Inc.

VanTassel-Baska, J., Feldhusen, J., Seeley, K. Wheatley, G., Silverman, L. & Foster, W. (1988). *Comprehensive curriculum for gifted learners.* Boston, MA: Allen & Bacon.

Vlog Nation. (2015). *Valuable YouTube tips and advice from Matthias.* Retrieved from http://www.vlognation.com/matthias-youtube-tips

von Stumm, S., Hell, B., & Chamorro-Premuzic, T. (2011). The hungry mind: Intellectual curiosity is the third pillar of academic performance. *Perspectives of Psychological Science, 6,* 574–588. doi:10.1177/1745691611421204

Vygotsky, L. S. (1978). *Mind in society: The development of higher psychological processes.* Cambridge, MA: Harvard University Press.

Westberg, K. L. (2010). Young creative producers: Twenty-five years later. *Gifted Education International, 26,* 261–270.

Wired. (2016). *The 12 greatest challenges for space exploration.* Retrieved from http://www.wired.com/2016/02/space-is-cold-vast-and-deadly-humans-will-explore-it-anyway

worldwidewebsize.com. (2015). *Daily estimated size of the World Wide Web.* Retrieved from http://www.worldwidewebsize.com

YouTube. (2015). *Statistics.* Retrieved from https://www.youtube.com/yt/press/en-GB/statistics.html

About the Authors

Angela M. Housand, Ph.D., is an associate professor and the coordinator of the Academically and Intellectually Gifted graduate programs at the University of North Carolina Wilmington. Over the years, her work has been presented internationally and published in the *Journal of Advanced Academics*, *Gifted Child Quarterly*, *High Ability Studies*, and *Gifted Education Communicator*, just to name a few. As a former teacher, Dr. Housand brings an applied focus to her instructional programs for in-service and preservice teachers and her research tests the effectiveness of the FutureCasting® framework. In addition to teaching and research, Dr. Housand serves the National Association for Gifted Children in both elected and appointed positions. The goal of her work is to support teachers as they challenge gifted students to achieve their potential. For more information, go to http://www.angelahousand.com

Brian C. Housand, Ph.D., is an associate professor, coordinator of the Academically and Intellectually Gifted Program, and recipient of the Max Ray Joyner Award for Outstanding Teaching in Distance Education at East Carolina University. Dr. Housand earned a Ph.D. in educational psychology at the University of Connecticut's Neag Center for Gifted Education and Talent Development with an emphasis in both gifted education and instructional technology. He serves on the National Association for Gifted Children's Board of Directors as a Member-At-Large. He researches ways in which technology can enhance the learning environment and is striving to define creative productive giftedness in a digital age. For more information, go to http://brianhousand.com

Joseph S. Renzulli, Ed.D., is a Distinguished Professor of Educational Psychology at the University of Connecticut, where he also serves as director of the Neag Center for Creativity, Gifted Education, and Talent Development. He is an international leader in gifted education and applying the pedagogy of gifted education teaching strategies to total school improvement. His work on the Three-Ring Conception of Giftedness, the Enrichment Triad Model, curriculum compacting, and the use of instructional technology to assess student strengths and match resources to students' electronic profiles were pioneering efforts to make the field more flexible and to place the focus on talent development. He has contributed hundreds of books, book chapters, articles, and monographs to the professional literature, many of which have been translated to other languages. The American Psychological Association named him among the 25 most influential psychologists in the world, and he recently received the Harold W. McGraw, Jr. Award for Innovation in Education, considered by many to be "the Nobel Prize" for educators.